College
Peer Groups

norc

**NATIONAL OPINION RESEARCH CENTER
MONOGRAPHS IN SOCIAL RESEARCH**

College Peer Groups

*Problems
and Prospects
for Research*

Edited by
THEODORE M. NEWCOMB
and
EVERETT K. WILSON

With contributions by
LEONARD BAIRD
BURTON R. CLARK
JAMES S. COLEMAN
WARREN O. HAGSTROM
ROBERT A. LeVINE
THEODORE M. NEWCOMB
C. ROBERT PACE
DAVID RIESMAN
PETER H. ROSSI
HANAN C. SELVIN
MARTIN TROW
BEN WILLERMAN
EVERETT K. WILSON

ALDINE PUBLISHING COMPANY
Chicago

LA
229
N4

This volume is based on the work of three seminars sponsored
by the Social Science Research Council, held at
Ann Arbor, Michigan, and Berkeley, California, 1959–60

First published 1966 by
ALDINE Publishing Company
320 West Adams Street
Chicago, Illinois 60606

Library of Congress Catalog Card Number 65–29033
Designed by Greer Allen
Printed in the United States of America

Theodore M. Newcomb is Professor of Sociology and Psychology, University of Michigan.

Burton R. Clark is Professor and Research Sociologist in Higher Education, University of California, Berkeley; Martin Trow is Associate Professor of Sociology and Associate Research Sociologist, University of California, Berkeley.

Everett K. Wilson is Professor of Sociology and Chairman, Department of Sociology and Anthropology, Antioch College.

Robert A. LeVine is Associate Professor, Committee on Human Development, University of Chicago.

Ben Willerman, now deceased, was Staff Associate, Social Science Research Council, New York, N.Y., on leave from his post as Professor of Psychology, University of Minnesota.

Hanan C. Selvin is Chairman, Department of Sociology, University of Rochester, Rochester, N.Y.; Warren C. Hagstrom is Associate Professor of Sociology, University of Wisconsin.

Peter H. Rossi is Director, NORC, and Professor of Sociology, University of Chicago.

C. Robert Pace is Professor of Higher Education, University of California, Los Angeles; Leonard Baird is research assistant to Dr. Pace.

James S. Coleman is Professor of Social Relations, The Johns Hopkins University.

David Riesman is Henry Ford II Professor of Social Sciences, Harvard University.

Preface

This monograph deals with one among many kinds of influences in contemporary American colleges and universities: that of students upon one another. Few students, we suspect, are immune to peer group influence, and we think such influence merits more study that it has received, for both teacher and social scientist have a stake in the matter. Their two concerns are as close as knowledge and action, theory and practice. And if, as we think, there may be grounds for pessimism — if peer group effects are very often irrelevant or even opposed to faculty-favored objectives, if the social psychological motors of student life are racing, disconnected from the wheels of intellectual advance — then we need to know it. We need to know to what extent and under what conditions peer group influences complement or contradict faculty and college aims.

The authors of this volume do not necessarily identify the intellectual advance of students with their attainment of faculty objectives. We even think that the latter may not be above reproach. But these are problems for another day, and meanwhile we may ask how teachers can take advantage of the facts (or, at any rate, the presumed facts) of peer group influence so that it may better mediate and reinforce the academic and intellectual influences which colleges are presumably capable of exerting. Thus our first objective — though in a somewhat remote sense — is the practical one of helping colleges use their own resources more effectively to achieve their own ends. All of the contributors are teachers. We not only share with large numbers of our colleagues certain misgivings about what is happening to the students entrusted to our tutelage, but we also think that one useful approach to the problem is by way of understanding peer group influence.

All of us, furthermore, are social scientists — a fact which both affects our approach to teaching problems and introduces another set of objectives. As social scientists we are interested, not in the mere assertion, but in the testing of generalizations about human behavior. But generalizations cannot be tested in general. They are tested, rather, by empirical findings in a variety of specific situations. The literature of social science is replete with general propositions relevant to the effects of students' membership in peer groups, but very few of them have been tested in the concrete context of the college. The gains for social science in doing so lie, not only in extending our knowledge of the range of applicability of the generalizations, but also in learning more exactly about the conditions under which they do and do not apply. These considerations, too, have strengthened our conviction that the problems dealt with in this monograph are important ones.

Since our central interests are in the improvement of education and in the strengthening of social science, we have concluded that we can make our best contribution through our professional specialties. To do this effectively, it is not enough to summarize the scant amount of documented evidence available concerning the role of peer group influence in student careers. It is more important, rather, to highlight special aspects of the general problem about which documented evidence is needed. We assume that educational practices can be more wisely—because more realistically—determined through documented information about the nature and extent of the influence of college students upon one another.

Hence our emphasis is rather upon fairly specific research problems than upon the theoretical conceptualization of the general problem. While all of us consider ourselves superbly competent to deal with such theoretical issues, we have restrained the impulse to do so except in the interests of putting research problems into meaningful contexts. But we have not, on the other hand, tried to make this a "how to do it" manual or a general treatise on the strategy of research. We have attempted to plan each of the separate contributions in ways likely to be helpful to those interested in carrying out research on the impact of peers upon the student. We have kept questions of this sort in mind: If the reader wants to conduct research related to peer group influence, what kinds of problems will he face? What are some possible ways of dealing with them?

Obviously we have had to face the problem of what to include in one brief monograph and what to exclude. Very early in our planning we abandoned the impossible goal of all-inclusiveness. Yet we have tried not to overlook matters of obviously prime importance. The following guidelines have helped us in determining what to include: (1) the areas of interest and competence of the contributors; (2) the significant, published literature relevant to the general problem; and (3) the present stage of theoretical and methodological development, on the basis of which further development may appropriately be projected.

Thus the plan of this small monograph stems from our common objectives and our several individual backgrounds of interest and experience. We (the members of three seminars in 1959 and 1960) have planned, in Part I, a set of papers providing a backdrop against which student experiences may well be viewed. In Part II, we present a series of more technical papers concerning problems of empirical research. Finally, we have asked Professors James Coleman and David Riesman to comment freely upon the manuscripts prepared for Parts I and II, so as to provide an overview at once critical and unifying. For despite our extended collaboration, our papers do not flow as from a single hand.

Historically, the monograph is an outgrowth of the Social Science Research Council's Committee on Personality Development in Youth, which in turn owes its being to Dr. Pendleton Herring, the Council's director. During the summer of 1959 and the following winter, this Committee sponsored three week-long conferences on student peer groups, attended by six of the writers — LeVine, Newcomb, Rossi, Selvin, Willerman, and Wilson. In addition, we were fortunate enough to have as participants Allen Barton (whose contributions to the general methodology of research on organization variables were particularly helpful); Richard Christie (who knows more than anyone else about the measurement of personality traits); and Frederic Mosher (who not only contributed to the substance of our thinking but helped us in many other ways). And, because of their wisdom and sophistication concerning the study of undergraduates, we have subsequently called upon Baird, Clark, Coleman, Hagstrom, Pace, Trow, and Riesman to add their contributions to those prepared by six of the original participants.

In addition to being grateful to Dr. Herring and to Dr. Ralph Tyler, the Committee chairman, we are indebted to the University of Michigan, the University of California at Berkeley, and to the Center for Advanced Study in the Behavioral Sciences (Stanford) for entertaining us during one or more of our seminars.

We thank Jean Block for preparing the Index.

T. M. N.
E. K. W.

Contents

List of Tables
and Charts

Part I

The Framework within Which Peer Groups Operate

1

The General Nature of Peer Group Influence

THEODORE M. NEWCOMB

SOURCES OF CHANGE AMONG GRADUATES

Not long ago a group of social scientists met to consider a set of problems which might be summarized in the question, "How can we find out what happens to students in American colleges and universities and why it happens?" Being social scientists, we soon found ourselves "categorizing" the "sources of variance" in "institutional output." What this really meant was that comparatively few kinds of things seem to be mainly responsible for the enormous differences that one can observe among students — within a given college or among many — as they leave ivied walls and cloistered halls. We guessed that graduating students are different because they were different on first coming to college, because they have met different kinds of faculty-administration influence, and because they have done different kinds of things to each other while in college. We may label them selection, tutelage, and peer influence.

Having categorized the sources of differentation, we then went on to rank them in terms of estimated importance. Somewhat to our own surprise, we found ourselves virtually unanimous. We believed that selection (i.e., all the things that students bring with them on arriving at college), more fully accounts for the final product than does either of the other sets of factors. We rated peer influences second in importance. Although most of us were college professors, we had no sense that by assigning these relative weights we were necessarily denigrating our own roles as educators. The factor of selection is important because students on leaving are very much like the same students on entering college; conversely, selection is important because some student characteristics, already present on entrance, make their possessors more likely to become different—in which case professors may provide the necessary mechanisms of change. As to the set of factors we rated second, peer influence is not necessarily opposed to faculty influence; it is at least possible that the latter is mediated and reinforced by the former—in which case, again, the professor's role is essential, even if not sufficient.

Whatever the facts of the matter, there is reason enough to conclude that on the contemporary American scene the effects of student peer groups are sufficiently important to justify the serious attention of social scientists. Everyday observation, theoretical expectation, and empirical investigation all point to this conclusion.

GROUP POWER OVER INDIVIDUALS

The theoretical bases for assuming that peer group effects should be rather considerable are not particularly abstruse. Essentially, the argument in its general form runs as follows. People respond to a situation, not necessarily as it "really" is, but as they perceive it to be. And they perceive all but the simplest situations—especially human ones—not as they have been preordained by their physiological makeup to perceive them, but as they have learned to do so. The matter of learning to perceive (acquiring habits of perceiving in one way things that might be perceived differently by others) is thought by nearly all psychologists to be a matter of acquiring habits as a result of successes and failures that follow from actions based upon "right" and "wrong" ways of perceiving situations. The notions of success and failure assume, of course, that individuals have motives—whether standard and universal or idiosyncratic—in terms of which success and failure are experienced.

At any rate, there are powerful reasons why groups have much to do with individuals' successes and failures, and thus with the kinds of perceptual habits that they acquire. This is true, first, because groups so often have it in their power to reward and to punish—by such actions as applause or shame or by the according or withholding of social status or of worldly goods. Group standards often seem arbitrary to members of other groups—and indeed they are and must be, in the literal sense, for in many areas of life it is the fact of consensus, not its content, that matters. One needs to know, dependably and in advance, what kinds of behavior will or will not be rewarded. Such standards come to have the psychological impact of ineluctability and are sometimes referred to as "social reality."

Successes and failures are matters of group life, second, because human beings want and need each other. (Perhaps I should add that groups may be small as well as large, informal as well as formal: A pair of lovers, for example, constitutes a group in almost every important sense of the term.) If we want and need other people, then their responses to us are potentially rewarding or punishing, regardless of whether our wants represent spontaneous affiliativeness or the calculated instrumental use of others. In either case, group members develop sets of consensual expectations about each other (e.g., husband, wife, and child all want and expect husbandlike, wifelike, and childlike behavior from the appropriate family member, as well as certain similar, rather than differentiated, kinds of behavior from all).

For the purposes of the present argument, the outcomes of these two bases of group power over its individual members are the same: individual members develop attitudes toward each other—most commonly favorable ones—and they develop consensual sets of expectations regarding each other's behavior and regarding important aspects of their common environment, by which their individual expectations of success and failure are guided.[1] Such consensual expectations of each other's behavior are known as norms. Baldly put, groups have power over their

[1] The prevalence of favorable over unfavorable interpersonal attitudes, as outcomes of interaction, is by no means limited to voluntarily associating group members. Witness the very common fact that most parents and children the world around have predominantly favorable attitudes toward one another, though they had nothing to do with choosing each other in the first place. The observation of Homans (1950) that interaction and interpersonal attraction tend to increase together is, in general terms, very dependable.

members because the same processes of interaction that result in the members' feeling favorably toward each other also result simultaneously in their adopting norms that enable them to aim at success rather than failure.

The final step of the argument, of course, is that student peer groups, as a special case of a general phenomenon, are subject to the general rules. A plausible case can in fact be made for the assumption that the general rules should apply a fortiori to student groups. College students (particularly in this country, perhaps) meet each other with a ready-made consensus constructed of needs for independence from parents in a setting where independence is relatively possible and of strivings for adult status in a world that treats them partly as children. These initial bases of consensus, together with the fact that students are inevitably thrown together in dining rooms, classes, and dormitories, result — and often rather quickly — in the joint processes according to which groups acquire power over their members.[2]

The empirical grounds for concluding that substantial peer group effects do in fact occur in contemporary American colleges are not as solid as many of us would like to believe. Within the bounds of student peer group studies, the following conclusions seem justified. (1) Under certain conditions (as noted later) there have been several demonstrations of marked changes in attitude, of consensual nature, during college or professional-school years (Jacob, 1957; Newcomb, 1943; Sanford *et al.*, 1956; Merton *et al.*, 1957). (2) A much larger set of studies fails to show any such changes (esp. see Jacob, 1957). Almost without exception, however, these studies have made no attempt to study differentiated peer groups. Their data have generally come from samples (more rarely, from whole populations) of certain college classes, with no attention to group membership beyond the assumption that entire classes, or even entire student bodies, constitute membership groups. (3) Many, and probably most, of this larger body of studies have quite understandably concentrated

---

[2] More substantial bases for the general position outlined above may be found in the works of Festinger *et al.* (1950), Newcomb (1950), Asch (1952), Hare *et al.* (1955), Gardner and Thompson (1956), Sherif and Sherif (1956), Tagiuri and Petrullo (1958), Schachter (1959), Thibaut and Kelley (1959), and Cartwright and Zander (1960).

upon the kinds of attitude changes that educators consider desirable. As an educator, I consider it deplorable that some of the kinds of changes that I think should be occurring in contemporary American colleges are not, apparently, occurring. This conclusion—if justified—is, however, almost irrelevant to the question of the nature and extent of college peer group influences. Here, as elsewhere, the weekday job of social scientists is to discover and to understand what is in fact going on, leaving till Sundays and holidays the delights of personal evaluation.

In sum, I believe that the theoretical reasons for expecting important peer group effects within American colleges are very convincing, and that the expectations have been well supported when they have been put to the proper tests. Let me now suggest certain conditions of peer group influence that have emerged, or hypothetically would emerge, from such "proper tests."

SOME CONDITIONS OF PEER GROUP FORMATION

It is, of course, "natural" for people with common interests to associate with one another, and in our own society at least, not only early but also late adolescents (including most college students) seem to have strong needs for acceptance by age and sex peers. But this fact leaves the entire matter of selection unexplained. Even in very small colleges, everyone does not associate with equal frequency or with equal intensity with all of his peers. There are, moreover, wide differences among individuals; some are under- and some overinvolved, in terms of local norms. Furthermore, there are many possible bases for peer group formation, ranging from chance propinquity, through more or less casual common interests, to shared concerns of great moment. And so, in order to gain our primary objective of understanding the effects of peer group experience, we must examine such specific questions as why it is that particular peer groups get formed in the first place. I am, of course, making the social scientist's usual assumption that things happen in orderly rather than in "uncaused" ways and that, in any college community at any given time, if certain conditions had been different the consequences for peer group formation would have been different.

We may consider three kinds of factors as of primary im-

portance and as independent—i.e., as contributing to the formation of particular peer groups.

Precollege acquaintance
Particularly during the early college experience, previous
acquaintance, especially as established in secondary schools,
may form the basis of college peer groups. One study of high
school seniors' preferences among colleges (Coleman and Rossi,
1960) found that a small proportion of high school friends hoped
to attend the same college. Neither this study nor any other
known to me, however, provides much information about the
subsequent fate of precollege friendships. It seems probable that
many if not most of them are superseded by others developed in
college with previously unknown persons. In the presumably
rare cases in which they do persist through a significant proportion of the college years, it seems more likely that they reinforce
existing attitudes and values of the individuals involved than
that they mediate new ones acquired through college experience.

Propinquity
One cannot very well develop peer group relationships with
persons whom one has never met. Neither does one develop
them with all of the persons whom one has met. But propinquity
determines the probability of any two persons' meeting; and, in
particular, early propinquity in college—when most other individuals are relatively indistinguishable, since most of them are
strangers—determines the probability of early meeting. This
basic statement of statistical probabilities, together with a rather
basic psychological consideration, has important consequences
for peer group formation. This consideration, somewhat over-
simplified, is that a currently known source of reward is not likely
to be valued less than an alternative whose reward value is less
certain (cf. Murphy [1947] on "canalization"). Existing sources
of reward enjoy a kind of squatter's right, and peer group acceptance is likely to be rewarding. This principle, the consequences
of which are in a certain sense conservative, must of course
compete with other and sometimes overriding principles, and
therefore it describes a probable rather than a required state

of affairs. But the two kinds of probabilities together result in a frequency, considerably greater than chance, of persisting peer group relationships that originated in "chance" encounters facilitated by propinquity, as in dormitory residence or classroom attendance.

In view of the fact that marriage rates—even within a single city—vary directly with residential propinquity of marriage partners (as Bossard showed in 1932), we should scarcely expect that the formation of less intimate peer group relationships would be immune to the same considerations, and the known facts support the expectation. Festinger (1950), for example, has shown that in a housing project for married students the closest interpersonal relationships (in a statistical sense) developed not merely on the part of those whose apartment entrances faced the same court, but also, in particular, among those who used the same stairways and other facilities. A more recent investigation (Newcomb, 1961) shows that, even within a small, two-floor house accommodating only seventeen students, there were at first (but not following intimate acquaintance) significantly more close relationships among the eight men on one floor and among the nine men on the other than between men on the different floors. Roommates, whose proximity to each other was greatest of all, were particularly prone to developing close relationships.[3]

Insofar as we are interested in the study of formal peer groups (which are much easier to identify than informal ones), it seems clear, from these and other findings, that they are likely to be found wherever local arrangements—of living, dining, studying, engaging in student activities—result in very frequent associations among a given group of students. Not all individuals whose associations with each other are frequent will necessarily be subject—and certainly not in equal degrees—to the effects of the norms that inevitably develop under such conditions, but a large proportion of those who are influenced by such norms can probably be thus discovered.

---

[3] The finding concerning same-floor and different-floor relationships holds even when roommates, whose relationships were generally close, were excluded from consideration. I should add that all of these seventeen men were total strangers to each other on entering the house, and they had nothing at all to do with the choice of their roommates.

Similarity of Attitudes and Interests

Birds of a feather do flock together, and the kind of feathering that seems to be most essential for the human species is clearly marked by common interests. This fact both rests upon and illustrates some crucial principles concerning human interaction. People are most likely to interact (and thus, in terms of probabilities, to develop close relationships) when shared interest in some aspect of their common environment brings them together. The earlier principle (Newcomb, 1961, pp. 3 ff.) that interaction tends to create consensual attitudes should not obscure the equally important one that interaction tends to begin on the basis of existing interests that are shared. The two principles, together, imply that interaction may lead to new (and often widening) kinds of shared interests.

A combination of contiguity and common interests (or, at least those assumed as common) seems to account for the beginning of most peer group relationships. An initial basis may be provided by the common features of the shared environment, but the selective association that usually occurs within large groups, all of whose members have an environment in common, is likely to be based upon shared interests that are not inherent in the immediate situation, such as preferred sports, hobbies, or tastes in music or sex partners. In my own study of the process of acquaintance on the part of small populations of college men, common interests in sports or college majors often served as a basis for early clique formation, but these did not necessarily persist; changes tended to occur with further opportunity to explore each other's interests. Closeness of interpersonal relationships after four months of acquaintance was in many (though not all) cases determined more by sharing of general values (religious, perhaps, or aesthetic) than by more specific interests held in common.

The common interests that are so essential to the formation of peer groups may or may not extend beyond those which students bring with them to college or beyond those which they share with their contemporaries outside of college. If not, the consequences of membership in such groups may be quite unrelated — or even opposed — to the distinctive objectives of higher education as commonly assumed by educators. I suppose no one really knows how generally it is true that peer group effects are essentially irrelevant, in this sense, in the contemporary American scene. In the following section I discuss some of the conditions under which such irrelevant outcomes most probably occur.

Meanwhile, to pursue the question of how common interests contribute to the formation of student peer groups, it is well to remember that the interests of groups, like those of individuals, may change. There is a well-known principle in psychology according to which motives that are initially instrumental to the gratification of some other, overriding motive may take on a life of their own, independent of the goal to which they were at first subsidiary.[4] Means often become ends. An analogous principle may be applied to groups. A group already character-ized by consensus of interests and attitudes, and by interpersonal attitudes that are favorable, may persist as a group on the basis of the latter set of attitudes even though the former set has become dissipated. A group that has acquired considerable interpersonal solidarity may prove to be autonomous, in this sense, but it does not follow that a subsequent basis of consensus can be dis-pensed with entirely. If the original common interests have dis-appeared, they tend to be replaced by others. If not, interpersonal solidarity is likely to decline, leaving nothing to hold the group together. The social psychological fact seems to be that group continuity is fostered by high levels of consensus of both of two kinds: first, favorable attitudes toward each other, and second, similar attitudes toward things of common importance – though most groups can tolerate less than a perfectly solid front.

In any case, the educator who despairs at the irrelevancies of student peer group influences may take heart over the fact that yesterday's poisonous irrelevancy may, in the same group, be-come today's relevant meat. He may even anticipate that, as students "reassort" themselves, old groups giving way to new, some of the emerging groups will form around his favorite relevancies. He may, in fact, regard such possibilities as special challenges to his educational skills.

---

[4] Among various formulations of this principle, that of G. W. Allport (1937) has perhaps been most influential; he uses the term "functional autonomy."

SOME CONDITIONS OF PEER GROUP INFLUENCE

As I have already tried to show, it is the student's attitudes, rather than his general skills or specific capacities or basic personality characteristics, that are most likely to be directly influenced by peer group membership. Let me first indicate a little more clearly what I mean by that term and then point to some conditions under which attitudinal effects are most likely to take place.

Attitudes, as social psychologists commonly use the term, refer to the ways in which an individual has learned to assess things with which he is more or less familiar. "Things" include any entity—cabbages or kings or concepts—that he recognizes and distinguishes from other entities. Assessment refers both to the qualities that he attributes to the thing in question and to his evaluation of it in view of these qualities—evaluation, that is, in ways such as liking, fearing, approving, or their opposites. We generally think of attitudes as varying in intensity or strength, in sign (favorable *vs.* unfavorable), and in generality (i.e., the inclusiveness of the entity to which the attitudes refer: one may have attitudes toward a specific man, toward men in general, or toward human beings in general). We often refer to highly generalized attitudes, especially toward non-concrete entities, as values.

Groups have power over their members because two processes tend to occur together as group members continue to interact. Members become more favorable toward each other, and they come to adopt as their own certain group-shared attitudes, or norms, and to feel that those norms are right and proper. Both of these consequences (placing a measure of trust in others and accepting their assessment of things) involve in important ways the yielding to others of power over oneself. But it is the second —which I have described as the sharing in group norms—that is of primary interest as an outcome of educational experience.

The import of these considerations seems to me to be as follows. Insofar as we are interested in what college experience does to students' attitudes we must, because of the nature of attitude formation and change, be interested in the groups to which students (wittingly or not) yield power over their own attitudes. Most attitudes — and particularly those in which educators are interested — are, as social psychologists like to say, anchored in group membership. Let me hasten to add that this statement in no way represents an advocacy of conformity as opposed to personal independence and a critical attitude. The latter represents a kind of value (highly prized by most social psychologists, incidentally) which, like most others, is nourished by group support, however narrowly selective. The assertion that, as a matter of empirical observation, values and other kinds of attitudes are nourished and even created through group membership carries no implication that any given instance of the general phenomenon is to be applauded or decried.

Insofar as the proposition is correct, however, it is heavy with implications for educators. How can we direct such kinds of influences in accordance with, rather than irrelevantly or in opposition to, our educational objectives? This question is really a double-headed one. It invites both scientific and "applied" replies, i.e., both statements of conditions under which the presumed effects are most likely to occur and prescriptions for creating those conditions. I shall touch only lightly on the latter.

At least four conditions that facilitate the influence of student peer groups upon their members' attitudes appear to be well enough established to deserve mention. No one of them is an essential condition; perhaps any single one of them, under exactly the right circumstances, might prove effective in the absence of all of the others. Most commonly, however, several or all of these conditions exist together when marked effects have been noted.

Size of Groups

Perhaps the most obvious of these conditions has to do with group size. Membership in very large populations is not likely, of itself, to bring about the strong interpersonal attitudes that are so important an ingredient in peer group effects upon attitudes. Small groups, in which such interpersonal relationships can be established, often mediate the attitudes for which a larger population (like "the college") stands, but membership in the latter without the mediation of the former would probably not be very effective. From the point of view of formal arrangements which result in group formation, however, relatively large groups have the advantage of making it possible for individuals to be selective in their more intimate associations. From this point of view, the formal group should not be so large that most of its members cannot recognize one another yet so small that it discourages the formation within it of spontaneously formed congenial subgroups. The combination of strong interpersonal attitudes engendered by the latter, and the strength of support provided by the more inclusive group of which the subgroup is a representative, is often an effective one.[5]

Homogeneity

A second condition involves relative homogeneity of group members. Homogeneity of age, sex, social class, or religious affiliation contributes to effective peer group influence primarily because of the homogeneity of attitudes that tends to go along with such similarities. The more readily observable forms of similarity without their attitudinal counterparts will hardly suffice for the formation of effective groups. The fact that existing homogeneity of attitudes is so important to group solidarity has, of course, implications of conservatism: if group solidarity depends upon the similarity of members' attitudes, its continuing solidarity is likely to be threatened by lessened similarity in those attitudes. But the same fact also provides the possibility of exactly the reverse. As the late Professor Kurt Lewin used to say, apropos of the effectiveness of "group decision" under certain conditions, "it is sometimes easier to change the attitudes of an entire group than of a single individual" — simply because group support may be mobilized for change as well as against it. At any rate, if a group is not relatively homogeneous with regard to some existing attitudes of importance to its members, it will not have much power to change its members' attitudes.

---

[5] Witness, for example, the colleges within Cambridge and Oxford universities, the houses at Harvard and Yale, and small colleges like Antioch, Bennington, and Reed, all of which have formal arrangements resulting in groups of a few hundred that have proven capable of arousing effective group loyalties.

Isolation

A third condition, relative isolation from groups having divergent group norms, is closely related to the second. Either the fact or the illusion of a membership homogeneous in attitudes may serve to strengthen the conviction that those attitudes are "right." It is communicative rather than physical isolation, however, that I have in mind. In a college community which I once studied from the point of view of freshman-to-senior attitude changes (Newcomb, 1943), I found no students so untouched by the prevalent patterns of decreasing political conservatism as those who, together with tiny groups of close friends, were so insulated from the majority of their fellows that they were quite unaware of the dominant trend that was so conspicuous to others. Let me add, again, that to point to a condition of group effectiveness is not necessarily to approve of it. But whether one approves or not, there are many institutions of higher education, and many kinds of formal student groups within still more of them, whose policies of admission together with their selective drawing power result both in attitudinal homogeneity and communicative isolation. The effects of the combination are indubitably conservative and also indubitably effective.

Importance to Individuals of Group-supported Attitudes

A final facilitating condition for peer group effectiveness is also an obvious one: the importance to individual members of the group-supported attitudes. Other things being equal, the greater the importance to them of the attitudes for which the group stands, the greater the solidarity of the group, regardless of whether the sense of importance preceded or has been engendered by group membership. Again, the implications appear to be conservative, but they are not necessarily so. It does not always follow from the fact that group members feel that something is very important that existing attitudes toward it (even consensual ones) are immutable. It may follow from the same fact that its very importance requires accurate assessment of it, and group power may be mobilized toward recognizing new facts or widened perspectives from which changed attitudes follow. If so, the same group influence which previously resisted change now comes to support it.

In sum, groups become more effective influencers of their members under some sets of conditions than under others. The effective combinations of conditions are frequently present in contemporary American colleges, whether or not by design of their educational architects. Very often, too, they are not met —and perhaps fortunately so. The educator's objective is not necessarily that of maximizing peer group influence, but rather that of understanding how, when, and why it occurs, in order that its effects may be consonant with his purposes.

A FRAMEWORK FOR RESEARCH

It often happens, particularly in the world of human affairs, that the consequences of any event are more fully understood by viewing that event in the light of the circumstances of which the event itself is a consequence than by viewing the event as "un-caused" (though for many purposes this procedure is unnecessary or even impossible). The study of peer groups is a case in point. Peer group formation is an outcome of antecedent events; the nature of a member's experiences, and thus the effects of those experiences may be profoundly influenced by the circumstances attending the group's emergence. And so (in the language of contemporary social scientists) it is necessary to

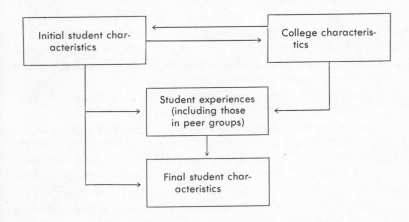

Chart 1.1 Schematic Diagram Illustrating Interdependent Influences upon Final Student Characteristics

consider peer groups, alternately, as dependent and as independent phenomena. More specifically, the nature of student peer group experience is sure to be influenced by the various factors categorized as selective, and these in turn are influenced by, and (in time) they also influence, both the actual and the perceived nature of the college itself. In very direct ways, furthermore, various kinds of institutional arrangements (e.g., student living arrangements) influence peer group formation. Chart 1.1, in which arrows indicate presumed directions of influence, suggests the kinds of interaction effects which must be taken into account. The chart suggests a framework, at the heart of which is "student experiences" — and in particular, peer group experiences. These latter are the focus of attention in succeeding chapters, as we look into the question of how peer group membership influences the college product.

Corresponding to this framework, the following two chapters deal with college characteristics and with those of the entering student, respectively. They represent antecedent conditions which, in their conjunction, contribute to the within-college experience. This experience, then, is viewed as a form of socialization in Chapter 4.

All of Part II (which is primarily concerned with more specialized problems, including procedural ones involved in research) also has to do, directly or indirectly, with student experiences. Chapters 5 and 6 deal primarily with formal peer groups — the former doing so in terms of some generic problems of field experiments, while the latter treats the problem of developing a useful and theoretically relevant classification of formal peer groups. The groups considered in Chapter 7 are more informal ones (if, indeed, groups of peers are peer groups). The human subenvironments in which student experiences occur are considered in both Chapters 7 and 8, though according to somewhat different procedures. Throughout all the chapters, including the final invited comments by Professors Coleman and Riesman, there appear at least indirect glimpses of final student characteristics as outcomes of college characteristics, initial student attributes, student experiences, and the interaction among all these.

2

The Organizational Context

BURTON R. CLARK
and
MARTIN TROW

In recent years social scientists have turned their attention to the colleges and universities in which most of them work.[1] Among the speculative questions which they are transforming into research problems is the perennial one: "What effect, if any, does their college experience have on students?" One approach to that question directs our attention to the relationships of students with one another. This has long been a central theme in the reflections of men concerned with higher education in America. Woodrow Wilson (1925), writing half a century ago, made the following observation.

The real intellectual life of a body of undergraduates, if there be any, manifests itself, not in the classroom, but in what they do and talk of and set before themselves as their favorite objects between classes and lectures. You will see the true life of a college . . . where youths get together and let themselves go upon their favorite themes — in the effect their studies have upon them when no compulsion of any kind is on them, and they are not thinking to be called to a reckoning of what they know.

[1] An earlier version of this paper appeared in unpublished form (Clark, 1960a). Parts of the earlier paper, in revised or abridged form, have appeared in works of Broom and Selznick (1963), Clark (1962), and Trow (1960, 1962).

We know from many sources that relationships among peers affect attitudes and behavior in a variety of ways; the subject is a continuing thread in sociological discourse and has been studied in many different contexts.[2] Work on this topic in the colleges has dealt primarily with the structure and processes of student groups and secondarily with their effects on members and on the larger systems of which the groups are part. Less well studied are the social forces and conditions that shape such groups: the features of social organization that generate and sustain the subsystems of student life. Our interest in this chapter lies precisely in these determinants. We want to know the bearing of larger social structures on student life and relationships. From this perspective we shall view the college peer group as the locus for a set of processes which intervene between the larger social systems and the outcomes of college education.

Two broad sets of factors shape the nature of the orientations and relationships of students in college. The first set flows from the character of the larger society. Students come to college with certain resources — material, moral, intellectual, emotional, and cultural. These resources are largely determined by the life experiences the students have had, and these in turn are shaped by the statuses they and their parents have held in the larger society. The prior social locations and experiences also shape aspiration: the kinds of lives the students envision for themselves in a rapidly changing society.

The second set of determinants derives from the nature of the colleges themselves: their historical development, their value climates, their structural features, and the shaping environment thus provided for student life. A college is not simply an aggregation of students, teachers, and administrators. Although the character of a college is greatly influenced by the nature of its staff and students, it also has qualities and characteristics which are to some extent independent of the people who fill its halls and offices at any given moment.

Throughout our analysis the one particular outcome of college upon which we wish to focus is the intellectual and cultural de-

[2] For reviews of the literature, see Katz and Lazarsfeld (1955) and Bales (1959). The classic work in education is that of Newcomb (1943). See also the articles in *The School Review* (*School Review* staff, 1963).

velopment of the adolescent and young adult. This analytical touchstone relates to the purposes of colleges. Colleges profess to be, and often are, civilizing agencies; they work to develop and refine the powers of intellect, perception, and feeling. Some students in some colleges "discover a new range of sensibility" under the influence of forces which "raise to the status of virtues certain humane feelings and actions which had until then been regarded as unimportant and even unmanly" (Nicholson, 1955). But to what extent does the civilizing process occur—for what kinds of students, under what conditions, and with respect to what sentiments and perceptions? Students bring to college a variety of interests and sentiments; in college they find support among their fellows for some of these and indifference or hostility toward others. But which are supported and which discouraged —subtle or crude ways of thinking, original or conventional conceptions, fresh or routine feelings and perceptions? And what forces in society and college affect the balance of influences that students have on one another?

TYPES OF STUDENT CULTURE

Instead of working with the formal properties of informal associations among students, we will focus on their normative content. Let us consider some of the orientations toward a college education which are represented on American campuses and which may be in competition on any one campus. These orientations are defining elements of student subcultures, in which they appear as shared notions of what constitutes right attitude and action toward the range of issues and experiences confronted in college. We will first distinguish several leading types of subcultures, then discuss some of the forces, both internal and external to the college, that shape the strength and distribution of the subcultures on any particular campus.

In passing, we wish to caution that the following are types of subcultures and not types of students, despite the fact that we often describe these subcultures by characterizing their members. First, an individual student may well participate in several of the subcultures available on his campus, though in most cases one will embody his dominant orientation. Second, these types of subcultures are analytical categories; the actual subcultures that flourish on any given campus may well combine elements of more than one of these types. Third, as will be seen, the analytical types simply break dimensions in half and hence oversimplify. These dimensions could be divided into a greater number of more homogeneous categories and combined in blends not here discussed or anticipated. Finally, we would not like to encourage the game of naming subcultures and then pigeonholing individuals, groups of students, or colleges. Rather, we think of this typology as a heuristic device for getting at the processes by which social structures shape student styles of life in different kinds of colleges.

Collegiate Culture

The most widely held stereotype of college life pictures the "collegiate culture," a world of football, fraternities and sororities, dates, cars, drinking, and campus fun.[3] A good deal of student life on many campuses revolves around this culture; it both provides substance for the stereotypes of movies and cartoons and models itself on those stereotypes. Teachers and courses and grades are in this picture but somewhat dimly and in the background. The fraternities have to make their grade-point average, students have to hit the books periodically if they are to get their diplomas, some gestures have to be made to the adult world of courses and grades which provides the justification for the collegiate round.[4]

In content, this system of values and activities is not hostile

[3] For a description and analysis of campus subcultures, see Angell (1928), Johnson (1946), and McConn (1928). For an early (1909) classic indictment, see Wilson (1925). For a recent sociological analysis of this student world, see Goldsen *et al.* (1960).

[4] Goldsen *et al.* (1960, p. 73). The following are quotations from interviews with fraternity men in their sample.

Lots of pledges come in with the idea that fraternity life means all fun and no studying. We quickly educate them. Not that we want grinds — no — we try to get them to maintain a respectable average. Nothing very glittering, of course, just respectable.

We try to keep our house's grades up to standard. There's plenty of help for the brothers who fall behind. We have files of old examinations in almost every course that they can use in studying. We even assign certain men to tutor any brothers who need help. They don't have to get super grades. After all, when you get out of college nobody asks what your grades were. Just maintain a decent average.

to the college, to which in fact it generates strong loyalties and attachments. It is, however, indifferent and resistant to serious demands emanating from the faculty for an involvement with ideas and issues over and above that required to gain the diploma. This culture is characteristically middle- and upper-middle class, for it takes money and leisure to pursue the busy round of social activities,[5] and it flourishes on, though it is by no means confined to, the resident campuses of big state universities. At other institutions, part-time work, intense vocational interests, an urban location, commuter students, all work against the full flowering of a collegiate subculture, as do student aspirations for graduate or professional school or, more generally, serious intellectual or professional interests on the part of students and faculty.

Vocational Culture

The countervailing forces of student poverty and vocationalism, on the one hand, and serious intellectual or academic interests, on the other, are strong enough to make the collegiate culture relatively weak on many American campuses which otherwise differ greatly. In the urban colleges which recruit the ambitious, mobility-oriented sons and daughters of working- and lower-middle-class homes, there is simply not enough time or money to support the expensive play of the collegiate culture. To these students, many of them married, most of them working anywhere from twenty to forty hours a week, college is largely off-the-job training, an organization of courses and credits leading to a diploma and a better job than they could otherwise command. These students have little attachment to the college, where they buy their education somewhat as one buys groceries. But like participants in the collegiate culture, these students are also resistant to intellectual demands on them beyond what is required to pass the courses. To many of these hard-driven students, ideas and scholarship are as much a luxury and distraction as

[5] In eleven universities across the country, fraternity members were found on the average to come from considerably wealthier homes than do independent students. In 1952 only 24 per cent of the fraternity men as compared with 46 per cent of the independents reported their fathers earning under $5,000. Computed from data of Goldsen *et al.* (1960, p. 71, Table 3.3).

are sports and fraternities. If the symbol of the collegiate culture is the football and fraternity weekend, the symbol of this vocationally oriented culture is the student placement office.

Academic Culture

Present on every college campus, although dominant on some and marginal on others, is the subculture of serious academic effort. The essence of this system of values is its identification with the intellectual concerns of the serious faculty members. The students involved work hard, get the best grades, talk about their coursework outside of class, and let the world of ideas and knowledge reach them in ways that neither of the foregoing types does. While participants in the collegiate subculture pursue fun, and the job-oriented pursue skills and a diploma, these students pursue knowledge: their symbols are the library and laboratory and seminar. If the faculty members who embody these values also represent the college as a whole, then this academic subculture is identified with the college. For these students, the attachment to the college, often as strongly felt as that among the collegiate crowd, is to the institution which supports intellectual values and opportunities for learning; the emotional tie to the college is through the faculty and through campus friends of similar mind and temper. This is the climate encouraged at the colleges that are academically strongest, and when colleges aim to upgrade themselves, it is the students already oriented in this direction whom they seek to recruit.

The products of this culture are typically aiming at graduate and professional schools; it is not surprising that they identify so strongly with the faculty and internalize the scholarly and scientific habits of mind and work as part of their anticipatory adjustment to future professional roles. These students are often oriented toward vocations but not so directly or narrowly as are the lower- and lower-middle-class commuters who hold the consumer-vocational values described above; they choose "a basic general education and appreciation of ideas" more often than "provide vocational training" as the goal of education most important to them (Goldsen *et al.*, 1960). In any case, it is not necessary to decide whether they are concerned with their studies more for the sake of learning than because of their career ambitions. The distinctive qualities of this group are, first, that they are seriously involved in their coursework beyond the minimum required for passing and graduation and, second, that they identify themselves with their college and its faculty.

Nonconformist Culture

It is in this latter respect, identification with the college, that "nonconformist," "intellectual," "radical," "alienated," "bohemian" students differ from their serious academic classmates. Some kind of self-consciously nonconformist subculture exists in many of the best small liberal arts colleges and among the undergraduates in the leading universities. These students are often deeply involved with ideas, both the ideas they encounter in their classrooms and those that are current in the wider society of adult art, literature, and politics. To a much greater degree than their academically oriented classmates, these students use off-campus groups and currents of thought as points of reference, instead of the official college culture, in their strategy of independence and citicism.[6]

The distinctive quality of this student style is a rather aggressive nonconformism, a critical detachment from the college they attend and from its faculty (though this often conceals a strong ambivalence), and a generalized hostility to the college administration. The forms that this style takes vary from campus to campus, but where it exists it has a visibility and influence far beyond its usually tiny and fluid membership. Its chief signifi-

[6]Jencks and Riesman (1962). The academic, in their usage, refers to the pursuit of knowledge within some scholarly or professional discipline by experts and specialists (or their apprentices), whereas intellectual inquiry is the pursuit of wisdom—answers to perennial problems of living—through the play of intelligence rather than through specialized learning. As they observe, the official view holds that "the intellectual and the academic are largely synonymous," and they are concerned with those student organizations at Harvard that "have emerged to defend intellectual concerns against overt or covert pressures from the curriculum." Our typology to some extent cuts across this distinction: the academic cultures we speak of include students with genuine intellectual interests as well as "grinds" submissive to the demands of the faculty. In our typology, the members of the academic subcultures tend to link their interests to the curriculum; the nonconformists pursue theirs outside it.

cance is that it offers a genuine alternative, however temporary, to the rebellious student seeking a distinctive identity in keeping with his own temperament and experience. In a sense it provides some intellectual content and meaning to the idealism and rebelliousness generated in adolescence in some parts of American society. While the preceding three types of students pursue fun, a diploma, or knowledge, these students pursue an identity, not as a by-product, but as the primary and often self-conscious aim of their education. And their symbol is often a distinctive style — of dress, speech, attitude — that itself represents the identity they seek.[7]

The nonconformist subculture eludes easy characterization. It may, in fact, constitute a residual category, concealing within it quite different kinds of attitudes and orientations, some of which are on the rise, some of which are declining in their importance. Here, next to the fashionable bohemians and the compulsive rebels are those who already exhibit in college the radical cosmopolitanism and skepticism, the commitment to abstract ideas, and the alienation from merely "institutional" attachments that are marks of the intellectual.

The types of subcultures we have been describing emerge from the combination of two variables: the degree to which stu-

[7] Nonconformist subcultures may provide opportunity and support for some of the processes of identity play discussed by Erikson (1956, pp. 56–121). The relatively little attention given to nonconformist cultures in this essay reflects our ignorance about them and not their relative importance for American life and education.

	Involved with ideas	
	Much	Little
Identify with their college — Much	Academic	Collegiate
Identify with their college — Little	Nonconformist	Vocational

Chart 2.1 Types of Orientations of Four Most Distinguishable Student Subcultures

dents are involved with ideas and the extent to which students identify with their college. If we dichotomize these variables, the above four types of student orientations, which provide the content of the most important and distinguishable student sub-cultures, emerge in the pattern shown in Chart 2.1.

These subcultures are fluid systems of norms and values which overlap and flow into one another on any one campus in ways that challenge the effort to distinguish them analytically. Yet that effort, for all the violence it does to the complexity of social life, appears justified by the light it promises to shed on colleges and their effects on students.[8]

Having distinguished these elementary types of subcultures, we can now raise some questions about the ways in which these subcultures are linked to the larger social structure and to the essential characteristics of colleges.

1. In what strengths and combinations are these orientations found in different types of colleges? Among the 17,000 under-graduates on the Berkeley campus of the University of California, all these systems of values are represented in some strength; among the large number at a nearby state college, the collegiate, academic, and nonconformist subcultures are weak compared with the predominantly vocational orientation of the great majority. At small, academically elite schools, the academic subculture is clearly dominant, with nonconformist values represented, while both the vocational and the collegiate are weak. And at a large number of colleges, large and small, of average rank, the older collegiate values still reign supreme, tempered perhaps by an academically oriented minority but with the leaven of nonconformists almost wholly absent.

2. What are the social characteristics of the typical members of these different subcultures? Where do they come from in the social structure, and what are the links between their prior ex-

[8] This simple typology does not take into account other dimensions of student orientations which may be important for understanding the specific forms that student subcultures take. Research aimed at applying, extending, and re-fining this typology is currently under way at the Educational Testing Service, Princeton, and in Berkeley at the American College Testing Program as well. For a report of a study employing this typology, see Gottlieb and Hodgkins (1963).

perience and their college orientation? There are distinctive patterns of experience that heavily condition the qualities and characteristics that students bring with them to college. Behind patterns of life experience lie social class, racial and ethnic ties, and religious identifications; it is the subcultures in the general population and their values, orientations, and aspirations that shape the orientations most students initially assume toward college.

3. How do these biographical linkages differ in different kinds of colleges? We have already suggested the connections between lower- and lower-middle-class origins, strong mobility aspirations, and vocational orientations toward college work. But some students thus oriented will find themselves in a minority in, for example, an Ivy League college, while others will find themselves among the majority in, say, a municipal college. How do these "similar" students deal with their college experience in these quite different situations?

4. What are the historical and structural characteristics of colleges that affect the character of their cultural mix? The purposes of an institution, its size and rate of growth, its historical traditions, its sources of funds and faculty, its physical location, the images of it held in different parts of the population—these and other factors shape the character of the student life within a college. The task is to specify how these forces operate.

Clearly the problem is no task for an essay the length of this chapter. We will deal with it in a preliminary way, in part speculatively, in part through tentative analysis of data from a recently completed study (McConnell, 1963).

THE LARGER SOCIETY

Among the broad forces that affect colleges and student cultures are the values regarding higher education held in different parts of the population—notions of what a college is and ought to be. These values are very heavily shaped by changing requirements of the occupational structure, which in turn reflect the changing character of the society's major institutions. In the society as a whole, and especially in the strata that send their sons and daughters to college and hire the college-trained, there appears to be a long-range trend toward greater rationality, toward the bureaucratic virtues of prudence, calculation, and the acquisition of useful skills and knowledge.[9]

The immense growth of large-scale enterprise — big business, big government, big labor, big education — and the concomitant growth of the technical, managerial, and salaried professional occupations[10] affect the colleges that train the future occupants of offices. More students find that bureaucratic or professional career lines dominate the post-college horizon, and more plan to pursue postgraduate studies.[11] Corporation job interviewers in growing numbers show the same kinds of interest in the transcripts which record college performance as do the deans and graduate faculties reviewing the applications of would-be academic men and professionals.

The sobering effect on college activities and relationships of these anticipated scrutinies of college records is still escaped by some students. The boy who envisions a place for himself in his father's automobile agency or other small business can throw himself into the fun of the collegiate culture with a lighter heart than the boy whose record will be examined by the corporation recruiter or graduate-school dean. But the number of students who can afford to ignore the record is diminishing. As a result of this and other tendencies, the collegiate subculture, whose panoply of big-time sports and fraternity weekends has pro-

---

[9] For a recent summary of research on American values, see Kluckhohn (1958).

[10] Between 1950 and 1960 the total number of jobs rose only 10 per cent, while the number of "professional, technical, and kindred" workers increased by 48 per cent (*Monthly Labor Review*, 1963). This category of workers, it is estimated, is in the process of growing by an additional 40 per cent in the 1960's (Wolfbein, 1962).

[11] The proportion of college students who go on to graduate or professional schools is rising very rapidly in some colleges. For example, DeVane (1960), dean of Yale College, estimates that 77 per cent of the class of 1960 will continue. Ten years ago the figure was about 50 per cent, and in 1920, when he graduated, only about 20 per cent continued their studies. The proportions continuing vary greatly from college to college. Such seemingly different colleges as Dartmouth and City College of New York report that 60 per cent of their graduates will continue their studies. In contrast, only about 25 per cent of the male graduates of the University of Wisconsin will continue. But even there the proportion going on to some form of postgraduate education is rising very rapidly.

vided the dominant image of college life since the end of the nineteenth century, is now in decline.[12] While the collegiate sub-culture is in no immediate danger of extinction, especially on its state university preserves, the demands of large organization and the Cold War for bureaucratic and technical expertise are strengthening the academic and especially the vocational cultures, while reducing the prestige and appeal of the collegiate.

The vocational subculture is also encouraged by the extension of opportunities for higher education to lower social strata. Many of the young people of working-class and lower-middle-class origin who are going to college in increasing numbers see college in largely instrumental terms, as the place where they can acquire the skills and diplomas that will earn them good jobs in some large organization (Kahl, 1953; Trow, 1958). When these students go, as many of them do, to large institutions that do not have a strong tradition of intellectual playfulness or a serious commitment to ideas, then the vocational subculture flourishes. On those campuses the absolute level of student interaction is lower, and relations among students center on the shared training experience—friendships are shaped very largely by common departmental affiliations. Upper-middle-class students, on the other hand, more often can afford the luxury of an interest in ideas, as they also can afford the luxury of the collegiate sub-culture and its fun morality. Which way they go depends on the intellectual climate in their homes, their own academic skills, their experience with ideas, their occupational aspirations, and the kind of college they enter.

Thus three major social forces—the bureaucratizing of organization, the professionalizing of occupations, and the democratizing of higher education—are together influencing what students seek in college and how they use their college experience. The forces link to student cultures in part through their effects on student aspirations. Lower-middle-class origins and modest aspirations for security in a job predispose students to

[12]"As academic pressures are stepped up, students have less time to rehearse cancan numbers for variety shows, hunt down floodlights to illuminate fifty-foot homecoming signs, and fashion castles out of tin foil for floats. The result: any number of traditional extracurricular activities are being scrapped" (*Mademoiselle* staff, 1960). The article goes on to cite other illustrations of what a Princeton man calls "creeping asceticism." See also Goldsen *et al.* (1960).

taking a vocational stance toward their college studies; in the upper-middle class, aspirations for the intellectual occupations and professions that involve postgraduate study predispose students toward the academic cultures and the disciplines of learning.[13]

This picture grossly oversimplifies, and it probably applies chiefly to boys, though girls are likely to take part in college subcultures similar to those of the husbands they seek. Moreover, recruitment to those subcultures is affected by many other factors.[14]

For example, while students from working- and lower-middle-class origins are more vocationally oriented and less culturally sophisticated than are students from upper-middle-class and professional homes, these differences are less likely to be found among the students within any particular college. Our data show that at Antioch, Reed, and Swarthmore, the small minority of students from lower-class origins are indistinguishable in their cultural habits and orientations from the majority of students, who come from upper-middle-class and professional homes, while at San Francisco State the minority of upper-middle-class students are culturally indistinguishable from the students of lower- and lower-middle-class backgrounds. The effects of selective recruitment (through both self-recruitment and admissions screening) along lines of academic orientations and aptitudes are so strong that they wash out, or at least greatly reduce, differences in cultural and intellectual orientations that stem from differences in social origins among students within any one of these colleges.

[13] When working- and lower-middle class boys do go into a profession, it is likely to be one of the two — engineering and education — that require least postgraduate training (Trow, 1958; Rosenberg, 1957). In Great Britain, as well, "It is no accident that the technologies take in proportionately more young people of working class origin than any of the other faculties. If the proportion for the arts is also high, this is because of the function of art faculties in the modern universities as professional schools would be for grammar school teachers" (Halsey, 1958).

[14] This finding is supported by data collected by Hagstrom and Selvin (1960) among students at the University of California at Berkeley. Studying political tolerance among students, they found students from working-class origins even more tolerant than students from middle-class homes, despite the fact that in the general population manual workers are on the whole a good deal less politically tolerant than middle- or upper-class people.

There is clearly a very selective recruitment to the University of California of students from working-class backgrounds, one which washes out or reverses relationships found in the general population. This selective recruitment does not necessarily make the student community more homogeneous in its attitudes and orientations, but it does increase the importance of lines of cleavage other than class origin among students. This is even more likely to be the case in colleges which do not provide for residential sorting by wealth. But the critical linkage between these broad trends in the society and the distribution of student subcultures on American campuses seems clear. Insofar as skills and formal knowledge grow in importance, and as more and more students of lower-class origins go to college, the vocational and academic orientations grow in importance at the expense of the collegiate.

Types of Vocationalism
Two kinds of vocationalism—the first an interest in college as the source of usable skills and knowledge, the second an interest in college as the source of a salable diploma or certificate—are found side by side on college campuses, usually associated with different departments and majors, with different consequences for student development. On some campuses, the disillusionment of some of the students majoring in education, business administration, and the like, arising out of their sense of the practical irrelevance of their studies, leads to much time-serving. This disillusionment with vocationalism opens some to an awareness of the "importance" of general education and ideas, and for a relatively few is a genuine step toward a response to the intrinsic intellectual rewards of their non-vocational studies (Sanford, 1956). For many others, especially upwardly mobile students from culturally impoverished origins, "Culture" becomes the skill which they aim to acquire in college. The style of the college-educated man—a certain familiarity with ideas, a mode of speech, certain tastes in books and furniture and politics and music —becomes part of the salable package which students who will be selling themselves and not their skills prepare in college (Trow, 1960). When time and money allow, these same students

may seek to complement their "cultural" skills with social skills through participation in an approximation of the collegiate culture.

Skill-oriented students, such as engineers, while less likely to be bored or indifferent to college, are also much more stubbornly resistant to the appeals of "general education"; their styles and identities are more firmly crystallized. In many respects, they are not really in college, but already on the job. But for the large group of diploma-oriented students whose college training has no direct relevance to the work they will be doing, the lines between vocational, collegiate, and academic orientations become blurred. The blurring comes from their sense of the pointlessness of any of the available orientations toward college. The traditional justifications of liberal education sound hollow to them, the vocational courses irrelevant, the collegiate round expensive and trivial. Small wonder that college comes to seem an obstacle rather than an opportunity, an arbitrary and extended test of motivation, endurance, and general intelligence that leads to a qualifying certificate and a better job.[15]

But as we have suggested, the disillusionment with their "training" which leads some diploma-oriented students to mere timeserving also opens others to new interests and new influences. Which ways these students go, how genuinely liberating and civilizing their college experience is, therefore depends heavily on the organization of the college and especially on its success in

[15] Jacques Barzun (1960) has commented cogently on the tendency of colleges to serve as a screening mechanism for the occupational world through the translation of business routines into academic subjects:

> The chief characteristic of man's work in our time is that all occupations tend to become professions. And these professions, following the example of medicine and law in past centuries, tend to become academic subjects. That is, the practices become codified, they are written up in textbooks, courses are given, specialties proliferate, and degrees multiply. Work and study face into each other and are deemed equivalent. Young men of business toil at a Ph.D. in marketing, real estate operators write theses, personnel managers take and learn to give tests, accountants, diplomats, writers of advertising copy are taught in universities. In short, every worldly youth is poring over a book in hopes of passing into an office. That great aim is expressed by the verb "to qualify."

insulating its pursuits from occupational purposes while developing and sustaining a climate which supports enthusiasm for learning.

THE ORGANIZATION

We have discussed the support given the several student cultures by a few major features of the general society — support effected principally through the interests, sentiments, and occupational aspirations brought to college by student recruits. In turning to the campus context in which student groups arise, persist, and change, we inquire into organizational reasons for the forms that their cultures take. In part, we shall address the question: What are the organizational conditions of student commitment, indifference, or hostility to intellectual achievement?

We will not attempt to list exhaustively the characteristics of colleges that may affect student perspectives. Rather, we have identified a few features that appear to have major importance, these organized principally around the basic sociological categories of values, interests, and structures. We first discuss the institutional ethos, speculating briefly about the role of the historically derived purposes of the official college and the salience of its general character. We then examine some objective interests of faculty and administration that are induced by work and career. Finally, we inquire into four structural aspects of college organization — the distribution of authority, the size and complexity of organization, the requirements of membership, and the autonomy of the system.[16]

Institutional Ethos

A college has an official culture, historically derived and reflected in the present belief and practice of the paid staff. In any but the most splintered system, the student cultures are

---

[16]Between 1947 and 1961, enrollments in public colleges increased by 104 per cent and in private colleges by 30 per cent; the public colleges absorbed 77 per cent of the total increase in college enrollments in that period. At the beginning of the period, 47 per cent of all American college students were in public institutions; at the end of it the public colleges enrolled 60 per cent of all college students. That trend will almost certainly continue. Figures from American Council on Education (n.d.).

affected by, first, the type of purpose that the college has determined for itself or has had set for it by outside forces and, second, the distinctiveness of the character and image of the college.

Type of purpose. — Student cultures are located within larger systems that vary widely in purpose, for American colleges are up to quite different things. The most important division in purpose, in the middle of the twentieth century, is between colleges intent on providing a liberal education and those committed to serving diverse public interests. Most colleges that in practice restrict their effort to the liberal arts purpose are private, four-year institutions. The service enterprises are predominantly public, state, or municipal and include as major forms the state university, the four-year teachers or state college, and the two-year junior college. Although the service enterprises dominate the American scene in number of students enrolled,[17] the liberal arts colleges possess an older tradition and stand high in public esteem.

In the colleges committed to liberal education, the academic and collegiate orientations have long competed for the time and energy of the student, largely excluding the vocational and the nonconformist orientations. Students have readily identified themselves with these colleges; the conflict has come over whether they would study or play, be seriously interested in the traditional curriculum or develop their characters through sports, women, and leisure. The academic seriousness of these places has been commonly compromised by necessity. Liberal arts colleges have been enormously competitive, and, like small businesses, many have been pushed to the wall by lack of clients and shortage of resources. For example, only twenty out of some forty colleges established in Ohio by Protestant churches before the Civil War have survived. Until recently, the average college has had to recruit its small student body from a very small

[17] In 1961 – 62 the three big vocational fields, business and commerce, education, and engineering, accounted for almost half (48 per cent) of all the bachelor's and first professional degrees awarded by American colleges and universities. In that year the number of bachelor's degrees awarded in business and commerce alone outnumbered the first degrees awarded in English, history, and mathematics combined (American Council on Education, n.d.).

proportion of the adolescents in a delineated area. In this economy of scarcity, formal controls and expectations were adjusted to what the market would tolerate. Students came ready to prolong adolescent play; the authority of officials was checked by the need to hold their limited clientele if there were to be a college at all. Later we shall suggest other reasons, especially those of administrative interest, for the long-standing strength of the collegiate orientation.

The collegiate subculture has predominated in the liberal arts college during the last seventy-five to one hundred years, with exceptions occurring only where a stern religiousness has been maintained or where the college has been able to select and hold an especially serious segment of the college-going population. The ideal of the secular liberal arts college necessitated finding the kinds of students and patrons who would support the intellectual life in the face of the competing collegiate interests. As we will later see, a few colleges have built such bases through heroic effort. For most colleges, however, deliberate containment or reduction of the collegiate subculture has depended on a state of the market in which a high demand for entry into college makes selection for seriousness as well as ability a realistic alternative.

The colleges committed to servicing the needs of broad publics have long had vocational subcultures contending and mixing with the collegiate and the academic. Vocational values in the student body have been encouraged by these colleges' intention and practice of diversifying the curriculum to meet the training requirements of specific fields of work.[18] If we ask why large numbers of students in certain state colleges and universities are vocationally oriented, the first answer is that these enter-

---

[18] A recent vigorous statement by University of Wisconsin President Conrad A. Elvehjem (reported by University of California, 1959*b*) to this effect sees vocationalism as basic to the impact of college on the student and the nation.

It is almost a heresy, these days, for a college president or even an industrial leader to suggest the major effort of higher education should be to fit individuals to play a practical role in our society. The popular chant concerns itself with putting individuals "on the path of maturity and wisdom." This is a noble goal, too. But it is my contention, and I believe a basic tenet of the Land-Grant idea, that this can be accomplished, and accomplished best, while preparing the individual for a practical contribution to mankind.

prises are strongly and directly committed to occupational train-ing.[19] Students would need to deviate widely from the norms of their environment if they were to involve themselves in student academic subcultures while majoring in such fields as accounting, real estate, and hotel management.[20] The purpose and related practices of the service college are in large part a basic condition of student vocationalism.

Then, too, the curricula that are directly occupational have been not only more practical but generally easier than the liberal arts disciplines (the humanities, the natural sciences, and the social sciences). A college, and especially a university, is an aggregation of "hard" and "soft" fields. The "soft" majors reduce the academic pressure on students, lightening the work load for large numbers and allowing some to remain in college who other-wise would fail. In this way, the softer majors become impor-tant curricular props to collegiate culture, providing special sanctuaries for those primarily oriented to collegiate life, as well as those oriented to "diploma" rather than "skill" vocationalism. "Soft" majors and low standards in parts of the comprehensive service campus allow for a mass version of the gentleman's C. In brief, the nature of the curriculum affects student culture. This is most apparent and important on the diversified campuses where occupational fields have been the source and support of vocationalism and where fields low in intellectual content have supported the collegiate as well as the vocational culture.

Distinctiveness of character.—Colleges also vary markedly in the distinctiveness of their character. For example, Reed College is a special kind of place and is widely perceived as unique, while many state colleges are perceived indistinctly and

---

[19] "Such impressions, such challenges to a man's spirit, such intimations of privilege and duty are not to be found in the work and obligations of professional and technical schools" (Wilson. 1925).

[20] College football coaches are generally conscious of the extent to which sports are public relations and define themselves in part as public relations men. One of the best in the business, J. L. Kuharich (1960) offered this description: "A football coach has to touch so many bases and be so many things. . . . He has to be a psychologist, a public relations man and a philosopher, to mention only a few. He must have a fine conception of public opinion and be able to pacify the public. You might say it's a profession within a profession."

as more interchangeable with other members of a class. Degree of distinction plays an important part in shaping student culture, for distinctive colleges are more able to set the terms of existence for subcultures than are colleges of indistinct character. Special character thrusts the organization more deeply into the lives of its participants, in part because it offers a clearcut image with which to identify, and in part because special character is cause and effect of a unified system of action.

This point may be clarified if we look briefly at the historical development of distinctive character. A college may achieve distinctiveness through a slow, largely unplanned evolution; usually, however, a distinctive outlook is created quite purposefully within a brief creative period at the college's inception, or during a later moment of transformation and redefinition. Colleges with a sturdy, unified culture are generally able to point to a defining era when new purposes were set in motion over the obstacles of established thought and practice. And the student culture is caught up in the creation or change and deeply affected by it.

To take a specific example: the present distinctive character of Swarthmore College dates from the early 1920's, when a new president, Frank Aydelotte, introduced a modified Oxford program of reading for honors, recruited students nationally on open scholarship, and transformed the college generally from a local, family-oriented enterprise into a national intellectual center. The student culture of the college was transformed as part of the general change in character; indeed, the whole experiment would have failed if the students' style of life had not been radically altered. The student culture changed from predominantly collegiate to predominantly academic between 1920 and the early 1930's.

This was accomplished by means of a number of specific alterations that supported one another. The college sought out a larger number of bright, serious students, especially ones with a capacity for leadership. It rapidly expanded the number of students who were in the honors program in their last two years from a handful of students in 1922–23 to a fourth of the juniors and seniors in 1925 and approximately 40 per cent in 1930. The administration and the new student body together gradually but drastically modified student social activities, for example, eliminating freshman hazing, cutting down the number of fraternity dances, and, in 1933, abolishing sororities. The administration and faculty also gradually assumed control over athletics, eliminating an area of collegiate life in which students and alumni had had much influence by transforming a program of big-time intercollegiate sports into one of intramural and intercollegiate sports for the student amateur. Through these and allied changes, extracurricular activity was subordinated to and integrated with a life of serious study. Intellectuality became a virtue with much of the excitement of competitive sports transferred to the winning of academic honor. The dominant values of the student culture today stem from these considerable alterations made a quarter of a century ago.

Swarthmore illustrates the strength and integration of a distinctive institutional character; it also suggests ways in which a central college culture may become embodied in the structural foundations of the student subsystems. Central values are built into a college in tradition and legend, in administrative arrangements, in emphases of the curriculum. Crucial in influencing the tone of the student culture is the extent to which official values are reflected in the organization of the extracurricular. Swarthmore, as we indicated above, found it necessary to reorganize social and athletic activities to render them supportive rather than subversive of academic work. This entailed personnel and financial changes: a critical event at Swarthmore was a shifting between 1927 and 1933 of the financial support of the sports program from gate receipts to a college subsidy. The college put the extracurricular on a different foundation, one that robbed sports and social life of the dynamics that ordinarily tend toward independence and dominance. After reorganization, the extracurricular was no longer so extra to, or competitive with, the academic.

In the broad spectrum of American colleges, Swarthmore is an extreme case of academic purpose permeating and controlling the extracurricular. It throws into relief the common situation of the diffusely oriented college or university that is dominated by a strong collegiate culture, much of which is grounded in organized but non-academic segments of the system. Here, typically, many student activities are supported by income from big sports, chiefly football games, and are managed by professional personnel of the central student organization, e.g., the executive director of the "associated students." The extracurricular staff is a quasi-independent segment of the college that is strongly linked to the outside; for example, many interests of the athletic director orient him toward alumni and the gate. Much of the extracurricular is public relations and is covered in the sports section and social pages of the newspaper rather than in the educational news.[21] As a result, the extracurricular activities of many universities become hooked into the mass media and the entertainment world and take on some of their coloration, e.g., commercialism and the star system, with leading performers becoming valuable properties.

The major sports on the large comprehensive campuses are both a source and a symbol of the dominance of collegiate culture. Their institutionalization in revenue and personnel, as well as in the sentiments of students, alumni, and larger publics, resists any attempt to reduce the weight and thrust of the collegiate values. The sports and their related structural props represent the division of the college as a whole – the coaches and directors from the professors, games from classes, weekends from weekdays – that parallels the division between the collegiate and academic student subcultures. When the extracurricular is thus organized as a thing apart, it "represents" the official college culture principally in reflecting the attitude that constituencies must be allowed their social events and spectator sports to maintain their support.[22] This outlook allows for an exchange, largely undeliberate, whereby professors may go their own way while students and alumni go theirs: professors to research, and other activities free of student contact, and students and alumni to the collegiate round of life.

[21] The bearing of faculty and administrative interests on collegiate culture will be more fully discussed later.

[22] On the distinction between local and cosmopolitan orientations in college faculties, see Gouldner (1957). See also Caplow and McGee (1958).

The integration or non-integration of the extracurricular with the academic is thus an important aspect of the character of the college. The degree of this integration also affects the distinctiveness of the institution. Distinction has other important effects, notably upon the recruitment of students. A distinctive college projects public images that attract some students and repel others, cutting through the potential applicants to procure students of a particular orientation (Clark, 1960).

When the student culture on an American campus is dominantly academic, the strength of the academic will partly be founded in the impressions held by those applying for admission; serious students consistently find their way to a serious college as a result of self-selection steered by public image. A collegiate culture may also be based in part on a strong image, although generally today it is connected with a mixed institutional character and reputation, as in the case of the state university campus that appears as many things to many men. Finally, in colleges of non-distinction—extreme cases of the service enterprise—students are attracted because of geographic convenience, minimal cost, low standards, and an array of occupational curricula. Here, in the absence of a clear or distinctive image of the institution, the consumer-client comes to obtain his vocational training or diploma without much concern for the name of the college.

Objective Interests

From features of colleges that are parts of their historically derived ethos we turn to characteristics that reflect the real or natural interests of college personnel. The interests of men are affected by their position in the social structure—their social background, present role, and anticipated career. These material interests in turn shape their concerns, their definitions of what ought to be done. Here we try to suggest some ways that certain interests and related orientations of professors and administrators contribute to the major types of student subcultures.

Faculty interests and orientations. — In order to perform effectively, a college needs diverse orientations in its faculty; these include teaching, administration, and research and scholarly study. Colleges vary greatly in the distribution and relative strength of these different orientations and in the extent to which the orientations are rewarded. Four-year colleges largely reward attention to the student, and universities reward orientation to one's discipline or profession.[23] The kind of professor idealized in the small liberal arts college may be the teacher-scholar, the teacher-counselor-friend, or just plain teacher, but in any case the norm emphasizes teaching and points to the student. In these colleges developing the undergraduate is what the college is largely about. The university is involved in many other operations, being primarily a center of research, scholarship, and professional training; close attention to the education of the individual undergraduate student is not generally a prominent part of the professor model. There are few logs with anybody sitting on them in the undergraduate colleges of large universities (Kerr, 1962).

The point bearing on student culture is that faculty members' interests vary from a singleness of purpose in shaping the undergraduate student to a complex of interests in which the student plays a very small part. At one extreme there is the teacher who deeply involves himself in the lives of students, seeing them frequently and informally in diverse situations and being on call at any hour for advice and support. Here faculty interests encourage an interpenetration of faculty and student cultures. This may result in the faculty members' being "captured" by student collegiate values, as well as their introducing scholarly values into the student subcultures in which they take part.

At the other extreme is the professor who teaches as little as possible and then is off to interests that separate him from students, often but not always the pursuit of research and scholarly writing. These interests, reflecting an orientation to the cosmopolitan world of scholarship, science, and distant peers, and a

[23] "An emphasis on contributions to one's discipline as over against good teaching and concern with undergraduates pervades our university faculties and even some of our college faculties. It cannot be otherwise, since career advancement for faculty members depends far more on the former than the latter. As long as this situation prevails, the interest of faculties in undergraduates is unlikely to increase." (Sussman, 1960, p. 95). For the influence of major research programs on undergraduate education, see Orlans (1962).

career pattern of movement from college to college, tend to reduce faculty-student relations to interaction in the classroom.[24] Cosmopolitan interests are an important source of the schism between faculty and student cultures typically found in the state university. In pulling the teachers away from the students, the faculty's professional interests promote the rise and persistence of an autonomous student culture which is then filled in by student interests. These may be intellectual, as is often the case around many European universities, in which serious students model themselves after the distant, professionally committed faculty. In this country, however, such interests will more likely be vocational or collegiate. Then, especially in the case of the collegiate, the autonomy of the student culture blunts faculty influence.

In the strain between professionalism and localism in faculty interests, some faculty members effect a compromise wherein they have many avenues of contact with students while sustaining a professionally rewarding career. A few such men are found in the better small colleges and are afforded high status because they are both professionally competent and locally committed. They are also found in the large universities, where they rarely receive the highest esteem for their involvement with undergraduates.

In general, however, most faculty members do not balance these interests in a rough parity but come down heavily on the interests that are rewarded by the organization and are promising for a career. Thus, small-college faculties tend to be strongholds of personal and particularistic relations with students, and university staffs, centers of impersonal relations and universalistic criteria. The one generally produces some faculty understanding and penetration of student life; the other is based on and reinforces social distance between faculty and students. The university is also the home of the expert, and the academic and intellec-

---

[24] Lest this account seem suffused with small-college bias, we should point out that many small colleges are societies of containment, in which weak faculties go along with adolescent play in return for obedience to traditional belief and morality.

tual distance between the expert and the student is so great that it is only bridged with difficulty.

Within and between faculties, basic trends in higher education are producing a greater differentiation between those who attend closely to students and those who do not. There is increased professionalism in the university and in many liberal arts colleges, with the ideal of the expert in ascendance over the ideal of the cultivated man.[25] The training of students as experts requires little attention to their life outside the classroom and laboratory. Also, increasing size promotes greater division of function and interest within and between colleges; we may soon expect an even greater distance between faculties that are strictly liberal arts and those that are heavily vocational, as well as between the professors who have the highest academic status and those who man the undergraduate classroom.

Administrative interests. — What are the material interests of a college administration and how do these bear on students? Like management elsewhere, one interest lies in the orderly conduct of internal affairs — at the minimum, chaos reduced to confusion. College managers in this country are charged with regulating a system in which hundreds of young men and women are simultaneously clients, participants, and wards, with the result that the proper ordering of students looms large in internal affairs. Administrators also directly bear the brunt of demands made on the system by outsiders, from parental complaints about the care and feeding of a particular student to the often vigorous efforts of major interest groups, such as the alumni or local businessmen, to shape the outlook of the college as a

---

[25]Some forty years ago Max Weber (Gerth and Mills, 1946) made the following observation.

Behind all the present discussions of the foundations of the educational system, the struggle of the "specialist type of man" against the older type of "cultivated man" is hidden at some decisive point. This fight is determined by the irresistibly expanding bureaucratization of all public and private relations of authority and by the ever-increasing importance of expert and specialized knowledge. This fight intrudes into all intimate cultural questions.

These comments are not less relevant in America in the 1960's.

whole. The administration is also responsible for college finances and the recruitment of students. In short, it needs to be aware of the steps necessary to placate a public, find a donor, or cultivate a constituency.

The interests of the administration and segments of the faculty in financial support, student supply, internal order, and public approval have favored "conservative" student cultures in the majority of colleges—cultures that contain perspectives rather than stimulate and civilize them, cultures of custodial care rather than of intellectual ferment.

Collegiate cultures are ordinarily seen as frustrations of academic purpose that college staffs, administration and faculty alike, have long labored to overcome. But these collegiate cultures have certain conveniences: they are routine, predictable, and acceptable to important constituencies. Therefore, on many campuses, they are not only condoned but officially supported by administrators and influential segments of the faculty. Consider the relationship of administrative interests to student government in this regard. A collegiate student government is not very dangerous administratively, since it avoids controversial ideas and political action. Its main interests are social and it lends itself to the monitoring of student social activities.[26]

The surveillance of student morals that is expected of college administrations by outsiders is a time-consuming task, one that is generally delegated to an administrative unit, usually the office of the dean of students, that stands apart from the faculty. In turn, the routine work of policing student life is further delegated to the student council, the interfraternity council, the individual student house. The making and enforcing of rules at this level is supervised and coordinated through an officialdom of assistant deans, house mothers, and hall advisors. When student organizations are primarily oriented toward the routine social problems of the student community, they are likely to be a grass-roots arm of the official control apparatus.

[26] "The first half of the twentieth century saw student government evolve on most American campuses, but its function has been chiefly that of supervision of student social activities" (Klopf, 1960).

At most colleges, student government is either explicitly defined or implicitly considered by officials to be an integral part of the administration.[27] The collegiate and vocationally oriented students are more likely to accept this definition than are those who are intellectually inclined. The vocationals are not interested, the collegiates care only that their social life not be too greatly hampered. Academics and nonconformists, however, may or may not be interested in student government, but when they are they tend to relate it to outside issues, hence involve it in "politics." The tendency of liberal intellectual students to turn a student government into a political arena, taking stands on controversial issues, sharply conflicts with the desire of administrators to use it as an administrative unit, one that works only on campus and within prescribed areas of non-political activity. The kind of student government most threatening to administration is one entailing serious political involvement, for here a subsystem of the college will be taking stands and entering into alliances that irritate segments of the outside community, including those which are sources of financial and moral support.

Powerful traditions and outside groups work to convince college administrations, and often faculties, that collegiate cultures have their justification. The collegiate life has long prepared students socially for business and the professions; it has been supported by alumni associations, national fraternal organizations, and spectator publics. It has been the style of life expected of "kids" in college. Academic, nonconformist, and vocational subcultures, in contrast, have not had such widespread social and cultural supports. At the same time, internally, the collegiate culture has been a reasonably well-ordered system of adolescent play and training in social skills, which also generates only relatively minor collective transgressions (e.g., panty raids) that come to public view. A tradition that is publicly sup-

[27] The University of California (1959*a*), for example, makes an explicit definition: "Student governments are established by the University for the purpose of conducting student affairs on the campuses." The governments have their power through a "delegation of University administrative authority." This means, in respect to controversial issues, that "the student government, as any other integral part of the University administration, must also refrain from taking positions on such issues."

ported and internally orderly is not easily laid aside; unless powerful counterforces enter, there will be good reasons to condone it.

Administrative interest in internal order and external equilibrium has also supported the big-time sports aspect of the collegiate subculture. A big intercollegiate sports program centering around football serves several purposes. For one thing, it organizes and channels the energies and high spirits of young men in reasonably orderly and non-violent ways. The early history of American colleges, before the advent of organized sports, was full of student violence, directed at each other, at the faculty, the institution, and the "townies" (Earnest, 1953; Hofstadter and Hardy, 1952). Brawls, riots, even knifings and shootings, were common; the policing of student life, the sheer maintenance of order, was a major and onerous task of the faculties and administrators. Intramural sports drain off some of the high spirits and physical aggressiveness. Intercollegiate sports do that and more: they encourage strong feelings of local patriotism, of identification with the institution and against "the enemy," and thus focus aggressive feelings outward away from the college and its staff, at the same time that they confine it within the rules of the game.

Moreover, the powerful institutional identifications thus promoted become the basis of continuing ties between the institution and its alumni. For many alumni, particularly those in nonintellectual occupations, the football team is the most important continuing link to the alma mater. A loyal and active alumni, of course, is a primary source of funds for private colleges, and of both funds and political support for public colleges and universities. Since this is the case, only strong alternative sources of support, or strong purposes in conflict with big-time sports, will dispose an administrator to diminish an already established big-time sports program. Aydelotte, for example, had both when he de-emphasized football at Swarthmore.

Thus, in brief, student government that restricts itself to student social life, and a sports program that excites large numbers of students and outsiders, are both likely to find favor with administrators interested in reducing student disorderliness while seeking greater support among external non-intellectual groups. When intercollegiate sports first began, the reduction of student disorder was their principal basis for administrative support. But as they became spectator sports, public relations became the most important source of the encouragement the collegiate sub-culture has received from many college and university admini-strators. This support is probably most vigorous and enthusiastic when, additionally, the president shares some of the sentiments of his non-intellectual constituencies—their distaste for irrever ence, political radicalism, intellectuality, beards, and bare feet.

The foregoing analysis of a tendency for administrative in-terests to support collegiate values applies, we believe, to a large number of American colleges over the last seventy-five years. In a few cases, however, vigorous counterforces have made other interests dominant. Interests are shaped by values, and some colleges have become so deeply committed to the in-tellectual life that academic values determine the critical de-cisions of the administrator. For example, Reed College has been seriously academic from the day it opened its doors. An almost fanatical pursuit of academic quality, with sports and social life largely excluded, early became part of its character; the college's senior faculty became firmly wedded to this outlook and admin-istration has been shaped accordingly. It has not been reward-ing for Reed administrators or segments of the faculty to seek intercollegiate sports and a diversified social life for students, even though it has long been clear that these changes would have helped public relations and financing. Such moves are considered outrageously inappropriate to the college's true character, as seen by most of the staff and alumni and the students recruited by the academic image. In short, the college's historically de-rived and salient commitment to academic excellence steers administrative interests.

Administrative interests have also been decisively swayed toward academic quality in some colleges by virtue of a struc-ture of authority in which faculty are highly influential, if not dominant. Authority may be so extensively in the hands of the faculty that administrative impulses to adjust to outside pres-sures are restrained. When the faculty essentially determines what is to be done, then the need for administrators to adjust to faculty expectations outweighs the necessity of rapport with the trustees and the public. In some colleges the faculty defines itself as carrier of the college's traditional culture and sees to it that the administration does not deviate radically. A strong faculty, however, is usually a conservative force, and it may work to preserve a tradition of mediocrity and parochialism as well as an institutional commitment to scholarship and high intellectual standards.

The most important counterforce to collegiate adaptation by the administration and the faculty today is the greatly increased number of recruits. Many colleges are moving into a relatively permanent condition of student glut, a situation that diminishes their dependence on traditional constituencies. Before 1945, even the elite colleges of the country were generally constrained by the number of applications for admission. Prestige colleges before World War II had only three contenders for every two places; in 1959 they averaged about four applicants per place. Amherst, for example, had 371 applicants for 232 openings (0.6:1) in 1941, but in 1959 was able to choose among 1,677 applicants to fill 259 openings (6.5:1). Princeton had 925 candidates for 644 places (1.4:1) in 1941; 3,213 for 757 (4.2:1) in 1959 (Bloomgarden, 1960). Princeton officials have reported that from 1921 to 1941 the college essentially had no choice, never refusing admission "to boys with good character testimonials and adequate scholastic preparation" (Jacobs, 1958).

Now the colleges of modest to high reputation are in an economy of abundance that permits selection for high aptitude and seriousness and a stiffening of the requirements for completion. And colleges are encouraged to use academic aptitude and achievement as selection criteria because these measures are felt to be most legitimate in light of the democratic belief in equality of opportunity, the increased emphasis on utilizing talent, and the preference of college staffs for intelligent students.[28] By widening administrative discretion in selecting and retaining

[28] Voluntary contributions to American colleges and universities nearly doubled in the four years 1954–55 to 1958–59 (American Council on Education, n.d., p. 216). Insofar as this represents increased diversity as well as amount of support, it should also work to increase the freedom of colleges to define their own goals and programs.

students, heavy demand leaves administrators freer to respond to their own inclinations toward quality, to faculty desires for a tougher tone, and to public calls for the pursuit of excellence.

In addition, the national temper since World War II has encouraged college officials to become impatient with the traditional "rah-rah" form of collegiate life, which increasingly is seen as a foolish luxury that the seriousness of a permanent Cold War no longer allows colleges to afford. The collegiate culture has also lost some of its appeal as a mechanism for controlling student energies, as the academically and vocationally oriented students of today increasingly discipline themselves.

Authority Structure

We now turn to several major structural aspects of colleges, the first being the distribution of authority. Authority in academic organizations has been little explored, and we do not propose a general analysis; our limited purpose is to discuss briefly two ways in which the structure of authority shapes student culture. One is through the support given to different values and interests; the other, through the involvement of students in college affairs.

Support of values and interests. — Authority takes many forms in academic communities — control by traditional constituency, lay trustee, autocratic or charismatic president, bureaucratic official, or academic colleague. The secularization of American higher education has been accompanied by a change from traditional and autocratic forms of authority, such as the church and the college president, to the bureaucratic and colleague types: the administration and the faculty as a whole. The latter two types now actively contend with one another; today the conflict appears principally to take the form of the administration and governing board on the one side appealing to a bureaucratic principle of a legally based hierarchy of authority, and the professors on the other holding to the principle of a self-governing body of academic colleagues. In the main, faculties have won some control over the content of the curriculum and are increasing their influence in the selection and retention of faculty personnel (Clark, 1961). But colleges are exceedingly diverse in authority structure, ranging from complete control by trustee and president to a middle ground where the faculty has some important decision-making power, to an extreme where the faculty chooses personnel and sets the budget as well as determines the curriculum.

There is apparently no binding connection between types of authority and types of student culture. Strong play cultures are found on campuses where faculty control is strong as well as where it is weak. Dominating presidents may support vocational or academic or collegiate student interests. Even so, certain tendencies and typical connections may be observed.

1. The four-year state colleges that are characterized by student vocationalism tend to have strong presidential authority and a bureaucratic structure. This often stems, in part, from the state colleges having been in the past a normal school and then a teachers college, earlier stages when the faculty was exceedingly weak. It is also related to close supervision by the state legislature or department of education, and to conceptions of efficient utilization of teachers in which scholarship and research are viewed as luxuries. But as the state college attempts to move beyond a narrow vocationalism to the status of a comprehensive college with some commitment to the liberal arts, the faculty tends to challenge the hierarchy of control. The faculty begins to compare its privileges and responsibilities to those of the faculties at the state university and leading private colleges. It wants an academic senate and control over the curriculum, and soon some faculty members are even proclaiming that administrators are incompetent to judge professors. The administrators also come to learn that able scholars will not remain in a barony, and in the push to become a liberal arts college and then a university they accommodate to some faculty authority. Broadly, vocationalism and size urge "efficient," hence bureaucratic, organization, but liberal education and the push for academic status and quality press for a "community of scholars."

2. The private liberal arts colleges that are characterized by academic student cultures and high status tend to have strong faculty control. Many such colleges have been pulled from a traditional localism to national prominence by vigorous, even

charismatic, presidents, undergoing a transformation in character under a benevolent dictator. This is transitional authority. After the revolution comes consolidation; succeeding presidents are expected to preserve and administer the successful experiment. The faculty recruited by the charismatic leader, or attracted by the changes he made, takes over after he leaves. Their self-appointed role is to insure the continuity of the new character of the college, and their authority takes on this conserving function. Often a faculty council, or some other representative body of the faculty, becomes the key policy-making unit. In other cases, authority becomes lodged formally and informally in the hands of department heads and senior department members.

In either case, strong faculty control henceforth plays a role in attracting and binding faculty. Some men come because they are impressed by the college's combination of high status, distinctive name, strong faculty government and correlated freedom from administrative and lay control; they remain, in part, because the running of the college becomes "their" business. In a sense, a faculty that captures control is also captured in return, committed by involvement in policy-making—after a half-dozen years, a man has often invested too much of himself to leave. These tendencies can be of enormous advantage to a college in attracting and retaining a good teaching faculty despite a poor salary scale. This binding effect of faculty control appears to work in the direction of supporting vigorous academic subcultures in the student body by holding on a campus faculty members with serious intellectual interests.

3. The universities that are characterized by enormous size and a marked bifurcation of faculty and student interests are also the systems in which authority has the least consistent relationship to student culture. In some state universities the faculty has strong control while in others they have only weak authority and afford little protection for the individual. As noted above, the extent of faculty authority affects the quality of staff recruitment. But the locus of authority in the university does not matter to the same degree for the attraction of students and the nature of their undergraduate life. Weak or strong colleague control, for example, may coexist with a collegiate student culture. As we

previously remarked, the undergraduate student and the professor largely go their separate ways in the university; the distribution of authority among trustees, adminstration, and faculty little affects this underlying divergence of interest.

Faculty authority is most likely to be reflected in the student world when faculty influence encourages a tougher selection and retention policy; but faculties and administrations perhaps do not diverge so greatly in their wish for a general upgrading, and strong faculty authority probably changes the pressure in this direction only in modest degree on the large, comprehensive campus. In any case, changes made under the authority of the administration or the faculty will generally work around the edges of student life, changing selection slightly or establishing an honors program for a small segment. Such moves may eventually have large consequences, but in the university, with its impersonal relations and its wide divergence in faculty and student interests, the strength of the various student subworlds — academic, collegiate, vocational, nonconformist — is more dependent on basic commitments and general social trends than on who has power within.

Involvement of students. — A second important aspect of academic control is the extent to which authority becomes lodged in the hands of students. Again, the variation on the American scene is great, extending from student governments that are no more than playful mockery to ones in which students have a dominant voice in a wide range of affairs and serve on committees of the faculty and the administration. The modal type is one in which student government is given the appearance of authority but in fact has little control, the college being either unable or unwilling to stand the costs of error and controversy. As suggested earlier, colleges and universities that have long accommodated to collegiate play have not found it equally rewarding to suffer strong student government. Weak student government supports the tendency for student involvement in the running of campus affairs to be minor. American students, little disposed by background and orientation to enter campus politics, turn further away when student government is seen as superficial. Weak student authority, we suggest, thus closes a main avenue of involvement—a road that encourages identification with the college and involvement with ideas, hence supports academic subcultures.

The effect of involving students actively in the formation of policy at the high and middle as well as the lowest levels of administration may be observed in such a college as Antioch, which has had a "community government" in operation for over a quarter of a century. Here student government is ideologically and structurally linked to the running of the whole enterprise, supporting and partly redeeming a definition of the college as community. According to doctrine, students, faculty members, and administrators participate as equals in the community government. Although this is not fully realized in practice—the faculty being more equal than the students—the students have the majority vote on the community council and in the committees of the community government. Their minority membership on faculty committees also insures, at the least, that they are informed on affairs of the official college and that their views are heard. The elaborate system of committees found in the college's several overlapping governments has the function of involving students and providing avenues of participation for interest groups. Political militants can find their way to a civil-rights committee, for example, and there badger the faculty about their excluding students from the faculty lounge as well as to mobilize concern about segregation in the South. The joint student-faculty membership on committees insures that some students relate closely to some of the faculty outside the classroom and, at least part of the time, on meaningful issues. By offering actual participation in campus decision-making to some students and the symbols of that participation to all, Antioch's political structure becomes a dragnet of involvement, encouraging civic interest and helping to commit students deeply to the college. With a bright, liberal student body, it is also not unrelated to their involvement with serious ideas.

The colleges of strong student vocationalism appear generally to be at the other extreme in the character of their student government. The working, commuting student at the state college has no time for interest in campus matters, social or political, especially if he is supporting a family as well. Also, control over all important matters tends to remain in the hands of such distant authorities as the state board of education and with the top members of the administrative staff who are held accountable by the higher state officials. Thus one of the principal means of involvement is largely shut off, with little likelihood that identification with the college will be generated by civic participation or that interest in ideas will be excited by contact with genuine issues of social and political action.

Size and Complexity

We turn now to a quite different matter, the effect of organizational scale. The trend in western society toward increasing size and complexity in formal organization is nowhere more apparent than in American higher education: a large college before the Civil War had 600 students, and most were much smaller, while today central campuses of state universities run to 30,000. Large scale in college organization is permanently with us. Campuses of several thousand students or more will soon accommodate the overwhelming majority of college students. For the form and content of student life, nothing appears to be of greater consequence.

In any large organization that works on people rather than on products, thousands of invividuals must be admitted, classified, treated, and ejected. This is generally done by routinizing procedures and processing people in batches. In the large university, impersonal batching is reflected in the registration line, the objective test, and the mass graduation. With increasing size, there is also a tendency for the faculty member to face more students in the classroom than ever before and to interact less with the individual student outside the classroom. With the TV camera and taped lecture, students may need a special appointment in order to meet the man. This mass processing does not seem to encourage a serious concern with ideas on the part of most students. Routinized classwork, for example, can be completed without serious thought. Increasing scale, it would appear, is most appropriate for a consumer orientation toward college and primarily promotes vocational subcultures. The tendency for increasing size to weaken social ties, turning groups into aggregations, leads toward the atomized vocational subcultures.

Conversely, vocationalism encourages growth in size and complexity. Business associations, professional bodies, and other interest groups that see the college as a training center encourage colleges to proliferate occupational curricula. Students mindful of upward mobility seek occupational preparation in a host of fields. Occupational training in a complex society is indeed efficiently handled by large enterprises tooled to train large numbers in diverse fields.

If increasing scale primarily promotes vocational subcultures in the student body, it secondarily supports the continuation of the collegiate life, principally through a weakened connection between the academic life and leisure. Large scale tends to separate work from non-work, teaching and learning from what goes on outside the lecture hall. In a society where intellectual values have a marginal existence, it is not to be expected that the interests of the majority of entering students are intellectual; and many of those so inclined seek the small schools that have a liberal arts image. Those finding their way to the large institutions have predominantly a vocational interest, but some are also inclined to have fun, college-style, before work and marriage. Also the faculty members typically do little in these large places to determine the shape of the student's social life for, as previously pointed out, it is not in their realm of interest or authority. The collegiate world, in its less rah-rah forms, will continue to receive some administrative support in the very large places if for no other reason than that it helps the administration to handle the overwhelming problems of student housing and social life. The collegiate life also helps to soften the harsh contours of vocationalism, offering some leisurely play around the edges of the campus, and making the large college or university appear more like its smaller, historical antecedents.

Small size in college organization usually inhibits impersonal processing, for participation in smaller systems is more likely to have community qualities. Size and residence, the latter to be discussed later, appear to be the most important determinants of where colleges fall along a continuum from community to bureaucracy. At the extreme of community, approached principally through small size and residential facilities, the interaction of students, faculty, and administration is intense and informal, and judgments are particularistic, as faculty and students respond to one another as personalities ("she's bright but erratic and would profit from work with . . ."). The individual is known across the system; e.g., death is a campus event. Importantly, social and academic activity are integrated. Here the faculty has some chance to shape student culture and educate liberally through personal influence and example. But for occupational training in a complex society, such colleges are expensive, inappropriately oriented, and relatively unspecialized.

The bureaucratic end of the continuum is reached chiefly through large size and off-campus living. Here interaction is formal and segmented, universalistic criteria are used throughout the system, and academic activity is separated from the social. Teaching and studying are jobs, the personality of the student is little involved, and death is an announcement in the newspaper. Here the conditions are favorable not for liberal education but for occupational training, for such a college can offer expert instruction and service in a large number of fields.

The absolute size of colleges and universities may be a seriously misleading factor, however, because its effect on interpersonal relations and student cultures changes markedly with the nature of the organization substructure. Harvard's house system clearly "reduces" its size, and some state universities are psychologically and socially smaller than others of similar size because of the way that campus subunits ("colleges," "houses") substructure an otherwise loose aggregation. An effective substructure provides groups small enough to encourage networks of face-to-face relationships and to prevent the "we-they" dichotomy between the students and the faculty that inheres in large scale. It offers systems of action that are within the human scale of observation and comprehension, especially the limited scale of the adolescent and inexperienced adult. At the same time, when the smaller systems are part of a large college or university, the larger setting may also offer a cosmopolitan environment in which students can explore a wide range of experiences (Riesman, 1960).

Important to the psychological and social effectiveness of

organization substructure are the criteria on which it is based; most important may be the homogeneity or heterogeneity of interest. The diversity of interests and orientations found in the total college may be reproduced in the subunits by random assignment of students. Then the large is writ small, no small change in itself. Alternatively, the substructure may be formed along broad lines of shared interests, causing subgroups to be different from the whole. We suspect that the interest substructures, rather than those that mirror the whole, provide the more meaningful centers of interaction and identification, since the subunits can then acquire a distinctive character. Certainly, diversity in a student group or residence hall may contribute to the liberal education of its members, and may break down the parochial ties of class, field of study, or the like; this apparently is one function of the Harvard houses, as Jencks and Riesman (1962) describe them. On the other hand, without the tutorial system and the other mechanisms through which Harvard's houses link leisure to learning, the "diversity" resulting from random assignments to residence halls may lead to a common culture rooted in the lowest common denominator of student interests, and so prevent the development of intellectual communities among the students. Groupings based on natural common interests appear to be viable bases for intense interaction and interpersonal commitment; drama and art students illustrate this point on a number of campuses. The problem is to hook the substructure into natural interests (engage motivation institutionally), while at the same time leaving participation sufficiently voluntary and open so that the subunits do not encapsulate the student.

In the main, the universities whose size threatens the viability of student subsystems, especially the academic, have attempted little substructuring along these or other lines. Faculties have not been markedly interested, and college managements and outside supporters have held to logics of economy and efficiency that favor standardized procedure. College comptrollers, for example, do not like to work with diversely organized subunits.

At the same time, many small colleges worry about the consequences of large size every time they contemplate expanding by one or two hundred students, concerned that the character of the campus, especially the closeness of personal relations, will be changed. One answer now being offered to the problem of how to grow and yet stay small is a federation of colleges—essentially a multiplication of small, distinct units rather than the continued growth of one. The five colleges of the Pomona-Claremont complex are one such example, Wesleyan University's "College Plan" is another.[29] Wesleyan is attempting a reorganization that will allow the enterprise as a whole to grow larger, while newly established "colleges" involve the student in smaller systems of activity focused on a set of related disciplines. Of course, all universities have units called colleges, but in most cases these are largely paper assignments for students. Substructuring makes a difference when it actually changes the nature of involvement. A set of subcolleges on a comprehensive campus may enable students and faculty to keep one another in view and share some academic interests, important conditions for an academic student culture in a society in which collegiate fun and vocationalism come naturally.

Another aspect of college scale is rate of growth, one especially important as the public colleges of the nation move into a period of rapid expansion. Slow growth permits the assimilation of the new to the old: for example, new faculty members may be enculturated slowly and spontaneously to the special values and customs of a college. Rapid growth, on the other hand, reduces this possibility. New faculty come along so fast that there is neither time nor energy for the old staff to orient the new, and the student cultures are likely to be similarly overwhelmed. Administrative time and energy is also pre-empted by the operational problems of growth, e.g., recruiting personnel and expanding facilities to accommodate an annual increase in enrollment of 500 to 1,000 or more. The student cultures that are disrupted may have been primarily academic or primarily collegiate, but the outcome of rapid growth is predictably an increase in the vocational-consumer use of college, centering on the means of career achievement in the general society.

[29] See Subcommittee (1958). The most impressive effort in this direction is being made on the new campus of the University of California at Santa Cruz.

Requirements of Membership

The demands made by colleges on their client-participants also shape the strength of the several subcultures. What does it take to get in, survive, and get out in good standing? Selectivity in American colleges varies from none to severe; length of time in the system, for students in good standing, varies from a semester to four years or longer; and the standards of performance for retention range from subliminal to savage.

Relatively high selectivity seems a necessary but not sufficient condition for the dominance of academic subculture. Selectivity brings a clientele that has the potential ability for difficult study and vigorous intellectual life; the college may also select for seriousness. By contrast, the unselective college will contain a large number of students whose limited ability restricts serious attention to complicated issues and ideas and who have not been encouraged by the rewards of high performance to take on academic values.

The extremes of selection are now found in the public junior college, where open-door admission permits students of all levels of ability and achievement to enter (Clark, 1962), and in the several dozen elite private colleges and universities where applicants outnumber vacancies over four to one and virtually all students are in the upper twenty per cent of college students in ability. The possibility of sharp selection adds greatly to the power of the official staff in shaping student cultures so that they embody academic values. Restraint by recruitment is perhaps the most important means of control by college officials over the values and practices of students.

The length of time that students in good standing spend in college systems also varies enormously. In the elite private colleges, typically 75 to 90 per cent of the students graduate in four years. In state universities, 30 to 60 per cent generally survive. Then there are some state colleges, e.g., in California, that lose over 80 per cent of their students in the first *two* years, and the typical length of stay for students in public junior colleges is from one to one and one-half years. The length of uninterrupted time on campus undoubtedly affects the content of student subcultures as well as their viability. Where students remain in the same college for four years, relationships can grow and ripen. If this is combined with certain other conditions, especially small scale and faculty involvement, it means four years of community-like participation. At the other extreme, relationships are fleeting and are further attenuated by the realization that oneself and one's friends are here today and gone tomorrow to another college, marriage, or a job. Colleges of short duration and heavy dropout take on some of the atmosphere of a distribution center; they resemble the army's replacement depots in which people are classified and sorted.[30] The brief span of time students spend in these colleges virtually precludes the possibility of strong academic subcultures.

Performance standards work similarly. As discussed earlier, low standards of work allow heavy participation in collegiate life. High standards of performance, conversely, make hard work a condition of remaining in the system.[31] Perhaps this simple, obvious fact of academic life should not be obscured by elaborate sociological analysis of student subsystems. Faculties have the means, in the quality and amount of work they require, to weaken seriously the competition of the sidelines and the side shows. The danger here, of course, is that very heavy academic demands can crush the intellectual and cultural play and pursuits that students sustain outside the official structure, alone or in nonconformist subcultures. This is what seems to happen in the best engineering and professional schools.

Autonomy of the System

Academic systems vary enormously in their integration with the environment. Some colleges are almost of another world in their immediate surroundings, geographically detached, intel-

[30] Characteristically, the army replacement depots in World War II destroyed prior institutional loyalties, freeing the soldier for new attachments to his next regular outfit. But no loyalties were generated within or to these organizational decompression chambers (Merton and Rossi, 1957, pp. 225–80). This "degrouping process" makes sense for colleges which are pre-employment training centers, and which are not attempting to socialize students in the special values and perspectives of liberal education. As we might expect, student attachments to San Francisco State are much weaker than comparable ties of students at Reed, Antioch, or Swarthmore.

[31] For a case in which the demands of the curriculum generally predominate over student output norms, see Sussman (1960, p. 44).

lectually alien, and committed to a distinctive style of life; for example, Antioch in conservative southern Ohio, Bennington in small-town Vermont. In contrast, some municipal colleges are continuous with the sidewalk and at one with the environing city, and students in some junior colleges and state colleges have never left high school and home.

A central feature of the campuses that are closely fused with the general society is the considerable extent to which the student is a role, not a personality. This state is most likely to come about where the student does not sleep or play or work, for the most part, at the college. The student living at home, working, and commuting generally attends classes in the role of student-visitor.[32] At San Francisco State College, a typical urban non-residential college, 60 per cent of the students live more than fifteen minutes away from campus, with 30 per cent spending over an hour a day traveling to and from the campus. Only 8 per cent walk or ride a bicycle, while 26 per cent come by bus or trolley and 68 per cent by automobile.

With his life lived off campus and his time and attention caught up in off-campus roles, neither the campus nor the classroom has much chance to engage the student's personality, other than in the special cases in which institutional purpose is unusually striking or student motivation unusually strong.

Physical location plays a role in the autonomy of some colleges, but by no means is the essential condition. Reed in the suburbs of Portland, Harvard in industrial Cambridge, and City College of New York in metropolitan New York are cases of physical contiguity in which bright students, able faculty, and an aura of distinction and challenge have combined to hold the environment at arm's length. In extreme cases of autonomous colleges, much seems to flow from the sense of holding to values quite different from those dominant in the bordering community and the larger society, even to the point of an ideology that divides mankind into the two worlds of "them" and "us."

The concept of intellectual autonomy sums up many impressions we have of the optimum conditions of academic impact.

---

[32] See the study of Columbia University's School of General Studies reported by Zetterberg (1958).

Colleges in this country are most likely to move students toward the ideal of the liberally educated man when (*a*) they self-consciously hold to values different from those of society at large and (*b*) the campus constitutes a community. In the first respect, the ideal of liberal education is a marginal rather than a central value of modern society and is strongly held by colleges only at the price of being different in a number of related ways, such as believing that knowledge is a value in its own right, that a life of study is meaningful, that amateur sports are for amateurs, that seventeen-year-olds should be defined as adults. In the second respect, men are shaped in college toward this ideal when they are so encompassed by the campus social system that they are made aware of the norms that define the ideal and participate in activities in which the ideal is, in fact, lived out. The most potent instrument of value change in education is the quasi-total institution, where members sleep, play, and work in the same place (Goffman, 1958). Intellectual autonomy and academic impact are thus generally dependent on the autonomy of ends, i.e., the purposes of the institution, and the autonomy of means, i.e., the internal conditions making for the involvement of the student.

The extent to which colleges in the United States have accepted the custodial role has greatly reduced their autonomy, for a college that stands *in loco parentis* to students deals with children rather than adults and is expected to guide unformed minds along conventionally approved paths. Where students are defined as adults, the college is freer to encourage independence and skepticism, qualities which are subversive of received truth at the same time as they are aspects of the ideal outcome of liberal education.

Residential colleges are commonly expected to assume the parental functions of nurture and guidance, and the freshman girls at coed residential colleges exert a pressure, both as fact and symbol, against intellectual boldness and innovation on many campuses. But the commuter colleges that are free of this expectation do not, by and large, translate that freedom into serious commitments to liberal education. For reasons we have discussed, they are vocational in orientation; they stand less as the specialized surrogate of the family and more as the pre-employment training arm of industry and government. The exchange, however, does not necessarily increase the autonomy of the college to pursue educational purposes which are different from, and sometimes at variance with, the socialization of children or the training of employees.

Despite the dominant philosophy of service which minimizes the autonomy of many public non-residential colleges, however, in some cases the relative freedom from the custodial function has permitted the emergence of adult liberal undergraduate education. At a few commuter colleges, especially those in large cities which recruit able and sophisticated students and faculty members who have independent connections with local intellectual and artistic circles, the larger worlds of politics, literature, and art find an institutional home in some segments of the college. These groups of faculty and students create their own nonconformist cultures around shared interests, sometimes in the institutional nooks and crannies of what are predominantly vocational enterprises. The art and drama departments at San Francisco State are an illustration of this phenomenon: these departments are in some ways more closely connected to the cultural life of San Francisco, and thus to larger cultural movements, than they are to the college itself. Within them, there is a good deal of direct relationship of faculty to student and the creation of a genuine cultural community with strong involvements, at variance with the impersonal and fleeting relationships typical of much of mass higher education. Although the non-residential character of much of the public section of higher education makes the development of institutional autonomy more difficult and tends to reduce the degree to which the majority of students are encompassed and affected by their formal education, the same factor may free parts of such colleges from their custodial responsibilities and thus allow them to develop pockets of adult undergraduate education which have impact on a minority of their students. The rapid growth of public commuter colleges increases the need for additional study of such developments. In 1958 only 30 per cent of all college students lived in college housing. A third lived with parents or relatives while over a quarter made their own living arrangements (American Council on Education, n.d., p.121).

VOCATIONALISM AND LIBERAL EDUCATION

The Triumph of Vocationalism

In discussing the determinants of student subcultures, we have dealt with a number of forces that work in one direction. We suggested earlier that vocationalism, as an orientation toward college and learning, is growing relatively stronger at the expense of both the collegiate and the academic. It is worth recapitulating some of the forces behind this tendency to see their mutually reinforcing effects.

1. *Expansion of higher occupations.* — In considerable part, the expansion of higher education is a response to the growth of professional, managerial, and technical occupations which require advanced training. As a result of this change in the occupational structure, and also contributing to the change, the growth in the college population in recent years has been very largely in fields of study that are directly vocational, such as business administration, engineering, and education.

The big three vocational curricula — business administration, engineering, and education — which account for nearly one-half of all undergraduate degrees, grew nearly twice as fast as the total number of college graduates in the four years between 1954 – 55 and 1957 – 58; the number of degrees earned in these fields increased by 49 per cent as compared with an increase of 27 per cent in all bachelor's and first professional degrees. Between 1957 – 58 and 1961 – 62, however, business and engineering stood relatively still in numbers, and only education, of these three fields, continued to grow rapidly. Training for the higher occupations is, of course, involved in the work of all the disciplines, in mathematics as well as in engineering (American Council on Education, n.d., p. 92).

2. *Education as the means of mobility.* — Formal education has been the chief ladder of mobility for aspiring lower- and lower-middle-class people in America for many decades. Their movement toward college continues the secular trend toward more and more education which saw the growth of nearly univer-

sal secondary education in the thirty years between 1910 and 1940. People of lower social origins now increasingly see college as the prerequisite for the economic and social advancement of their children, and these perceptions are reflected in the rapidly growing college enrollments. When education is primarily an instrument for the achievement of higher status, rather than a way to maintain and legitimate it, it is defined in primarily vocational terms—as a way of getting the training and diplomas which are needed for the better-paying jobs.

3. *Responsive character of public colleges.*—This rapid expansion of college attendance among job-oriented children of lower social origins has been very largely in the public colleges. These colleges are generally free, conveniently located, and generous in admission. They are responsive to state and local demands and willingly train for the expanding array of occupations that require advanced skills. Comprehensively organized, they take on many characteristics of a large service enterprise. Their commitment to liberal education is partial rather than total.

4. *Bureaucratization of academic organization.*—These comprehensive colleges are typically people-processing institutions, whose administrative staffs must deal with and organize the scattered activities of great numbers of students enrolled in a variety of programs. Relations between teachers and students under these conditions are typically in the mass, usually fleeting, and largely impersonal. Additionally, teachers' involvement with students is lessened by commitment to research, profession, and off-campus service. This tendency toward impersonal relationships among students and between students and faculty members fits vocational education, which aims to transmit technical information efficiently.

5. *Withdrawal of student involvement.*—An increasing proportion of college students are enrolled in colleges that are largely non-residential. Living at home and holding part-time or full-time jobs, students visit the college campus to attend class or use the library; they drop in and out of college, some finishing in six to eight years while many do not finish at all. In brief, the student role is narrowed to formal coursework and is squeezed in among other roles that are oriented off campus.

All these forces which are on the rise in American higher education tend to reduce the impact of college on the student in the older academic sense. Increasingly, students with narrow vocational interests enroll in colleges whose faculties and administrators are neither able nor strongly motivated to modify those interests and orientations.

The small distinctive colleges of high academic achievement, filled with talented upper-middle-class students headed for graduate school, are in another world. The academic subcultures which flourish in those colleges require a high average level of cultural sophistication, the inclination and leisure to cultivate intellectual interests, the help of personal attention from a devoted and able faculty, and the luxury of having merely to maintain rather than newly achieve high social and economic status. These schools will continue to play a role, especially in the country's intellectual life, out of proportion to the numbers of their graduates. But despite the worries of their presidents and professors about their effectiveness, these schools do not now pose the most difficult questions regarding the bearing of student life on higher education. It is in the large public colleges and universities, where vocationalism looms large, that the contribution of student life and its relationships to education becomes most problematic.

These problems do not arise solely in the United States. In every industrial society, recent immense advances of science, organization, and industry exert great pressures on higher education to become "the training institutions for the skilled manpower required by a complex technology" (Halsey, 1960). The USSR has gone farthest in making education an arm of the state and the economy. The Russians want no part of liberal or general humanistic education. They want no generalists – only specialists. Their main objective is to offer functional education so as to train, to mold, to develop the skills, the professions, and the specialists required by their long-run development programs – specialists who are capable of performing the tasks of running the industrial and bureaucratic machinery of the communist state. And in order to accomplish this, the Russians were, are, and will be training an army of scientists and technologists. "Although professing the aims of general and well-rounded education, the Soviet educational system in reality is uniquely geared to the training of specialized manpower" (DeWitt, 1960).

Even in England, where the university (and aristocratic) tradition of the cultivated man is strongest, the decades since the War have seen a greater emphasis on vocational and professional studies, especially in science and technology, although this movement has been slowed and contained by the elite conceptions of the university in that country (Halsey, 1960).

The great conflict on American campuses over the past fifty years has been between the academic and the collegiate subcultures, with the faculty upholding the intellectual values and the majority of students successfully opposing those with their own non-intellectual or anti-intellectual interests. Increasingly, however, the struggle will be between the vocational and academic subcultures, with the cleavage more nearly vertical—that is, with proponents of each set of values found in the faculty as well as in the student body. Both the vocational and the academic orientations are "adult" in a way that the collegiate culture is not. While collegiate values and practices were widely condoned by college authorities, few adults in college were prepared to defend them as an adequate definition of the college experience. By contrast, the vocational orientation as the *primary* orientation to college is upheld in respectable quarters, finds expression in books on educational philosophy, and has many spokesmen both among college teachers and administrators. Thus the expanding conflict between vocational and academic values is not likely to be as dramatic as the old, because the symbols are less clear.

The collegiate symbols were sufficiently outside the workaday adult world to be instantly recognizable in a cartoon or film, and their romanticization of adolescent vitality and irresponsibility made that world seem exciting, full of freedom and fun and unearned money. The academic subculture has its prestigious symbols: the academic procession and cap and gown, books, the library, the laboratory, and the classroom. But the vocational subculture is almost an adjunct of the adult world of jobs and work; it has as yet no defining symbols which distinguish it as a special college subculture, unless it be the engineer's slide rule in its orange case swinging from the belt. But it is inherently too humdrum and work-oriented ever to be very glamorous, a fact which affects both recruitment to it now and its fate as an alternative image and definition of higher education in the future.

The fact that the vocational orientation has no symbols of its own, but nevertheless is serious and is oriented to the adult world of work, allows it to borrow the traditional symbols of academia: so a picture of a college lecture hall or of students hard at work in a library can as easily be signs of vocational training as of liberal education. But the common use of the same set of symbols for vocational and academic subcultures makes it more difficult for issues between them to be joined, though the conflict is at the heart of fights over admissions policy, curriculum, and standards on many campuses. Although the cleavage between these cultures within colleges is not so sharply drawn along the traditional lines of academic status and rank, the outcomes of the conflict promise to be equally consequential, both for the experiences of students in college and, more broadly, for the nature and functions of higher education in America.

Student Cultures and Administrative Action

The forces we have described are deeply embedded in the structure of the society and the values of its members. The changing occupational structure, the immense expansion of the college-going population, and the vocational orientations of many who contribute to the increased enrollments provide the basic conditions for the development of mass higher education. At the same time they are largely beyond the influence of the colleges themselves. The forces which are not directly manipulable by educators create many of the problems with which educators grapple.

In our view, the central problems of mass higher education are not the problems of measuring and identifying talent, financing expansion, or raising faculty salaries, to name a few that have dominated the attention of educators in recent years. Rather the central problems are student boredom, their indifference to ideas, and the irrelevance to their education of their associations and relationships with other students. To a considerable degree, these attitudes and feelings in the individual students and in their subcultures flow from the fact that hundreds of thousands of students from culturally impoverished backgrounds and with narrow vocational interests enter college as a step toward qualifying for the many jobs and occupations which now call for college diplomas, but they do so without any marked enthusiasm, curiosity, or involvement with ideas and learning. And these qualities of mind are rarely created by experience in the big impersonal vocational colleges.

Nevertheless, the organization of the college as a community has profound effects on student life in ways that have been given too little consideration by administrators and too little study by scholars. The possibilities in this respect vary with circumstances, but what we have said about the effects of size and impersonality, of the dilution of intellectual interests among great numbers of students and their neglect by a faculty which deals with students fleetingly and in the mass, suggests that structural innovations working against these anti-intellectual forces might contribute to the growth and maintenance of academic and intellectual subcultures among at least a significant minority of students. The main thing is to get such students together so that they can stimulate and support one another's often precarious commitments and to provide direct and personal encouragement and rewards for such commitments by similarly committed faculty members. This requires serious effort by the administration and at least a part of the faculty to minimize the "people processing" aspects of mass higher education. In our section on the substructuring of student bodies, we suggested that the *effective* size of an institution can be reduced, even without a reduction of its absolute enrollment, by creating what are in effect distinctive smaller communities within the larger organization, communities which include both students and faculty, which have a sense of identity, and, above all, whose members share interests and commitments which can be supported and furthered, rather than diluted and discouraged.

Such communities cannot be called into being by proclamation; they have to have structural definition and support, formal membership, physical place for meeting and working, and insulation against distracting and competitive interests and appeals.

They must be small, stable, and reasonably homogeneous with respect to the values and interests represented so that members can center their relationships around these shared and developing interests, rather than, as in the collegiate cultures, around the static interests of the youth culture, which comprise the lowest common denominator of student life (Trow, 1959). In short, these have to be genuine intellectual communities, rooted in residence halls or groups of departments or in some other combination of structured interactions and shared intellectual interests. In colleges like Swarthmore and Reed, where the academic subcultures pervade the student body, the residence halls themselves come to define these academic communities, especially after self-selection has increased the homogeneity of interest and temperament within them. In universities where the academic values are by no means predominant but compete with vigorous collegiate and vocational orientations, the division of a student body in the residence halls may simply reproduce the heterogeneous and atomized mass of students in smaller units. The structural definition of a community is present but not the essential commonality of interest and value. That at least seems to be the case on a campus like Berkeley's. But as yet little is known of the nature and determinants of student communities and of the role which action by the administration can play in the creation of the best of them.[33] Here, if anywhere, a call for research is not mere ritual: the potential gains both for organizational theory and educational practice are great.

Conclusion

In the quotation with which we introduced our discussion, Woodrow Wilson spoke of "the true life of a college . . . where youths get together and let themselves go on their favorite themes." But Wilson (1925) also recognized that student peer groups cannot themselves sustain the intellectual life of a college.

The comradeships of undergraduates will never breed ths spirit of learning. The circle must be widened. It must include the older men,

---

[33]A notable and stimulating exception is the recent study by Selvin and Hagstrom (1960) of the living groups on the Berkeley campus.

the teachers. . . . So long as instruction and life do not merge in our colleges, so long as what the undergraduates do and what they are taught occupy two separate air-tight compartments in their consciousness, so long will the college be ineffectual.

Among the types of student subcultures here distinguished, we see the academic, and some of the nonconformist, subcultures as most likely to contribute to liberal education. There may well be many exceptions and qualifications: academic orientations can be mere conformity to faculty expectations and a kind of vocational training for intellectual professions; nonconformist subcultures can be mere rebellion and exhibitionism, shared symptoms of emotional disturbance. Vocational and collegiate subsystems may indeed offer some liberal education, more than we have made out. Such uncertainties call for detailed knowledge of the actual forms of student cultures in American colleges and their consequences for education. Above all, we wish to encourage painstaking analysis of the societal and organizational forces which *shape* these student cultures, not only for the light that may be shed on the interaction between our society and its institutions of higher education, but also for purposeful action toward strengthening the liberalizing and civilizing forces in the mass higher education that lies ahead.

3

The Entering Student: Attributes and Agents of Change

EVERETT K. WILSON

The student entering college is a congeries of characteristics, many of which are about to be altered in some degree – by his own design, by experiences contrived for him (as in the classroom) and by means unplanned and even unwittingly experienced. The traits he brings include aspirations and vocational plans, political and aesthetic preferences, knowledge and skills. To these last we customarily pay much attention; to the others rather little. We measure knowledge and skills at point of entry and intermittently thereafter (on the assumption that teachers and books are instrumental in changing them).

Although we have some crude information about what happens to a given input of knowledge, neither about knowledge nor, more emphatically, about his other attributes do we know with any precision where, when, how, or to what degree change occurs. If higher education is to be something more than a holding operation or an ill-considered act of faith, we need to know with what traits a student enters and leaves, and what accounts for any change. Or, in more formal language, we need (1) measures of input, (2) measures of output, and (3) an identification of those agents of change responsible for differences between input and output. To know the extent and direction of change, the first and second are necessary; to know how it came about, all three are necessary.

If our ignorance is impressive, from a practical point of view, it is scarcely less so from the perspective of the social sciences. The sociology of education has so far yielded little reliable knowledge about the informal organization of college life. Ever since World War I, psychology has produced a wide variety of tests, but the agents responsible for changed test scores over a period of time remain ambiguous. Social psychology—especially in its development of reference-group theory—has provided some clues suggesting the influence of informal change agents in the college setting (Sherif, 1936; Newcomb, 1943; Asch, 1952). But we have far to go, and it is time in any case that we know more certainly what we are doing in so formidable an enterprise as today's higher education. This volume is directed toward that end, and this chapter directs attention to the raw material presented by the entering students and to the agents of change, especially teacher and peer, as they modify the input of attributes characterizing the newcomer.

ATTRIBUTES AT TIME OF ENTRANCE: THE MEANING AND USE OF INPUT (AND OUTPUT) VARIABLES

To assess the impact of any agent of change upon the student we must know what he was like at time of entrance. For unless we know what is put in, we cannot know the part played by the peer group in producing a given output. If a student enters a group with ten units of something and leaves with fifteen, we might estimate that the group has by some means effected the difference (on the testable assumption that these five units would not have been acquired in the absence of the group). Hence any study of peer group influence must deal with those attributes which describe the student when he commences his college work and which are likely to be altered under the influence of his peers. We may call such attributes "input variables." In the most general sense an input variable is a discrete or continuous quality (represented either in discrete or continuous distributions) which characterizes units of the system being investigated at their point of entry into that system. Examples are IQ scores, number of siblings, family income, frequency of church attendance, scholastic aptitude test scores. For our purposes, input variables may be described as any attributes of the person, either achieved or ascribed, which characterize him at the time he enters college and which are subject to change or mediate change in this setting.

From one point of view this definition is too restrictive, in that there are many points of entry. Every day's participation might be viewed as a new entry. And from the same perspective, the organization entered is constantly changing. Furthermore, if the investigator wishes to cut into the problem of peer group influence at several points during a college career, the person's changed attributes (e.g., his information) at each successive tapping can be regarded as input variables affecting subsequent outcomes.

How many points of entry are necessary or desirable would seem to depend on several things. First, there is the matter of the mutability of the variables dealt with. The sex role (or pressures toward redefinition of the role) might be deemed relatively constant, whereas variables of skill and information might be expected to change more readily. Second, the number of points of entry (or waves, in a panel design) would depend upon the organizational arrangement of those peer group exposures whose expected influence should be tested. If the student enters a fraternity at the beginning of his second year, end-of-first-year measures would be necessary to assess the impact of his fraternity membership. Finally, and most generally, the number of waves will increase with the need for a detailed record of change and precise identification of agents of change.

The significance of input variables stems from two sources: first, as conditions of "exposure" to agents of change, and second, as providing the basis for adequate research design. Theoretically, they constitute a complex of traits which condition entrance into and participation in successive peer groups.

Illustrations of this first point come readily to mind. The student's religious identification, or that of his parents, may lead to affiliation with a given fraternity and thence to a dating pattern, campus activities and an intellectual orientation that are distinctively different from the pattern of peer group contact characterizing a student of another faith. Or religious identification may condition the choice of college in the first place. The conscientious Catholic will prefer Ohio State University to Oberlin, Antioch, or Reed—and Notre Dame to Ohio State. Similarly, students whose fathers' occupations are upper white collar will enter a private university in preference to the state university and the latter in preference to public junior colleges (Clark, 1960*b*, pp. 54, 55, 186).

After entrance, variations in socio-economic status, scholastic aptitude, wealth, parental occupation, and sex—to take some obvious and fairly objective attributes—are sorted out in accordance with the differentiated structure of the organization. The passive construction is not meant to imply a passive actor. The sorting occurs at the conjunction of one person's preference and another's need (or demand). The result is that attributes are distributed non-randomly in the many categories of the college structure: the various living groups, those majoring in the same subject, cliques of friends, extracurricular activity groups. In this process, peer groups may be conceived as filters, screening out those whose attributes do not fit.

With some groups the mesh is relatively loose and open; with others, discriminatingly tight or finely woven. For the analysis of peer influences, the most significant input variable is that which points unerringly to a given initial location in the peer group structure. None does, but perhaps sex comes closer than any other attribute—i.e., accounts for more of the variance in the behaviors associated with the student role than any other single variable.

Methodologically, the significance of input variables derives from their use as (*a*) independent variables; (*b*) controls; and (*c*) as base measures which, when subtracted from output measures, give us some notion of the power of intervening influences—among them, peer group influences. From another point of view, input variables may be seen as dependent on characteristics of the institution. The fact that a college is church-related may emphatically influence the distribution of church affiliation among applicants for admission.

Student attributes at point of entry may be dealt with as independent variables. Thus the socio-economic status of the student's family might be seen as an antecedent condition of peer group affiliation or, once removed, of political preferences as filtered through peer influences. Similarly, measures of initial attitudes might be used to study their connection with choice of field and with the selection of an intellectual or occupational peer group. For example, Rosenberg (1955) finds that students with "people-oriented" values tend to remain committed to teaching as a career, and so continue to expose themselves to the influence of like-minded peers. Those lacking such values tend to abandon the field. Parallel effects were reported for students having or lacking the dominant value complex that is characteristic of businessmen.

For analysis of peer group effects, measures of input variables are obviously necessary as controls. We may, for example, wish to test the hypothesis that different types of peer groups will influence the student's aesthetic preferences in predictable ways. Clearly we shall have to know the student's initial and current aesthetic views, the position characteristic of his group, and the degree of congruence of the individual's and the group's views over a period of time. But it is equally clear that the choice of group in the first place, and susceptibility to or independence of group influence, may be conditioned by long-standing characteristics of the student and his background. Parental education, religious affiliation, and political preference are examples of such attributes. In comparing changes presumably induced by different peer groups on a given campus, such variables as these must be held constant, as between the groups whose differential influence is being assessed. Similarly, selected point-of-entry characteristics of the student must be controlled for intercollege comparisons of peer group influence. One might suppose, as an illustration, that the influence of a fraternity on the student would depend on the size of the institution. In this case, the influence of fraternity membership upon, say, political preference of students having the same input characteristics would be measured, while varying the size of the institution. Even in the best of circumstances, matching a cluster of characteristics of an experimental group member with a similar cluster for a control group member is a difficult business. It usually involves a discouraging attrition in number of cases. We should note, however, that with college students as subjects, we approximate the best of circumstances, for these subjects constitute a self- and college-selected cohort of relatively homogeneous subjects. Even so, in the illustration given, the investigator may be reduced to using comparable frequency distributions as between peer groups (fraternities) in colleges of differing size.

The difference between freshman input and senior output provides a first gross measure of the impact of a complex set of intervening experiences. One would wish to interpose, within cost limits, intermediate measures, each of which would serve to represent input for subsequent measures. Simple before-and-after testing serves to reduce the range of ignorance somewhat. But without some sort of panel design we cannot know about shifts in direction of change, when change occurred, or through what specific agencies it occurred. While measures of initial input and final output are necessary, they are minimal, rather than optimal.

Quite clearly we cannot consider output variables independent of input variables. Presumably they bear the same name, as far as content goes. They are measured along the continuum of a specified dimension. And what is an output variable at one point in time may be regarded as input for subsequent measures of change. To learn anything about change and the agents of change which are influential we need both measures on a given variable. Most colleges have a rich supply of input measures, but even with the relatively recent emphasis upon Graduate and Advanced Graduate Record examinations, the output measures are scanty and inadequate. On the other hand, retrospective study such as that made by Havemann-West (1952) errs in the other direction, lacking input measures. Among their cohort of college graduates, 36 per cent were favorably disposed toward the political orientation implied by the New Deal and 64 per cent were opposed. But we know almost nothing about the extent of change, if any, which occurred in these students' political views, when it occurred, and who or what the responsible agents were. Both publicly and professionally these are important questions. If we are to get the answers, research people—and the foundations and institutions supporting their work—must so order the gathering of data through admissions, registrars' and testing offices as to provide the indispensable base point (input) measures. Parallel output measures must also be available.

Finally, changes in input variables—especially where we are concerned with intercollege comparisons—must be seen in the organizational context. Colleges vary enormously: there are church-related and independent schools; large ones and small ones; state-supported and private; men's and women's and co-educational; Negro, white, and integrated schools; rich schools for the rich and poor schools for the poor; commuter and residential colleges; metropolitan and rural; those with restricted offerings and others covering an encyclopedic range. A college may be organized to serve as a decompression chamber for over-aspiring, "latent terminals" (Clark, 1960*b*). It may be vocationally oriented or militantly liberal arts. The organizational posture may stress transmission of information and skills enabling the student to fit snugly into a given slot in the labor market. Or the college may be organized to develop broad understanding—a logical mind and a critical spirit leading to innovation rather than accommodation. The organizational emphasis may be one which underlines the poor man's *noblesse oblige*, the duty of dedicated service to others. In these contrasting organizational settings, both the attributes sought in the incoming student and their elaboration in succeeding years must be affected.

But whatever the organizational context and whatever the emphasis peculiar to a given college, it is generally assumed that academic achievement is the critical variable. Measures of success in absorbing the standard lore and aptitudes for broad classes of occupations define and limit the variables that are consistently and conventionally emphasized.

TYPES OF INPUT VARIABLES CONVENTIONALLY USED

The measurement of input variables as customarily practiced is in the hands of a college or university office of tests and measurements. (Admissions and other departments will of course have biographical data, preadmissions test data, and the like.) A cursory review of testing programs reveals the following.

1. The emphasis is overwhelmingly upon intellectual gains (and losses). Variables such as the following are not systematically used: status, aesthetic and political preference, religious beliefs, plans and expectations, attitudes toward minority group members, attitudes on international issues, views on socialism, capitalism, communism, capacity for critical thinking, and the like. Such data are, of course, sporadically available for parts of a college population—typically data from sociological and psychological research. There is, indeed, a rich and growing fund of research findings which we are disregarding in this section, not because they are unimportant, but rather because the effort here is to suggest in rough fashion the common, routine practices in assessing change in student attributes.

There is a tension between research and application—between what is done and what might be done if we knew better. The following pages emphasize the great limitations of present practices in identifying significant dimensions and agents of change in the college student.

2. Certain measures are quite commonly used, leading to the impression of a convergence in testing patterns with some of the leading schools serving as national bellwethers (American Council on Education, 1959; Riesman, 1956).

3. Beyond a core of instruments, widely used, there is great variation in tests used and variables measured. There are a number of works which survey and appraise instruments which might be useful in the study of peer group influence. The reader might find one or more of the following helpful: Buros (1959), Guilford and Lacey (1947), Anastasi (1954), Cronbach (1957), Thorndike and Hagen (1955). These treat, variously, tests of intellect, information, reasoning, verbal and mathematical abilities, judgment, foresight and planning, temperament, motivation, etc.

Instruments commonly used may be sorted into five categories, measuring (1) general scholastic aptitude—tapping native ability and/or prior training; (2) special aptitudes (clerical, musical, mechanical, physical); (3) achievement (both information and comprehension) in specific or general course areas; (4) personal interests—the extent to which students' interests correspond to those of successful practitioners (e.g., Kuder Preference Inventory and the Strong Vocational Interest Blank); and (5) personality—inventories, measures of personal and social adjustment (e.g., the Minnesota Multiphasic Personality Inventory).

Finally, the uses to which these instruments are put may be classified as (1) admissions; (2) placement and counseling, both at freshman level and subsequently; (3) waiving/exempting from course requirements, and as exit hurdles; and (4) input-output measures necessary for program evaluation.

Among the nine colleges and universities whose testing programs are summarized in this chapter, more than ninety tests and inventories were reported. (Sixteen of these instruments, however, were used for a special purpose—program evaluation—at San Francisco State College.) The ones most frequently mentioned are listed in Table 3.1.

There is, of course, no reason to assume that these nine testing

Table 3.1 Most Frequently Used Instruments in Nine College Testing Programs

Test or Instrument*	Number Reporting Use of Specified Measures	College or University†
High-school rank	6	A, Ch, D, L, M, Mn
ACE Psychological Examination	6	C, L, M, Mn, P, S
Cooperative General Culture Test	5	A, Ch, L, Mn, S
CEEB: SAT	4	A, C, D, Ch
Cooperative English Test	4	L, Mn, P, S
Wechsler-Bellevue Intelligence Scale	4	L, Mn, P, S
Strong Vocational Interest Blank	4	L, Mn, P, D
MMPI	3	D, L, Mn
Kuder Preference Inventory	3	A, L, Mn
Cooperative Test: Chemistry	3	A, L, M

* ACE: American Council on Education; CEEB: College Entrance Examination Board; SAT: Scholastic Aptitude Test; MMPI: Minnesota Multiphasic Personality Inventory.
†A: Antioch; C: University of Chicago; Ch: Chatham; D: Dartmouth; L: University of Louisville; M: University of Michigan; Mn: University of Minnesota; P: Pasadena City College; S: San Francisco State College.

programs represent nationwide practices. And we should note that while these were the instruments most .commonly mentioned, they were not necessarily used for all students for the same purposes. There is also some evidence of inadvertent failure to report commonly used instruments such as the College Entrance Examination Board (CEEB) achievement tests, especially that in English composition.

This suggests some of the difficulties encountered in trying to discover what instruments are used, how frequently, and for what purposes. Many measures are used for more than one purpose. For example, the same measure may be used for advanced placement in courses, for waiving requirements, for assigning students to special sections, and for course grading. Furthermore, it may be used for all or part of the student body. The instrument may be one contrived locally or a nationally used test. The tests used may change from year to year; few of them seem to be used consistently over a period of years. Instruments used in evaluative programs (for research on outcomes of specific educational procedures) may also be used in the regular testing programs.

Such conventional measures are obviously essential for educational quality control. They may also be useful as measures of input and output where one is concerned with the intermediate effect of differing peer group influences. But for research purposes these conventional measures suffer the twin defects of being developed for purposes only coincidentally relevant to the assessment of peer group influences, and of covering a very small part of the conceivable range of relevant input variables.

Table 3.2 summarizes most of the input variables on which data were gathered at nine colleges in 1958–59, classified by type of variable and the uses to which these measures are put. It should be viewed as only roughly accurate.[1] Having now touched upon the variables commonly dealt with, let us consider the agent generally assumed to be responsible for changes in them.

---

[1] This discussion is based largely on the study by the American Council on Education (1959), supplemented by correspondence with college and university examiners.

able 3.2 Input Variables Measured at Nine Colleges and Universities, 958 – 59[1]

Measure[2]	Admissions	Uses		Exemption and Exit Tests	Program Evaluation
		Placement and Counseling			
		Freshmen	Sophomores–Seniors		
eneral scholastic aptitude					
CEEB: Scholastic Aptitude Test	A, C, D, Ch	A, C, D	D		
High-school rank	A, Ch, D, L, M, Mn	D			
ACE Psychological Examination	C,[3] L, S[4]	M, P	L,[5] M, S[6]		
Minnesota Scholastic Aptitude Test	Mn	Mn	Mn		
General Aptitude Test Battery: U.S. Office Employment		P[7]	Mn		
Wechsler-Bellevue Intelligence Scale		L,[8] S,[4] P[7]	Mn, L[8]		
School and College Ability Test (SCAT)	S, L	S[9]			
Ohio State Psychological Test	S[4]		Mn		
Henmon-Nelson Test of Mental Ability	S[4]				
Leiter Adult Intelligence Scale		P[7]			
ACE Test of Critical Thinking	Ch				
ACE Test of Science Reasoning and Understanding	Ch				
Yale Educational Aptitude Battery— III, IV, VI, and VII (I and V used only where CEEB-SAT lacking)		A			
pecial aptitude measures					
Layton Engineering Aptitude Test		Mn[10]	Mn[10]		
ETS Medical School Test	M, Mn	Mn	Mn		
University of Minnesota Medical School Test			Mn		
ETS Law School Test	M				
chievement (information and comprehension) in course areas: general and specific[11]					
Cooperative English Test	L, S	Mn, P, S,[9] L	L[12]		
Cooperative Reading Comprehension Test	C	D, M	Mn[13]		
Quantitative Reasoning	C				
Reading test		Mn, P[7]			
Algebra test		Ch	Mn[10]		
Cooperative General Culture Test	L		Mn, L,[12] S,[9] A		
Physical Ability Test		D			
Iowa High-School Content Examination	Ch,[8] L	Ch			
Cooperative Test Battery designed for Sophomores		L	Ch[14]		

(Table 3.2 continued)

[1] A: Antioch; C: Chicago; Ch: Chatham; D: Dartmouth; L: University of Louisville; M: University of Michigan; Mn: University of Minnesota; P: Pasadena City College; S: San Francisco State College.

[2] For a number of these institutions an interview with the student and a letter of reference from the high-school principal are used as "measures." These practices are not tallied in this table.

[3] Given as part of the General Education and Entrance Test battery to accelerants only, who must be at least twenty-five years old.

[4] Occasionally used for retesting in case of doubt.

[5] Used for program for training elementary teachers.

[6] For entering laboratory technician program.

[7] Administered as requested or needed.

[8] Given locally, to a few.

[9] Used, *inter alia*, to test level of competence of elementary- and/or secondary-school teachers.

[10] Taken for Institute of Technology.

Table 3.2 *Continued*

Measure[2]	Admissions	Placement and Counseling		Exemption and Exit Tests	Program Evalua- tion
		Freshmen	Sophomores— Seniors		
High-school English record		L			
Cooperative English Test, B	L				
Chemistry		A,[15] L, M[16]			
Language		A, Ch, L, M			
Graduate Record Area Examination			Ch,[14] S	A	Ch[14]
Advanced Graduate Record Examination: Field				A	Ch
Content area tests in social sciences, humanities, natural sciences, mathematics, English, foreign languages		A,[11] C	A,[11] C[17]	Ch	
College Board Achievement/Placement tests, or local alternative, in languages, American and European history, mathematics, chemistry, physics, biology, and English	Ch[18]	A, Ch, D,[19] L,[19] M	Ch, D[20] (lang.)	Ch	
Oral/written language tests for teachers			S		
Speech		Ch, P	Ch		
Library		P			
Listening	D,[21] Ch, P	Ch			
Lado English Language Test for Foreign Students		P[16]			
USAFI: Interpretation of Reading Material in Social Sciences		Ch		Ch	
USAFI: Correctness and Effectiveness of Expression					Ch
Nelson-Denny Reading Test		Ch			
Michigan English Proficiency Test		M			
College Qualifying Test: Numerical		M			
Michigan Mathematics Placement Test[22]		M			
National Teacher Examinations					Ch

[11] Unless otherwise indicated, tests are locally constructed for purpose suggested by name and location in this table.

[12] Used for admission to senior college

[13] Taken by education students.

[14] Used occasionally for transfer and other special categories of students, or required of all seniors in alternate years.

[15] Antioch uses CEEB Chemistry. Others appear to be locally devised tests.

[16] For placement in chemistry sections.

[17] These are advisory tests to help the student assess his position and prospects. Six-hour comprehensive terminal exams are administered later for each general-education course.

THE AGENT ASSUMED TO BE EFFECTIVE IN ALTERING CONVENTIONAL VARIABLES

The emphasis upon such conventional variables as those summarized in the preceding section derives not only from the accepted academic goals of colleges but also from the conviction that teachers make the difference. The site is the classroom, the dependent variable, academic achievement (measured generally in terms of readily testable information gains) and the agent, the

Table 3.2 *Continued*

Measure[2]	Admissions	Placement and Counseling		Exemption and Exit Tests	Program Evaluation
		Freshmen	Sophomores–Seniors		
Personal interest					
Kuder Preference Inventory		A, L, Mn	L,[2] Mn		
Strong Vocational Interest Blank		D, L,[7] Mn, P[7]	L,[7] Mn		
Personal History/Future Plans form	Ch	D, Mn, A		A	A
Personality inventories: personal and social adjustment					
MMPI		D, Mn	L[2]		
Minnesota Teacher Attitude Inventory			L,[13] Mn[13]		
Allport-Vernon-Lindzey Study of Values		D[23]			
Omnibus Personality Inventory					A
Health inventories[24] (Cooperative Test, ETS)					S[25]
English Structure Test (U. of Michigan)					S[25]
Iowa Silent Reading Test		L			
University of California Subject A Examination					S[25]
Diagnostic Reading Test (Educational Records Bureau)					S[25]
Bell Adjustment Inventory					S[25]
Mooney Problem Check List					S[25]
Edwards Personal Preference Schedule					S[25]
Personality Inventory (self-insight)					S[25]
Bills's Index of Adjustment of Values					S[25]
California Auding Test					S[25]
Hills Economics Test					S[25]
Sociometric Tests					S[25]
Watson-Glaser, Critical Thinking					S[25]
Individual Inventory (self-insight)					S[25]
Attitude scales (Miami University)					S[25]
Degree of interest scales (Pennsylvania State University)					S[25]

[18] In addition, two other CEEB achievement tests are given, depending on student's choice.

[19] Local tests are used in some cases instead of CEEB. The tests mentioned are for selected groups.

[20] Used as one-hour of the final examination in courses above beginning level.

[21] Dartmouth uses listening tests for placement in language courses: French, German, Spanish.

[22] For placement of engineering students in mathematics sections.

[23] About 90 per cent of each class.

[24] These are not classified like the foregoing because of their peculiar use and character.

[25] These tests are employed at San Francisco State College in evaluating outcomes of teaching with and without television.

teacher. To ask seriously about peer group influence on intellectual gains must therefore strike some as being either irrelevant or irreverent. It might be conceded that political or religious views come under the influence of the student's peers, since the latter fill a vacuum created by the noncommittal academician. But if, as the instructor is disposed to think, variables relating to intellectual gains are the crucial ones; and if, as he may believe, he is the agent almost solely responsible for shifts through time in the values of these variables, then discussion of peer group influences must seem gratuitous.

But the social scientist operates under a mandate to question common sense. It is his professional prerogative to question whether in fact it is the teacher who teaches. And for our purposes the impertinent question about the effective agent of change is important from another perspective. For, assuming change has occurred, the probability of peer influence is increased to the extent that influence from other sources is shown to be inoperative.

Now if we are to follow this tack of estimating peer influence through elimination of other sources of influence, the obvious point of departure is that agent of change whose influence appears most certain—the teacher.[2] Coincidentally—but under pressures not immediately relevant to the problem of differential influence—there has been an effort to minimize student-teacher contact, or, as it is usually put, to increase teaching efficiency. Where such programs have been examined we can find some evidence bearing on the significance of the teacher as an agent of change and, therefore, the influence of the residual category of non-teacher agents of change including the student's peers. Let us look briefly at some of this evidence.

In 1956–57, frequency of teacher-student contact was experimentally varied in five courses at Antioch College. Because the college, operating on a work-study program, has two populations it was possible to give a specified course in the conventional lecture-discussion fashion and in a comparable experimental group, to reduce teacher-student contact by 60 to 80 per cent. The gross design for time and treatment is shown in Table 3.3. The two populations were matched by frequency distribution on initial knowledge of subject matter and on such background variables as sex, scholastic aptitude, major field, and year in college.

---

[2] When I speak of eliminating the influence of the teacher, I mean a reduction in amount of direct interaction with his students. But it is quite conceivable, as Professor Morris Keeton has pointed out, that teacher influence remains strong, if less obvious, in the design of learning experiences which may include, among other things, calculated exposure to peers and reduction of teacher-student contact.

Various types of gain — direct, anticipatory, accumulated, and over-all — were measured on multiple-choice tests, essay examinations, attitude scales, outside reading records, and the like. Both reliability and validity of test instruments were checked and found adequate.

The findings based on hundreds of statistical tests and reams of data indicate that "differences between control and experimental groups reflecting different treatments for twelve weeks are by and large insignificant" (Churchill, 1957).

Building on this initial inquiry, six instructors worked during the summer on a study for the succeeding academic year. Eight different courses were involved and for each a design was developed allowing extent of teacher contact to vary. Some of the courses, for example, were taught three ways: (1) the conventional lecture-discussion method under the continuous surveillance of the teacher; (2) small discussion groups having sporadic contact with the instructor; and (3) lone wolves studying — with the guidance of the syllabus — quite independently. Two courses were taught twice, so that a total of ten different classes was used in the study. Below is the central finding (Antioch College, 1958, p. 27).

What emerges clearly is that there is no proof that any teaching procedure [*read:* differing amounts of teacher-student contact] . . . is any better than any other for helping students attain objectives related to working independently. And this lack of difference is so, despite the marked preference on the part of the students for lecture-discussion procedures.

Table 3.3   Reduction of Teacher-Student Contact

Population	Period (in Weeks)								
	4	4	4	4	Christmas Vacation	6	6	6	6
A	*a*	*b*				*c*	*d*		
B			*e*	*f*				*g*	*h*

/// : Control (conventional lecture-discussion method).   ▒ : Experimental (teacher contact reduced by 60 to 80 per cent. Comparable course content (identical readings, some lectures, etc.) in *a* and *e*; *b* and *f*; *c* and *g*; and *d* and *h*.

Two more pieces of evidence may be adduced which test for differences in attitudes and learning related to variations in teacher-student contact. The first has to do with intellectual gains in a course on fundamentals of mathematics handled in the one case as a large lecture course (seventy students) with a student assistant conducting laboratory sessions. The control group was taught conventionally in smaller sections, the instructor handling all of them in the usual lecture-discussion way. Gains in understanding, knowledge, and skills did not differ significantly with variations in student-teacher contact (Churchill, 1958).

Similarly, in a different subject matter, the hypothesis was tested that, with two comparable groups of students in French I, an experimental group with three (rather than fifteen) class hours under the tutelage of the instructor and an additional six hours with student assistants using audiovisual aids would, first, learn as much French and, second, be as satisfied with course and instructor as would a control group conventionally taught. Gains were measured by the CEEB achievement test in French reading, the Antioch Language Placement Test, the Cooperative Listening Test, and tests of dictation skills, reading ability, and speaking ability. Again, the findings failed to reveal significant differences in learning as extent of contact with instructor was varied.

Similar reports come from studies at Oberlin and Vanderbilt. "As far as conventional measures of course performance go, the experimental and control groups appear to have learned equally well" (Oberlin College, 1958).

I have been at some pains to present evidence which suggests that teachers may not be teaching what they or we think they are teaching. I conclude that the teacher (or the student's peers) may have the greatest impact on variables other than those conventionally dealt with, and that the student's peers may be of unsuspected and underestimated importance for the student.

OTHER VARIABLES AND AGENTS OF CHANGE

We have argued that the probability of peer group influence is increased as the influence of other agents of change is diminished. Such evidence as we have suggests that on conventional measures the conventional agent of change (the teacher) is not as influential as is commonly assumed—or in the way commonly assumed. Indeed, as we vary the degree of student-teacher contact in a wide variety of settings the only conclusion so far justified is that it makes little or no difference on the variables we have tried to measure.

It may now be worth viewing this issue from the perspective of the person presumably affected, the student. Although there is something novel and perhaps naïve in the straightforward approach of asking the student himself, we are not constrained to lean heavily upon the accuracy of the senior student's response to the question, "As you reflect upon your four years in college, what do you see as significant changes in yourself which have occured during this period?" For as he names the kinds of changes he thinks he has experienced—the ones he deems of some significance—we may, however tentatively, learn something useful about the range of variables relevant to peer group influence. If, in addition, we ask the question, "How did these changes come about?" we may get some clues as to the relative significance of peers and other agents in inducing these changes.

Acting upon these notions, we performed the following: (1) a content analysis of twenty-five college senior papers, extracting all statements bearing on change, direction of change, time, place, and agent of change; (2) development of a questionnaire, the first part an open-ended inquiry about changes perceived in self, the latter part an ordered check-list of the ninety-eight change items previously revealed in the analysis of senior papers; (3) interviewed a pilot group of fourteen seniors with the questionnaire; and (4) interviewed a systematic random sample of fifty-three students among the remaining seniors. Their responses are summarized in Tables 3.4–3.6. The data suggest answers to these questions. Who are the agents of change cited by these students? Where do his peers stand among these agents of change? What are the kinds of changes which such senior students deem significant—changes pointing to variables which might prove of interest in research on peer group influence? How does strength of peer influence shift from one type of variable to another?

First, who or what are the agents of change? More than

Table 3.4 Agents of Change, by Category, Reported by Fifty Antioch Seniors, May, 1960*

Agent of Change	Total: All Types (Per Cent)	Intellectual (Per Cent)	Development of Interest in New Fields (Per Cent)	World View and Personal Philosophy (Per Cent)	Personality Development (Per Cent)	Social Development (Per Cent)	Career Plans and Choices (Per Cent)	Attitude toward Antioch (Per Cent)
Course	17	21	35	17	13	6	22	1
Work experience	15	9	8	11	18	16	30	19
Self-development, maturation, growing up	13	15	10	16	16	15	9	9
Fellow student	10	6	11	11	12	15	4	14
Teaching faculty	8	16	6	8	3	4	11	4
Antioch atmosphere, community program	7	6	7	6	3	7	2	19
Antioch "Education Abroad"‡	5	—	7	6	8	8	4	4
Don't know agent or not ascertained	4	5	3	3	8	2	2	5
Spouse	2	2	3	1	2	2	1	1
Book/author not course-related	2	2	1	5	1	—	3	—
Department extramural instructor, faculty member	1	1	—	—	—	1	—	10
Physician, minister	1	1	—	4	1	1	—	—
Relationship with others generally	1	—	—	—	2	6	—	—
Family, employer, fellow employee, special project	2	3	2	2	2	3	4	1
Other: miscellaneous	11	14	7	11	10	15	9	13
Totals§	99	101	100	101	99	101	101	100
Total number of changes mentioned	1,412	233	232	229	220	193	161	144

*Based on data from structured part of interview schedule.

†See the accompanying tabulation "Categories of Change" for explanation.

a dozen of the possible agents are noted in Table 3.4, and these condense a far longer list. Of the 1,412 changes mentioned, 10 per cent were attributed to the influence of respondents' peers. For some of us it will be reassuring to see that 17 per cent of the changes are accounted for by the impact of a course. If we add to this the proportion of all changes attributed to the teaching

---

Categories of Change   (Tables 3.4–3.6)

Intellectual. — Includes changes in desire for knowledge for its own sake, for its usefulness as a means to other ends, in academic indolence, excitement in learning, amount of outside reading, number of books owned, ability to integrate ideas, originality in thought, critical abilities, ability in logical analysis, importance of good grades, importance of getting a degree, and the like. Changes in a direction which the academician would deem bad are few in number. For example, out of 272 changes in the intellectual sphere reported by our two pilot groups (N = 20) only 7 were in the "wrong" direction; and this despite the interviewer's encouragement to report the bad with the good. Of course, this raises serious questions, both in theory and in methodology.

Development of interest in new fields. — Includes awakened interest in national and foreign affairs, interest in politics, religious interests, religious conviction, music appreciation—jazz, classical, and popular—understanding of and interest in the plastic and graphic arts, interest in the physical sciences, understanding of physical sciences, interest in sports, participation in sports, interest in life sciences, understanding of life sciences, breadth of interest.

World view and personal philosophy. — Includes clarity of life goals, plausibility of life goals, clarity of plans, importance of material goals, frequency of philosophical speculation, clarity of values, optimism, belief in effectiveness of individual actions, degree of commitment to a given political viewpoint, similarity of outlook to that of other students, to faculty, to people at home.

Personality development. — Includes degree of perceived introversion, tendency toward introspection, extent of self-knowledge and self-awareness, self-confidence among other on campus, in academic work and on the job, feeling of personal responsibility for own actions, ability to make decisions, sense of security, frustration tolerance, ability to relax, general feeling of efficacy, etc.

Continued

Continued

Social development. — Includes ability to deal with others, frequency of friendly association, ease of social relationships with faculty, with family, ability to work with others, leadership ability, modification of behavior in terms of anticipated social consequences, identification with student body, with a religious group, concern with conformity, interracial tolerance, interfaith tolerance, etc.

Career plans and choices. — Includes certainty about future occupation, clarity about degree requirements, extent of interest in career, extent of relatedness between academic "major" and career, personal qualifications for chosen career, change in career choice, etc.

Attitude toward Antioch. — Includes all responses which reveal a change in appraisal of or attitude toward the college as a whole, some department or subdivision of it, or with certain persons taken as revealing the college's assets or liabilities.

Table 3.5 Perceived Changes, by Category, Reported by Antioch Seniors, May, 1960

Type of Change*	Per Cent of All Changes Falling in This Category†
World view and personal philosophy	40
Personality development	25
Intellectual	12
Development of interest in new fields	8
Social development	7
Career plans and choices	5
Attitude toward Antioch	3
Total	100
Total number of changes mentioned	718

* See the accompanying tabulation "Categories of Change" for explanation.

† Indicates frequency with which seventy-three Antioch seniors reported perceived changes in themselves in answer to the open-ended question: "Will you please tell me, briefly, what you regard as the most important changes in yourself which have occurred since you came to Antioch as a freshman?" This query was preceded by the statement: "We are asking for your help in understanding more fully the significant changes in themselves which Antiochians have experienced during their years at college." The query was followed by the statement: "We are trying to find out what attitudes, values, and personal characteristics have changed, the direction of the change, the time and place of the change, and the agent of change (e.g., a book, a person, a critical situation)." The interviewer was then instructed as follows: "After the respondent has gone as far as he is able to along this tack, the interviewer should revise the approach, using some such words as the following: 'Undoubtedly certain people and events stand out in your memory as being major influences. Perhaps there were certain critical times during your career at Antioch which were turning points. Can you tell me about such people (names are not necessary) and such events?' As these agents of change are enumerated, record in each case the kind of change involved, its direction, and, insofar as possible, the time and place of occurrence."

faculty (.08) the total influence from these conventional sources mounts to 25 per cent—a disenchanting estimate of academic power.

In the intellectual sphere the influence of fellow students drops: his peers are held influential in 6 per cent of the changes in this category, whereas teachers and classes, together, are held responsible for 37 per cent of the intellectual changes, and simple physical maturation is felt to account for 15 per cent of such changes.

Courses and teachers, taken together, account for 41 per cent of new interests, tastes, and appreciation developed. But even here a student's peers are significant as influences, for they are listed as the responsible agents of change in 11 per cent of the cases. Except for influence on career choice and planning (4 per cent) the frequency with which peers are mentioned as effective agents is above 10 per cent in every case: changes in world view and personal philosophy, in personality development, in ability to work, play, and deal with others (social development), and in attitude toward the college. These "agents" do reveal— and this is the significant matter here—the very considerable range of influences which must be taken into account if we are to understand what happens on a given variable between the points of college entrance and exit.

Table 3.5 suggests the kinds of changes which were salient in seniors' minds when they were asked to reflect on their college careers and report the changes they deemed most significant. (In the second, structured part of the interview [Table 3.6] more changes were elicited, the spread of response was increased, and the percentages reported in Table 3.5 were altered. But the data in this table are reported as suggesting an order of salience.) Changes in world view and personal philosophy appear of overwhelming significance and, together with perceived changes in personality and intellectual growth, embrace more than three-fourths of all changes reported. On the other hand, changes in career plans appear relatively insignificant as a change category. This table suggests a range of variables on which, customarily, we have few if any input measures or output measures and virtually no knowledge as to the agents effective in inducing change.

A final set of data (Table 3.6) suggests the way in which peer influence may shift, depending on the content of the influence (the change category). Peer influence, as reported by these seniors, was strongest on matters of developing new fields of interest, of personal philosophy and world view, and of development of personality and learning to deal effectively with others.

Although these data are exploratory in nature, this preliminary inquiry into changes and agents of change retrospectively judged important by senior college students suggests the following conclusions quite forcefully. First, there is a wide range of agents of change and of relevant variables. Second, the effective agent of change may vary consistently with different types of change. Finally, customary appraisal procedures neglect all but a very narrow segment of the change spectrum.

TYPES OF VARIABLES AND THEIR RELEVANCE IN THE STUDY OF PEER GROUPS

Student attributes relevant to peer group influence are infinitely numerous. Hence it may be useful to contrive some simple system of ordering them, for then we can comment more economically on related classes of variables and sample certain of the propositions on peer group influence related to these classes of variables.

One approach is to classify the relevant variables along a continuum from the general to the particular — from those shared by major sectors of the population to those resulting from a particular configuration of attributes shared by fewer people. Almost everyone is male or female and each person shares his sex with about half the population. Almost everyone has, explicitly or implictly, some life view, but considerably fewer than half the population are existentialists, Seventh Day Adventists, or Presbyterians.

The classification of variables we are proposing moves, roughly, in this way, and from ascribed to acquired or achieved attributes. The former involve attributes typically dealt with as discrete distributions (gross differentiation — e.g., male-female, white-Negro) to those variables whose measures fall in a continuous distribution (implying a refined differentiation — e.g.,

Table 3.6 Distribution of Influence of a Given Agent of Change Reported by Antioch Seniors, May–June, 1960*

Agent of Change	Type of Change							Total	
	Intellectual (Per Cent)	Development of Interest in New Fields (Per Cent)	World View and Personal Philosophy (Per Cent)	Personality Development (Per Cent)	Social Development (Per Cent)	Career Plans and Choices (Per Cent)	Attitude toward Antioch (Per Cent)	Per Cent†	N
Course	20	33	16	12	4	14	1	100	244
Work experience	10	9	12	19	14	23	13	100	212
Self-development, maturation, growing up	19	12	19	19	16	7	7	99	188
Fellow student	9	18	18	18	19	4	14	100	145
Teaching faculty	34	12	17	7	7	17	6	100	106
Antioch atmosphere, community program	14	19	14	6	15	4	29	101	94
Antioch "Education Abroad"‡	1	20	19	24	21	8	7	100	75
Don't know agent or not ascertained	19	14	12	30	7	5	12	99	57
Spouse	19	23	12	19	15	8	4	100	26
Book/author not course-related	17	8	46	8	4	17	–	100	24
Department extramural instructor, faculty member	16	–	–	–	5	–	79	100	19
Physician, minister	12	6	53	18	12	–	–	101	17
Relationship with others generally	–	–	–	31	69	–	–	100	16
Family, employer, fellow employee, special project	19	13	13	13	16	19	6	99	31
Other: miscellaneous	21	11	16	14	18	9	11	100	158

*Based on data from responses on the structured part of the interview schedule.

†Totals may not add up to 100 per cent due to rounding.

‡Only twenty-one of the fifty respondents had undergone the Antioch "Education Abroad" experience. This is, therefore, an understatement of this change influence.

measures of knowledge, problem-solving ability, or position on a scale measuring religious behavior or belief). The former seem to be both early in appearance and pervasive; the latter, later in appearance and particular. The attributes on the basis of which roles are ascribed are those which most particularly must be held constant when we are concerned with the influence of different peer groups upon, say, changes in political preference. It seems a plausible notion that such a classification might accord with the individual's developmental sequence in which successive experiences serve to define life chances and aptitudes, to channel interests and specify the prospects.

In the following outline, each category is meant to imply the preceding one, while at the same time bearing on the succeding one. In short, such a classification should constitute a sort of developmental scale in which the value for a given variable implicates a cluster of antecedent variables. The four classes of variables are the following.

1. Biological attributes to which expectations as to belief and behavior are typically, or stereotypically, linked.
2. Social characteristics stemming from the student's categorical context (class, parental occupation, religion, and the like).
3. Social characteristics generated in the student's group context.
4. Personal traits presumably deriving from experiences implicit in the foregoing (Kuder preference scores, religious beliefs, aesthetic preferences, and the like).

These classes of variables may be seen as related to peer group influence since they condition (1) whether the person attends college, and thus exposes himself to the peer group influences there; (2) which type of college he attends — metropolitan commuter, Catholic university, ivy league, etc.; and (3) with whom he associates within the chosen college. As the classes of attributes move from gross and ascribed to refined and achieved, there is a roughly parallel change in the nature of peer group influence. Whether he goes to college is more emphatically conditioned by an ascribed trait, such as the student's race, than by most other attributes. Which college he attends may be influenced principally by a non-biological ascribed trait, such as the class of the student's family. (Clearly this bears on the "whether" issue, too, although it is not so determinative as race.) With whom the student associates — to whose influence he exposes himself within the college — is likely to be conditioned by the interest-and-attitudinal precipitate registered in his personality and built upon the antecedent variables. Thus, for example, a Negro from an impoverished background (low income, limited parental education, etc.) seeks distinction where he may. Achieving success in high school athletics he develops knowledge, skills, attitudes, and a career set which condition his location within the peer group "mix" at the university which recruits him.

The rest of this section is an expansion of this classification of variables, including a few propositions supported by more or less empirical evidence, and so ordered as to mesh with this classification.

Biological Attributes Commonly Linked with Expectations of Differing Beliefs and Behavior: Age, Sex, and Race

Behavior expected from and directed toward the person may be stipulated on the basis of age, sex, or race regardless of his particular social background or his personal achievements. That is to say, such behavior implies ascribed attributes. But the line between ascribed and achieved attributes is seldom clearcut. For example, the ascription of certain attributes, even though non-existent, may put in motion influences which lead to their realization — i.e., they become achieved attributes. "The difference between a Duchess and a charwoman," said Shaw, "lies not so much in the way they act as in the way they are treated." That is to say, the treatment elicits a correspondingly "proper" response. In the genesis of attributes the expectation precedes the response. A trait ascribed readily becomes one achieved. The point has been lucidly developed in Merton's "The Self-fulfilling Prophecy" (1948). We recognize the interaction between these several classes of variables — an interaction which results in differential exposure and sensitivity to the impact of the peer group. Thus we can think of a triangular interaction pattern between:

(1) ascribed traits like age, sex, or race, (2) a form of behavior like grade-point average achieved, and (3) the differing impact of contrasting peer group contexts upon such achievement (see Chap. 6). The interconnectedness of these classes of variables can be illustrated as we consider the matter of age.

At the undergraduate level (and barring the situation introduced by veterans) age might appear to be a non-discriminating variable because of the limited range of the distribution. But there is some evidence that age, sex, and parental occupation or socio-economic status interact. The older entering student may be poorer, from a blue-collar family; boys more often than girls may fall in this category. Hence age might represent a complex of traits relevant to peer group recruitment and subsequent effects (Hatch and Landis, 1942).

It is also quite conceivable that the significance of age may be strongly mediated by organizational characteristics. Where, for example, there is strong emphasis upon demonstrated academic ability, the variance of peer group members' age should be greater than elsewhere. This, of course, assumes that scholastic aptitude, interest, and perhaps achievement may vary independently of variations in age between seventeen and twenty-two. Thus for intercollege studies, in which within-year age variance is greater, one might detect the influence of an organizational arrangement celebrating intellectual achievement. But I doubt that these variables are, in fact, independent. It is more plausible that the relationship between age and achievement (indicated by grades) may be mediated by motivation, students above and below average age having stronger need for achievement. Hence we might expect to find, at a college or in a fraternity seeking to strengthen its academic standing, a disproportionate number of students who had entered at a younger or older age than the average (cf. Hatch and Landis, 1942, p. 258).

The general assumption underlying the interest in sex as a research variable is "that there exists a partial disjunction between the cultural worlds of males and females in contemporary American society, which gulf is greater than that between any other such pairs of status-categories" (Brown, 1952). To the extent that this is true, of course, it implies entrance and exposure to sex-differentiated peer groups and outcomes significantly different, by sex, in the college experience. But prior to college itself, this variable bears upon the fact of attendance.

There is some suggestion that girls, especially those from low-income families, are less likely to attend college than boys. Conversely, girls are likely to enter college disproportionately from professional and proprietary families (Hatch and Landis, 1942, pp. 224–25). In the second place, sex may condition the choice of college. But between the extremes of men's and women's colleges, it might be assumed that differences in the sex ratios of students' peer groups are related to differing outcomes —both in kind and extent of learning. Among their respondents Hatch and Landis (1942, pp. 223–25) found that entering women had an initial advantage over men in level of education achieved by their parents[3] and in their rank in high-school graduating classes. College women, it has been observed, are more likely to be overachievers than men (Milner, 1949; Veroff, Wilcox, and Atkinson, 1953). And Dexter and Stein (1955) found that among their women students high masculinity scores were positively related to leadership capacity and performance.

On the other side, male freshmen will have a higher mean age and will be more likely to have had other intervening experiences between high school and college. It is at least plausible that men will have a more instrumental orientation toward college education than women and should score higher on such instruments as Christie's Mach scale (which differentiates between persons having tough- and tender-minded philosophies of life).

What is the significance of such socially sex-linked traits as these? Simply this: sex conditions the peer group mix and hence the attributes flowing from peer group influence. As a specific example, if certain of the foregoing propositions are true, girls will be more likely to date downward, and boys to date upward, within the college population. This is, in effect, a cross-class confrontation. The outcomes in knowledge, attitudes, and values would be different were the attributes of this dyadic peer group differently mixed.

[3] But we should note that these investigators did not find a consistent association between college success and the amount of formal education of parents.

As with age, it might be argued that to the extent that ascribed traits are determinative, "earned" attributes such as scholastic achievement will be minimized. This would be attributed in part to the relative homogeneity of peer group influences and, conversely, to the absence of those psychic roadblocks which stem from confronting the unfamiliar, giving rise to creative resolutions — i.e., to thought.[4]

Similarly, race implies differing exposure to peer group influences. Connected as it is with the other classes of variables, it affects whether the person does or does not go to college, which one he enters, and with whom he associates within the college he does enter. It represents an emphatic gap between potential and aspirations, on the one hand, and probable rewards, on the other. As a point-of-entry attribute it suggests a personal dilemma which sharply differentiates the Negro student from the white. Again, the input variable reflects and affects the organizational stance and the character of the influence exerted upon the student. It might be assumed that between colleges, the greater the indifference to race as an input variable, as with age and sex, the greater the emphasis upon achieved attributes, academic or extracurricular, and the more diverse the peer groups to which the individual student will be exposed.

*Attributes Stemming from Those General Categories
to Which the Student's Family Can Be
Allocated*

Like the first class of variables, these refer to ascribed traits: nativity, place of residence, parental income, occupation, religion, education, and the like. But in this case they are not based upon biological attributes. They stand for influences characteristically felt by all persons ,who, by virtue of their families' positions, fall at birth into given categories. The principal stress

[4]Dewey (1922, pp. 178–79, 183) states: "The truth is that in every waking moment, the complete balance of the organism and its environment is constantly interfered with and as constantly restored. Hence the 'stream of consciousness' in general, and in particular that phase of it celebrated by William James as alternation of flights and perchings. Life is interruptions and recoveries. . . . *We know at such times as habits are impeded*, when a conflict is set up in which impulse is released [italics mine]."

implied in such attributes is upon a replication of parental experience. This conservative strain toward intergenerational redundancy may be viewed as a stabilizing influence, sustaining a social system. As input variables, these ascribed traits bear on peer group influence in several ways. They are matched against oranizational requirements at the point of admission. Thus they may be considered preliminary, gross filters conditioning the "whether" and "which" decisions: whether the student shall attend college and, if so, which one he shall attend—a state or a private school, church-related or non-denominational, a metropolitan or a country school, commute from home or go away to college, attend a Negro school or a men's or women's school or a non-segregated college. But in emphasizing the initial sorting-out function of these variables we should not minimize their subsequent significance in conditioning the groups joined and hence the particular peer influences to which the student is exposed after entering college.

I can illustrate the relevance of such variables in the study of peer groups by offering a few propositions as examples. Take, for example, the matter of place of residence. Mulligan (1953) found that size of home community was positively related to the proportion of students whose parents were in clerical, skilled, and semiskilled occupations. Thus, size of home community may be associated with student attributes significantly affecting the campus mix. On the assumption that such students from predominantly blue-collar families are using college as a social escalator, we might suppose that size of place in which one lives is positively related to an instrumental orientation to education. This might be expected to make for choice of a technical school over a liberal arts college or, within a college, of a vocationally oriented curriculum—business administration, engineering—over a liberal arts program.

Religion appears to be an ascribed trait of some significance in conditioning exposure to and influence by the student's peers. Some tentative empirical findings suggest that students from Catholic families will be underrepresented in the physical and social sciences and overrepresented in law and business administration (Cooper, 1945). Blau (1953) observed the connection between religious affiliation and participation in peer groups concerned with reform and civic issues. He found that the higher the frequency of church attendance among Protestants, the more active their participation in campus cause-oriented and civic activities. The case was just the reverse among Catholics and Jews. Since peer influence must be more effective as a given position is repeatedly reflected in associates' behavior, the following becomes an intriguing question: To what extent does a given college present a sufficiently clear public image to promote self-recruitment among religiously (or irreligiously) like-minded students, thus assuring a hard and homogeneous core of true believers who reinforce one another's predispositions?

Some research findings suggest the significance of parental occupation in affecting the input of student attributes and the subsequent peer group mix. For example, students whose fathers are farmers and blue-collar workers (in contrast to those whose fathers are in other occupations) show an interest in and enter teaching disproportionately (Moffett, 1929; Mueller and Mueller, 1949; Mulligan, 1951). On the other hand, students whose fathers are professionals appear to be interested in and enter fields of law, medicine, dentistry, and music in disproportionate numbers. Years ago Cattell (1906) turned up a direct relationship between father's occupational status and the student's academic achievement in the physical sciences.

One might assume, too, that parental education has a bearing on the input of student attributes. Drucker and Remmers (1951) report certain findings relevant to the civic views of entering students. Among 12,000 high-school students, those whose fathers had had a general education (in contrast to a special, or technical, or vocationally oriented education) had more correct or "better" citizenship attitudes than did their counterparts. They found the same to be true of Purdue University students. More "correct" meant, in this case, that students' responses to questions on world affairs, politics, civic relations, and government more nearly matched those of experts in these fields.

Social scientists have consistently found measures of class standing—occupation, income, and the like—to be effective predictors of belief and behavior. So we are not surprised to find that measures of parental status are positively related to the probability of: (1) attending college, with or without intelligence measures held constant; (2) attending a liberal arts college rather than technical schools or teachers' colleges; (3) attending private rather than public colleges or universities; and (4) fraternity membership (Mulligan, 1951; Strang, 1937; Warner, 1944).

Another set of findings is of great interest both theoretically and practically. McArthur (1955) found that for public school boys, in contrast to private school boys, attending college is an expression of need for achievement. They seem to be driven to achieve goals and glory eccentric to their family situations and for which the family offers no model. "Public" and "private" as used here seem roughly equivalent to middle- and upper-class families. Comparing students from middle- and lower-class families, Douvan (1956) found that the latter are likely to seek "payoff" situations and to modify behavior in terms of estimated yield, whereas students from middle-class families tend to continue striving to a degree independent of reward situations.

Another interesting outcome of parental status has been suggested by Goetsch (1940) and Mulligan (1953). The higher the parental income, the greater the distances travelled to college. This suggests a greater range from which colleges may select an appropriately homogeneous population. And this means a more homogeneous peer group to which the incoming student, from a well-to-do family, is exposed. Thus the input of student attributes may reasonably be expected to differ significantly by parental or familial characteristics: place of residence, religion, occupation, education, and class, to name a few.

Variables Related to the Student's Role in Precollege Groups

Let us shift our attention from the student's categorical context to the concrete groups in which he was involved before entering college. A new set of variables bears on this matter of exposure to and influence by college peers. Position in the family, relationships with parents, activity with precollege peers, size of school and achievement in it, frequency of moving (change in group affiliations) — all these may have something to do with the three decisions mentioned before: whether to go; if so, to which; and within which, to associate with whom. Consider some examples of propositions involving this third category of variables.

Allen (1955) found that being an only child (or the fact of a marked age difference between siblings) is positively related to success in college, "success" referring to a specific category. It might consist of those achieving a given grade-point average. But however success is defined, it seems altogether plausible that the effective peer group of the successful person will have a membership different from that of the unsuccessful. Further- more, the peer group may be the cause as well as the effect of "success." Hence it might be possible to link sibling position with type of peer group joined as well as with "success." The same applies to another of Allen's findings: the age when the person felt himself accepted as an equal by his parents is nega- tively related to success in college.

There is some evidence of a connection between precollege participation in the informal group life of peers and adjustment in college, where adjustment means absence of psychiatric re- ferral (Demorath, 1943). It may also be argued that past peer groups — or particular properties of them — condition member- ship in significant, successive peer groups. Assume that, in small colleges at least, fellow students concentrating in a given aca- demic field constitute a frequently interacting set of peers. What accounts for the sorting of students into these various fields? One aspect of this secondary recruitment process is, of course, the fit between difficulty of field and aptitude of stu- dent. And one likely factor in student aptitude is an interesting dimension of his antecedent peer groups: their heterogeneity. That is to say, the allocation of students among the several fields, from hard to soft (and their several, distinct peer groups) may depend in part upon degree of diversity in their past peer groups. For heterogeneity of group members' aptitudes and achievements is positively related to successful problem- solving. Hoffman's results (1959, pp. 28, 31), imply that a multiplicity of perceptions of a problem are productive of creative solutions. . . . [He] found that frequent contact between a scientist and other members of his research group was related to the scientist's productivity *only* in those situations when the other members of the groups were *dissimilar* from him in their work motivation and previous work experience [italics mine].

The significance of their high-school groups in defining students' goals and modifying their performance has been dramatically (and discouragingly) revealed by Coleman (1960). A study of ten high schools showed that it was not public bounty, the adequacy of physical facilities, or even high aptitude which led to academic excellence. Superior academic performance occurred only when the student's peers celebrated this sort of achievement—and this was not the usual case. On the contrary, since the social rewards went to athletic prowess and personal popularity, the able and astute achieved in these realms, sacrificing grades, while the mediocre students pulled down the higher grades. This study, then, gives us some impression of the power of the high-school peer group and the probability that its influence on those who go on to college will reverberate through succeeding years, affecting their choice of school and of peer groups, formal and informal, within the school.

Variables Which Measure Personal Traits Deriving from Experiences Implicit in the Three Foregoing Categories

These variables—and there are a host of them—lie in the realm of values, skills, knowledge, and attitudes. Except for matters of knowledge, they have been of interest, it seems, principally to guidance people on the applied side and to social scientists on the research side. Vocational hopes, plans, and expectations represent one important cluster of attributes of the entering student. Iffert's (1957) data show that certain vocational interests condition the type of institution entered. Among a sample of male students entering college in 1950 and reporting an interest in law, 62 per cent went to universities, about a third to liberal arts colleges. More than 60 per cent of those expressing an interest in medicine and accounting at the time of entering also went to universities, as did more than one-half of those interested in business administration and agriculture. Among those interested in education, about one-half went to teachers colleges, whereas 53 per cent of all students interested in biology entered liberal arts colleges. In short, certain vocational orientations lead the student to seek his training at one sort of institution rather than another, thus affecting the composition of peer groups and their reflexive influence upon the students.

There are many ways of viewing students' future plans and the connection of those plans with peer group influence. Blau (1953) found that the importance to the student of getting ahead in life was negatively related to association with liberally oriented peer groups and participation in their activities. Active participants in such peer groups may be the relatively able academic underachievers who enjoy enough self-assurance to preclude worrying too much about the future. Something of the sort is suggested by Owens and Johnson (1949), who report that underachievers will give more extroverted responses and indicate better adjustment to the college situation than will normal achievers or overachievers.

Plans for the future will, of course, condition the choice of academic peer groups. For example, students with high scores for managerial, persuasive, and aggressive traits were found to be underrepresented among those expecting to enter scientific professions (Astin, 1958). Early commitment to a vocation and identification with a peer group similarly oriented may be related to success in college work (Allen, 1955). Such a finding may be linked with the clarity of the student's self-image. Becker and Carper (1956) found that clarity of self-image varies inversely with the time at which an academic major is declared.

Anxiety is a necessary concomitant of problem-solving, and the college is an organization calculated to confront the student with problems, quite apart from the unsettling features of a novel setting and unaccustomed independence. So we might expect level of anxiety to be a variable of much interest in the study of student peer groups. As an example, Mills (1955) finds that abnormal psychology courses attract students of higher anxiety levels and more ambiguous self-images that do other courses. Here, then, is a possibility of self-recruitment for course (and career?) resulting in a peer group homogeneous for mild personality disorders. Other related findings touching on anxiety, sense of self-confidence, and independence of group pressures might be cited. Hochbaum (1954) reports that students' sense of competence is positively related to ability to resist group pressures. And Kelley and Shapiro (1954) find that students generally acceptable as co-workers to their peers are more able to deviate from group norms.

The matter of leadership capacity, to take one final example, seems intimately related to type and extent of peer group memberships. There is some suggestion that the student leader may be less instrumentally oriented than his peers, perhaps living more in the present and being more concerned with current and local rather than future problems, in contrast to his fellow students. Dexter and Stein (1955) report that demonstrated leadership ability among women students is related to indecision regarding, or rejection of, teaching as a career.

Limitations of knowledge and space prevent me from adequately sampling the range of problems involving the effect of peers upon personality variables and, of the latter, upon selection of and exposure to peer groups. These few examples must suffice. But any thorough consideration of personality variables would deal with the reciprocal interplay between peer groups and the following: motivation toward scholarly activity; aesthetic tastes; political preferences; originality; academic aptitudes; the student's attitudes toward his college and education generally and toward the future (as well as the past, including his parents and the values he ascribes to them); his attitudes toward aspects of the larger society and toward religion; his leisure-time habits and preferences; and his self-image. This is a suggestive rather than exhaustive list; the few examples I have cited are meant merely to imply the range of research possibilities in which personality variables are viewed as dependent on peer group association. The formation of such groups—and exposure to them—is seen as dependent on personality variables.

If the possibilities are great, so also is the need for such research. For if we are to know what changes occur in the student as a result of his college experience, we must know what he is like when he arrives and somehow disentangle the influential components of the subsequent experience. Thus the emphasis on input variables: we must know the relevant attributes of the entering student. But beyond assessing increments of knowledge by the use of conventional measures, assuming the while that the teacher is the sole significant agent of change, we had better cultivate an open-minded research attitude in considering other variables and other agents. Among these latter—and particularly for certain critical variables—the student's peers may be key agents of change.

I emphasize, therefore, the potential research yield in identifying and measuring those student attributes which condition the groups he enters, which then, as a result of such exposure, are altered. Such attributes span a remarkably broad range. For convenience I have ordered them in four categories of variables: socially significant biological traits, characteristics of the categorical context of the student's family, characteristics of the student's precollege groups, and finally, the precipitate of this seventeen-year trip through peopled time and peopled space, seen in a long roster of personality variables.

4

American College Experience as a Socialization Process

ROBERT A. LeVINE

This chapter is addressed to the following questions: What are the means by which the overt behavior and values of American college students are modified by their peers? What are the optimal conditions for such modification? How can behavior-modifying mechanisms in college peer groups be studied and their effects empirically assessed? One approach to these questions is to assume the relevance to the college situation of the principles of social learning that have been developed in laboratory experimentation on habit acquisition and applied to the acquisition of values in children (Miller and Dollard, 1941; Hill, 1959). The application of such principles can suggest variables in college environments that may have a direct effect on the behavior of students.

This set of principles can be stated briefly as follows. A person first performs a particular response as the result of verbal instruction, of observing another person performing it, or of trial-and-error behavior (Sears *et al.*, 1957, p. 369). The degree to which the response becomes habitual is a function of (*a*) the amount of motivation or drive the individual has toward certain goals, (*b*) the amount of reinforcement or drive reduction he experiences for each performance of the response, (*c*) the distinctiveness (or noticeability) of the cues or stimulus elements leading to drive reduction, (*d*) the number of times he performs the response in a reinforcing environment, or (*e*) the amount of reinforcement he sees other persons receive for performance of the response.[1] When the effective environment is a group that attaches a positive value to the response, we may refer to this process of habit acquisition as socialization.

There is one difficulty in applying this laboratory-based framework to college environments that is not encountered in its use for the study of child behavior in family environments — the factor of selective recruitment. Parents cannot select the infants they wish to rear, nor can the infant select his parents. The effect of this, with respect to acquired characteristics such as values, is equivalent to the random assignment of infants to parental environments and thereby approximates laboratory conditions. College students, however, are selected by colleges, and peer groups within colleges, primarily on the basis of acquired characteristics. Furthermore, some students are able to choose colleges and peer groups which are highly compatible with their existing orientations or which represent ideals with which they identify. Such students are already socialized to the values of these college groups. This means it is often incorrect to attribute behavioral variation among student groups to differential group influence, since it represents mainly the effects of differential selection and anticipatory socialization.

The danger of confounding the effects of selection with those of socialization makes the college environment a more difficult setting for the study of such mechanisms. The investigator interested in the mechanisms producing behavior change in fairly typical American college populations has to introduce numerous controls in order to test his hypothesis. But should he wish to study the maximal changes that can be wrought by various socialization techniques, the investigator can concentrate on situations of extreme discontinuity, such as student populations for whom the college environment presents a set of demands differing drastically from those of their precollege life. Such a situation is found in the small, progressive college with a nonconformist and politically liberal atmosphere but with

[1] For a discussion of the concept of observational learning, compare Campbell (1960).

students drawn mainly from politically conservative families and strict boarding-school backgrounds (cf. Newcomb, 1943). Protestant and Jewish students attending urban Catholic universities may provide another case of discontinuity. These discontinuous situations offer the best opportunities for uncovering mechanisms by which changes in behavior can be produced in groups of college students.

Whether or not a college presents its students with a sharply discontinuous environment, it is possible to detect peer group influence by charting the behavior changes that are exhibited by individuals during the course of their four-year college experience. At no college is selection so perfect that all the students recruited have orientations compatible with the dominant values of the peer groups in which they will find themselves. The study of Goldsen *et al.* (1960) illustrates several designs which separate socialization effects from preselection factors. They compare the admitted cheating of fraternity members at eleven universities with that of independent students at the same institutions, dividing them according to year in college (Goldsen *et al.*, 1960, p. 79). Since the difference in proportion of freshman fraternity members and freshman independents who admit cheating is slight, and differences are progressively greater over the years of college, Goldsen *et al.* conclude that the cheating of fraternity members is reinforced by their peer groups. Note, however, that this is not a longitudinal study of the same students and thus makes the assumption that seniors would have given the same responses when they were freshmen as did the freshmen that were tested. This challengeable assumption is eliminated in a panel design, such as the one used by the same authors to trace the changing political-economic opinions of fraternities at Cornell (Goldsen *et al.*, 1960, pp. 119–21). In the Cornell study, the same students were tested twice, and it was thus possible to ascribe changes in an individual's opinion to socialization by the peer group. The panel design has the unquestionable advantage of not confounding the learning of the individual with selective processes, such as dropping out and transferring from another college, that otherwise cannot always be controlled. It would be most desirable to divide the panel into subgroups on the basis of input variables (cf. Chap. 3, this volume) so that the interaction of input and college peer group variables could be detected.

VIEWS ON THE FUNCTION OF THE COLLEGE IN INDIVIDUAL DEVELOPMENT

Before proceeding further, it is necessary to set the research problems in perspective by stating some extant views of the role of college experience in the socio-psychological development of American youth. There are three basic positions that indicate the range of social science theory on the subject.

1. In college the individual acquires habits (including value-orientations) that are socially adaptive in postcollege life. This acquisition is part of adolescent personality development, and it is thus appropriate to study the college peer group as a social-izing agency much as one would study the family. In one version of this view, college experience serves mainly to reinforce habits acquired earlier; in another version, the discontinuity between precollege and college environments is stressed, indicating that entirely new habits must be learned. In either event, measurable and permanent changes in behavior are expected to occur during the college experience.

2. The college is one of several successive social environ-ments through which individuals may pass between adolescence and death. In each environment, the individual responds to immediate pressures but acquires few new habits that carry over into the next. Conformity occurs without internalization. The latter process — the acquisition of habits that resist extinction in environments differing from those in which they were formed — may be viewed either as peculiar to childhood or as unimportant in determining social behavior. In either event, what behavioral changes take place during college years are not seen as having any long-range effect, except insofar as an individual's having gone to college (or to a particular college) may help determine his place in adult society.

3. The individual's life in college is part of a transition from family life to adult participation in the wider social system. The transitional period is characterized by revolt against parents,

apathy concerning adult affairs, and the embracing of "youth culture." Behavior in this period is neither carried over from childhood nor socially adaptive in adulthood. Its function lies more in extinguishing childhood habits than in specific preparation for adult life. College experience, then, prepares a new *tabula rasa* for socialization in the adult role system of a complex society.

These three positions are not necessarily exclusive, and in some of the many varieties of American college experience each of them appears to hold true. It is the job of the social scientist to find out the extent to which each obtains for the particular colleges he studies, but their general applicability to certain types of environments will be indicated here.

The first view is supported by the findings of Davie and Hare (1956) in their study of "Ivy," an eastern men's college. Speaking of the peer group recreation pattern of "well-roundedness," they state the following (Davie and Hare, 1956, p. 15).

The pattern was seen (by undergraduate informants) as functional for upper class social life in the larger society since the well-rounded man is at an advantage among the country club set. It is also viewed as functional for future success in business where golf, bridge, etc., are some of the unofficial prerequisites for successful execution of the executive function.

The authors emphasize the continuity of this college preparation for adult life with the student's previous experience, the college environment providing mainly a strong reinforcement of certain previous habits and a definition of their appropriate place in life. The impression is one of an integrated folk culture in which males are sent to college to complete the socialization begun in family and boarding school and which will equip them for their adult roles. The college experience is compatible and continuous with precollege and postcollege life. This may indeed be the case among segments of the upper- and upper-middle classes in the United States. Another kind of life history is that of the upwardly mobile person, the child of a working-class family, for whom the college experience is drastically discontinuous but nevertheless provides him with skills and values that are necessary for him to adapt to adult life in a different subculture.

For many individuals, college experience seems to be ephemeral and to have little discernible effect. This is particularly true if the effects examined are those stated as official aims of the institution. It is less true if one considers the possible effects of peer influence as well as of the faculty and administration. But even considering a wider range of influences, there are many students whose involvement in college is slight and who emerge with their original values and attitudes intact. Perhaps this is most extreme in the case of the student who lives at home and attends a nearby technological institute. He may continue to have intensive contact with his parents and high-school friends and be relatively unexposed to the college environment outside the classroom. Even among those who are exposed to college environments, there are some who appear uninfluenced or who are only temporarily affected. The latter include, as an extreme, the campus bohemians from middle-class families who return in adulthood to conventional middle-class life. The apparently uninfluenced also include those students who select a college and/or college peer group closely compatible with their earlier training. Vassar graduates of this type are described in the report by Sanford *et al.* (1956). Change is a matter of degree, of course, and it is possible that they have been permanently changed in ways that only a detailed analysis of behavior would reveal.

There is considerable evidence indicating that, whatever the long-range positive effect of college experience, it often provides a transition from dependence on parents and parent-supervised activities to a life in which self-reliance and personal freedom are greater. This is most pronounced for students who leave their parental home for the first extended period when they attend college. Elkin and Westley (1955), reviewing sociological studies of precollege adolescents, conclude that in upper-middle-class groups, in which children ordinarily attend suburban public schools through twelfth grade, there are no signs of storm and stress, discontinuous socialization, or parent-child conflict.

It may be that such adolescents experience the first strains of personal independence when they become students in a residential college. The literature on emotional disorders of college students points to such a conclusion. For example, in an analysis of twenty cases of an "acute confusional state" in students at a residential college, Carlson (1958) found that the factors most frequently associated with the onset of this non-psychotic anxiety reaction were insecurity due to a new environment; first heterosexual commitment, with difficulty in achieving a satisfactory relationship; conflict with parents over choice of career and mate. Davie and Hare (1956, p. 18) report their informants' subjective feelings that "the transition from the secondary school to college tended to be a difficult one" and emphasize the new-found freedom and its concomitant responsibility.

Thus the college years are for some students an initiation period when childhood habits are eradicated and some self-reliance developed. Weaning from parents, choice of career, selection of mate, and broadening of social and intellectual horizons are features of the transitional character of many college careers. Although college experience as a dramatic personal transition seems generally to occur in those students at residential colleges who have left home for the first time, there may be special situations in which the break is even sharper (for example, students from severely restrictive boarding schools attending permissive universities or rural students at large universities dominated by urbanites).

Acknowledging that American college life can indeed be either an adaptive preparation for the adult role, a superficial experience leaving no permanent mark, or a break with past ties, it is possible to conclude only that college experiences differ so markedly that no single conception of the college as socializing agent can be adequate. Therefore, it is necessary to formulate the properties of college experience as variables that have different strengths in different situations.

AN EMPIRICAL MODEL

There are educational institutions, few of them colleges in the ordinary sense, that reportedly produce marked changes and even transformations in the behavior of their students. Such institutions exhibit certain of the conditions that are optimal for inducing behavior changes—conditions that are approximated in varying degree by college environments. An examination of them will help us translate the general theories presented at the beginning of this article into empirical variables measurable on the American college campus.

Examples of educational institutions with considerable impact are nurses' training programs and medical internships, Chinese thought-reform schools for intellectuals, Bennington College, and British officer-training schools. Thorner (1955) suggests that hospital training programs for nurses achieve "internalization of role personality" in their students. As evidence, he cites the emotional revulsion expressed by many trained nurses at the thought of deviating from expected role behavior by marrying a patient. He claims that such internalization is also produced by intern-training programs for physicians but does not occur in the training of dentists, pharmacists, and optometrists. The Chinese thought-reform schools have as a major goal a "shift in role behavior and personal identity from the filial son or daughter to the enthusiastic participant in the Communist movement" (Lifton, 1957, p. 15). They were apparently successful in many cases, although backsliding was frequent enough to supply Lifton with informants in Hong Kong.

Newcomb (1943) has documented the changes in the political and economic attitudes of female students from conservative families at Bennington, a progressive college in Vermont, during the 1930's. A journalist and graduate of a peacetime British infantry officers' training school claims that such schools take in middle-class students with no elitist values and turn them into arrogant officers who are convinced of "their absolute right to exercise unquestioned personal authority" and never lose their sense of being members of "a superior and order-giving class" (Raven, 1959, pp. 47–48).

What are the common features of these institutions that enable them to change the values and attitudes of young people? They may be considered under six headings: motivation, isolation, consistency of goals, explicitness of values and role models, practice of positively valued responses, and sanctions.

1. *Motivation.* — Since most of these institutions are specialized training schools with a voluntary attendance, it is reasonable to assume that their incoming students are highly motivated in the direction of institutional aims. Some of the Chinese thought-reform students were involuntarily attending the schools, but their motivation level was raised by coercive means, which are discussed below. Bennington College is the only one of the examples that is an unspecialized institution using no overt coercion to increase the motivation of its students. It is likely that its unusual program of progressive education and its value as an alternative to debutante life operated to provide it with students whose attachment to the college was unusually high. Thus a strong drive to complete courses, to conform to institutional expectations, or to achieve success in the school seems to be a condition for modification of behavior.

2. *Isolation from sources of influence outside the school.* — This is a striking feature of all the educational institutions under consideration. Lifton (1957, p. 12) states of the student in the Chinese thought-reform school: "He is living in a virtually airtight communication system: he does not leave it, no outside or contradictory ideas come through to him, and he never has the opportunity to weigh objectively a thought or attitude." Though this represents an extreme, the other institutions approach it. Thorner (1955, p. 537) attributes the influence of the training program for nurses and internship to life in the "isolated community" of the hospital. Newcomb also emphasizes the isolated setting of Bennington. Trainees in military training schools are characteristically isolated, as Dornbusch (1955, p. 317) states of the incoming cadet at the U.S. Coast Guard Academy: "For two months . . . the swab is not allowed to leave the base or engage in social intercourse with non-cadets." Isolation should facilitate learning, for distracting stimuli are absent, and the attention of the individual is not drawn away from the institutional environment.

3. *Intra-institutional goal consistency.* — In these schools the goals of the students are consistent with the goals of the instructors. Development of student subcultures in conflict with official

institutional aims appears to be minimal. In the Chinese thought-reform schools, this is formally controlled through the use of group leaders who receive orders to carry out in their ten-man groups and inform on their fellows to school officials. The lack of conflicting orientations between student peer groups and the faculty is particularly striking at Bennington, because it occurs in a non-coercive environment and because it deviates from the situation at so many American colleges. A consistency of goals among institutional subgroups may also be viewed as a condition isolating the individual student from distracting stimuli.

4. *Explicitness of values and role models.* — Each of these institutions presents a distinctive environment to its students, with little ambiguity about what kind of behavior is deemed desirable. In the training schools and thought-reform schools there is verbal instruction and indoctrination concerning expected role behavior, and individuals can also observe graduates or more advanced students performing the positively valued responses. At Bennington, although there was no program of indoctrination, the importance of political and economic issues in campus life made the college a distinctive environment for its students, and upperclassmen served as attitudinal role models for the freshmen. For most girls, there was no doubt about what political-economic attitudes were favored by the college as a whole.

5. *Practice of positively valued responses.* — In no case are the students passive agents simply absorbing verbal instructions; instead they are making responses and actively imitating their role models. At most of the institutions it could be said that repetition of expected role behavior is a feature of the training program, though not always a formal requirement. The length of the programs alone insures considerable repetition.

6. *Sanctions.* — Students are rewarded for performing positively valued responses and punished for performing incompatibly. Rewards include praise, higher group prestige, and privileges and positions within the student body. Punishments include expulsion, demerit systems, and criticism. Lifton (1957, p. 10) described the handling of Chinese thought-reform students whose manifest opinions are not changing as rapidly as expected.

Such a student becomes the target for relentless criticism in his group; and during odd hours he is approached by other students and cadres in an attempt to mend his ways. Should he fail to respond, friendliness gives way to veiled threats, and he may be called in to receive an official admonition from a class head. As a last resort, he may be subjected to the ultimate humility of a mass "struggle" meeting: in ritualistic form, he is publicly denounced by faculty members, cadres and fellow students—his deficiencies reiterated and laid bare.

In the institutions where the students' initial spontaneous motivation is high, they tend to be sensitive to sanctions from their instructors and supervisors. Furthermore, the enforcement power that supervisors and fellow students have by virtue of their intensive contact with the student combines with the isolation of the institution to make evasion of punishment difficult.

It is obvious that the typical American college environment does not closely approximate the conditions of the previously mentioned schools. Some of the most striking points of divergence are the lower motivation of the average American college student; the presence of peer values that oppose the official aims of the college; and the relative difficulty of maintaining isolation and enforcing rules. Despite these differences, the conditions found in the institutions that reportedly produce considerable change in their students can serve as a model and provide dimensions within which to study college environments and students.

SOCIALIZATION PATTERNS IN COLLEGE PEER GROUPS

Up to this point, discussion has concerned the influence on student behavior of widely varied aspects of the institutional environment. In applying this framework to college environments, however, the discussion will be limited to the influence of the student's peers. This is justifiable on several grounds. First of all, some evidence, such as that given by Jacob (1957), and the personal impressions of may observers, indicate that curriculum and faculty have little direct effect on student values at most colleges.[2] Second, American college life is characterized by the elaborate development of an autonomous under-

[2] See Chap. 3 of this volume, by Everett Wilson, for evidence concerning the effect of teacher-student contact in colleges.

graduate culture that forms the immediate environment of the student. It is likely that this immediate setting has the most influence on his behavior and that it weakens influences coming from the faculty and other parts of the wider environment.

Let me indicate at this point what kinds of modifiable behavior I shall be discussing. I shall be concerned with the impact of certain agents of change—among them, the student's peers—upon such matters as the following: (1) attitudes toward college academic performance (compared to social and athletic performance); (2) intellectual-aesthetic-scientific values (positive and negative); (3) attitudes toward sociability and group participation; (4) social class values (exclusiveness and snobbishness, conspicuous consumption attitudes, class-typing of personal behavior); (5) ethnocentrism, race prejudice, permissiveness concerning expression of strange or obnoxious ideas; and (6) political orientations, such as attitudes on domestic and international issues.

The list is by no means exhaustive, but to these values and attitudes should be added simple awareness of events, peoples, and institutions and of trends in the intellectual, aesthetic, scientific, social, political, and international worlds. This list covers the topic often referred to as "broadening of the student's horizons." A collection of the modifiable behavior of college students such as this is a mixed bag, partly because college students are not being prepared for a particular set of roles and partly because it represents the diverse topical interests of social researchers. Since the kinds of behavior involved are so varied, I will not attempt to analyze each of them in terms of stimulus and response. Note, however, that investigators such as Newcomb (1943) have more often found the acquisition of negative, or critical and skeptical, responses in college students than they have the development of positive orientations.

The following discussion contains suggestions for the measurement of peer group conditions that can serve as independent variables in research designed to study the effects of college experience. It follows the categories used for the examples in the previous section, with the exception of intra-institutional goal consistency, which is treated by Clark and Trow in Chapter 2 of this volume.

1. *Motivation.* — The degree and kinds of motivation of under- graduates vary widely and may be expected to relate to individual differences in susceptibility to peer group influence. For example, a high achievement drive might act to involve the individual in competition and striving for excellence within the peer group and thus render him more susceptible to its values. However, an equally plausible hypothesis is that strong achievement mo- tivation leads to a concentration on grades and career goals and insulates the student from peer influence. Such competing hy- potheses could be tested by comparing the degree of change in the values and attitudes of students who are high or low in their motivation to achieve. It might be that at some colleges the highly motivated students changed more in the direction of peer values, while at other insitutions the less motivated students changed more. This could provide an indication of the ability of the dif- ferent peer populations to influence students with high drive to strive for excellence within, rather than outside, the peer group.

Another motivational factor pertinent to undergraduate life is dependency. Many students describe themselves as lonely and isolated during their first weeks or months at college. This may be more pronounced for those who live on campus and are cut off from their families and old friends, but it can also be important for students living at home who may feel left out of the campus life. Such feelings of isolation can lead to a strong drive to be affiliated with, and dependent on, other students. One hypothesis is that the stronger the drive for dependency in an individual, the more his behavior will change with time by the influence of his peers. Sociability is yet another dimension of dependency. Some students come to college with a strong desire to meet people and have an active social life; it could be predicted that the greater this desire, the more change will take place.

An individual may be influenced not only by his own motiva- tion but by the drives of those around him. A student with a given drive level may react differently to a situation in which he is surrounded by high-achieving, highly anxious, and highly dependent students than to a situation consisting of students low on these factors. By giving personality tests to students in the "interpersonal environment" of the individual,[3] one could detect the influence of the motivations of other students on his change in behavior. It is also possible to form experimental groups on the basis of motivational factors.[4]

Several studies of college students that did not focus on peer groups demonstrate the importance of a motivational factor best described as ego-involvement. The findings of Selvin and Hagstrom (1960) and Goldsen *et al.* (1960) suggest that students vary in their susceptibility to influence by college environments according to how much they are interested in religious activity, public affairs, and ultimate success in career goals. Some of these interests tend to expose the student to college influence; others insulate him from it. It seems appropriate to attempt to measure the degree of the student's ego-involvement in goals and activities relevant to particular values and to compare the extent to which students with high and low degrees of ego-involvement absorb or resist the values present in their peer groups.

2. *Isolation.*—In the previous section, "isolation" referred to lack of contact with persons and events outside the institution. Here it refers to the isolation of students from sources of influence outside their immediate peer groups. Davie and Hare (1956, p. 20) report the following of "Ivy."

Since the evidence from the panel suggests that for the average undergraduate there is less continuous contact with other aspects of the college environment such as faculty and coaches, and with non-college aspects such as family and girl friends, than with the peer culture, it would appear that the culture is the most important single external factor in the student's experience. Most of his time is spent with his peers. The small size and relatively homogeneous nature of the student body tend to promote conformity and group solidarity and this tendency is reinforced by situational factors such as the geographical location of Ivy [isolated], the absence of cars, the presence of a fraternity system, and the fact that all students must live in university dormitories on campus.

[3] See Chap. 7 of this volume, by Peter H. Rossi.
[4] See Chap. 5 of this volume, by Ben Willerman.

Thus the peer group can be isolated not only from the world outside the college, but from non-peer influences within the college. Indeed Goldsen *et al.* (1960) refer to formal peer groups as "insulating subsystems." Not all college student bodies are as isolated from external influences as that of "Ivy," and previous examples lead to the expectation that greater isolation makes for more behavior change in students, a hypothesis which could be tested in a comparative study of colleges. Measures would include not only the geographical position of the campus, and the amount of student mobility off campus, but also the degree of student-faculty contact.

On the intra-institutional level, the degree of isolation can be determined by measuring the frequency of student communication with persons outside the peer groups, as well as by classifying them according to gross residential characteristics that affect their exposure to non-peer influence. Isolation from contact with parents would theoretically be one of the most interesting variables, since it relates to the question whether precollege parental influence continues into the college years and counteracts peer influence. (In both Bennington College and the Chinese thought-reform schools, absorption of school values was accompanied by rejection of parental values.)

The division of students into commuters and campus residents is a ready-made variation that can be exploited in research. Willerman and Swanson (1951, 1953) found many differences between the feelings of satisfaction, participation, friendship, and "belongingness" of sorority members who lived in the house and those who lived in town. This suggests that the conditions for exclusive socialization by the sorority were better for the house residents. The influence of parents on attitude change in the two groups within the sororities was not explored, but it could be.

Campus residents could be divided according to the frequency and content of their communication with their parents. Frequency might be gauged by how many times per week or month students saw their parents, communicated by letter, and talked to them on the telephone. Applicable information concerning parent-child communication would be whether the student discusses certain problems related to peer group concerns with his parents, to what extent he receives guidance from them, the extent of his financial dependence on them, etc. A most significant study would be one that indicated the parts that parents and peers had played in the making of the student's decisions during a specified period in college. These measures would provide a basis for classifying campus residents according to their degree of parent-orientation or peer-orientation.

An important supplement to data on parent-child communication would be knowledge of any precollege experience of the student away from home. For boarding-school graduates and veterans of military service, a high or low degree of communication with parents might have quite different meaning than for a student whose college experience was the first break with the family.

Students may have other off-campus contacts that are worthy of measurement. For example, married undergraduates (of which there are an increasing number) could be compared in their change in value attitudes with single campus residents. Some students continue to see their high-school friends off campus and to fraternize with townspeople; many date persons outside the college. All this outside interaction should be included in a calculation of the frequency and content of communication to yield a measure of the isolation of the student from influences outside the college peer group.

3. *Explicitness of values and role models.* — Although the typical undergraduate college does not have aims as narrow or explicit as a military training school or theological seminary, it can be a distinctive environment for its students. Furthermore, groups within the student body are likely to be highly distinctive, each with its own self-image, goals, and value-orientations (Goldsen *et al.*, 1960, pp. 64–66). The hypothesis here is that, other things being equal, the more distinctive, noticeable, and explicit the peer group stimuli, the more behavior change in the student.

Newcomb's study of Bennington College serves as a guide for testing this type of hypothesis. Having found that Bennington students became less conservative during their years at the college, Newcomb asked freshmen and seniors to estimate the attitudes of their own class and of the class three years above or below them. He found that seniors tended to overestimate the actual differences in conservatism between their own class and the freshmen, while the freshmen underestimated them. At Skidmore College, however, though seniors were slightly less conservative than freshmen, both freshmen and seniors underestimated the difference in conservatism between them, reducing it to zero (Newcomb, 1943, pp. 52–53). The difference in response between Bennington and Skidmore is clearly related to the fact that at Bennington political conservatism was a much discussed issue, a focus of student attention, while at Skidmore it was not. This suggests that the estimates made by students, especially seniors, of freshman-senior differences on a particular attitude or value can be used to obtain a measure of its importance or distinctiveness in the student environment. If they consider it important, the seniors will tend to overestimate the differences between themselves and the freshmen; if it is not a focus of their interest and attention, they will underestimate or deny the differences. This is a particularly appropriate device for a study of socialization because the seniors are the finished products of the socialization process and may act as role models for the freshmen.

The estimation of freshman-senior differences need not be limited to studies of entire student bodies or cross-college comparisons. One could take several formal groups believed to be different in their values (e.g., fraternities and sororities with contrasting reputations) and have newest and oldest members estimate the value differences between them. Presumably, the amount of difference estimated would vary across groups. The values and attitudes on which seniors overestimated the difference would represent the ideals toward which the newer members are being socialized.

Before doing an individual questionnaire study of this kind, it would be useful to interview informants from each group concerning their images of the group and their conscious ideals for the behavior of its members. This was not so important in the Bennington College study, because the values of the college environment were explicit and obvious to Newcomb. But few social scientists, faculty members, or administrative personnel have an accurate picture of the constellations of values and attitudes that pervade the undergraduate subcultures at their colleges. Often a particular attitude in which the investigator is interested can best be understood in its relation to an overall ideal such as "well-roundedness," "Ivy-league-ness," or "being cool." The informant interview gets at these general value-orientations and their relations to specific attitudes, providing material from which one can construct a better questionnaire.

The method of comparing estimated attitudes to actual ones is well suited to the measurement of the role-model attributes of seniors but need not be limited to such groups. Assuming that awareness of another's attitude is required for the emulation or acceptance of that attitude, studies could be done of the degree to which students are aware of the actual values and attitudes of others whom they seem to be emulating. For example, at colleges where there is a fairly distinct group of campus leaders, one could investigate the responses of these leaders as well as the estimates by other students of their responses to values and attitudes. It might be, for example, that the students outside of the leadership group have no idea where the leaders stand on political and racial issues, and therefore cannot be learning from them in this area of behavior. Such investigations, then, would indicate which aspects of the overt behavior and value-attitudes of campus leaders are salient stimuli for other students and which are not.

This method could be used wherever there is a group higher in prestige or one that tends to dominate campus life. One possible research design would obtain estimates by low-prestige fraternity or sorority members of the values of high-prestige group members; another would seek estimates by "independents" of the responses of members of Greek-letter societies. In all such studies estimates would be compared with actual responses, and the more accurate and agreed-upon the estimate, the greater expectation that students will be influenced and changed on that variable.

Visible symbols of subcultural differences within an undergraduate student body could be the subject of cross-college comparative study. For example, suppose an investigator were interested in the stimulus conditions that promote the development of social class-consciousness, and he compared two colleges. At college A there are many fraternities and sororities, ranked according to wealth, exclusiveness, size of house, etc. The wealthiest students have sports cars and new convertibles, less wealthy ones have ordinary and older sedans, and the poorest have no cars at all. The distribution of students from various income groups at college B is the same, but the administration prohibits fraternities, sororities, and student possession of cars on campus and requires all students to live in dormitories. At college B, the most visible means of stratifying the student body are absent, and though invidious comparison in dress may be present, it does not create sharp lines of cleavage among groups of students. The investigator would be justified in predicting, according to the hypothesis proposed here, that the students at college A will become more class-oriented, both in their awareness of class differences and in their evaluations of human differences in terms of class.

A similar design might be possible for the study of the development of political orientations. At some colleges political organizations have few members, and very few students identify themselves politically by group membership. On other campuses there are sizable poltical clubs of varying political ideology, and a larger proportion of the student body is affiliated with political groups. A comparative study should reveal that freshmen initially matched on political awareness, interest, and ideology change their political orientations more in those environments in which political affiliation and interest are more overt.

4. *Practice of positively valued responses.* — Learning theory indicates that frequency is one of the variables antecedent to acquiring habits. It has been noted above that activities in institutions that produce marked changes are often highly repetitive. The student is required to perform the desired responses over and over again in the course of his training. This suggests the value of studying how college students spend their time and how often they repeat various activities. The hypothesis pro-

posed is that those activities more often repeated will come to be more highly valued than those that are practiced less.

Davie and Hare (1956, pp. 15, 16) come closest to discussing this in their description of recreational patterns at "Ivy."

> One reaches the conclusion that, all in all, there is little new behavior added. What changes do occur seem to be changes in degree rather than in kind. Perhaps the major new aspect is the time element in recreation, where the student is freer than formerly to indulge in recreational activity at hitherto unusual times.
>
> In brief, the apparent effect of Ivy culture on the individual student's development in the area of recreation is to enlarge the repertoire of skills, increase his interests, and define the importance of recreation in relation to other areas of undergraduate life.

They make it clear that many students use their free time to perfect their skill in bridge and golf, which they will be using in postcollege life, and to practice an apportionment of time among different activities, something both highly valued in terms of "Ivy" cultural values ("well-roundedness") and functional in later life. The authors imply, although they do not attempt to prove, that the practice of undergraduate years leads to the acquisition of permanent recreational habits. Goldsen *et al.* (1960, pp. 70–71) found that fraternity members participate more in extracurricular activities, date more frequently, and drink alcoholic beverages more frequently than independent students, even when social class is held constant. Group membership requires fraternity members to participate more in such activities, and it seems possible that habits are thus developed that independent students as a group do not develop to the same degree.

Although it may prove difficult to avoid confounding the effect of repeated practice with that of interpersonal influence, the behavior-modifying consequences of response repetition by college students is well worth exploring. Experimental methods might be most fruitful in investigating this topic.

5. *Strength of sanctions.* – In a simplistic response-reinforcement approach to conformity behavior, the amount of reward

for conforming and amount of punishment for not conforming are major independent variables. To apply even so simple a pattern to the environment in a college peer group, it is necessary to know (*a*) what the rules are to which conformity is required; (*b*) what kinds of rewards are available; and (*c*) what kinds of punishments are possible. In my opinion, the investigator can most efficiently fulfill these prerequisites for his systematic research by conducting informant interviews with members of student groups, focusing primarily on the question of how much of a student's behavior is of normative concern to his peer group. Without exploratory work, a pencil-and-paper questionnaire on acts considered praiseworthy and criticizable is likely to miss many of the implicit rules of the peer group that are revealed in an informant interview. The latter technique also has the advantage of unearthing conceptual connections among rules.

The study by Davie and Hare is one of the few in which informant interviews were used to investigate undergraduate rules and attitudes toward deviance. The following finding concerning pattern of recreational activity is an illustration of the results (Davie and Hare, 1956, p. 15).

Using the majority who follow the pattern as a base point, men who exaggerate the pattern are identified as "goof-offs." At the other extreme are men who consciously do not follow the pattern and who are aware that they are a group apart; these are the "individualists." Between the majority and the individualist, are three groups who also deviate from the pattern, but to a small degree. The most acceptable group is that of the "jocks" (athletes) who are asked by their coaches not to smoke or drink during training and to get to bed early. Next in order of acceptability of motive would be the men whose interest in extracurricular activities or work for student employment prohibits full participation in the pattern of recreation. . . . Finally, the "grinds" have the least acceptable motive for not participating.

Goldsen *et al.* (1960) quote numerous explicit statements by individual fraternity members concerning the content of indoctrination at "shape-up sessions" (pp. 63, 66) and rules about studying (p. 73). The value statements concerning the academic side of life provide a meaningful background for their subsequent quantitative analysis of admitted cheating.

Once the investigator has established what the recognized rules of behavior are in a peer group and the group's response to various kinds of deviation from the rules, then it is possible to do a study of the effects of varying amounts of reward and punishment.

Reward in groups of college students is usually measured in terms of prestige. Newcomb (1943, p. 168) found that students who achieved prestige and social success tended to adopt college attitudes more frequently than those who were less successful. Later work by Homans (1950, p. 188) and Merei (1949) lends confirmation. Using this finding as a hypothesis, the investigator working in a more complex college environment than Bennington could devise at least two ways of testing it. First, taking as a sample the students entering a formal or residential group at a particular point, he could find out whether the individuals who achieve high prestige in the group change their values and attitudes more in the direction of group ideals. Second, by doing a comparative study of fraternities or sororities which are ranked by degree of consensus and by prestige (see Willerman and Swanson [1953] for measurement of group prestige), he could find out whether the freshman-senior differences on values and attitudes are greater in high-prestige groups than in low-prestige groups. The hypothesis would predict that an individual would derive more reward from being a member of a high-prestige group and that such a group would therefore be the more effective socializing agency. Ideally, one would want to measure change in attitude in individuals over the full period of their membership, but taking freshman-senior differences cross-sectionally might be an adequate substitute.

Other types of reward should be mentioned, though the possibility of measuring them must be determined empirically. College students are often dependent on their peers for emotional support, advice, and material goods that can be borrowed in times of need. These are rewards inherent in peer relationships, and it is possible that those who feel they have received more of them change more in the direction of group norms. One kind of help that has exceptional importance in peer groups is supplying members with dates and opportunities for meeting students of the opposite sex. Students who are satisfied with this aspect of their peer group membership may differ in attitude change from those who feel deprived.

Punishment is more overt than reward in student peer groups and thus easier to explore. Many college peer groups, especially formal ones like fraternities and sororities, have formal punishments for rule deviation; point systems and fining are common. Davie and Hare (1956) describe the effect of a formal but covert means of punishment: Members, even those who have done little drinking before, tend to drink at "Ivy" fraternity parties because they have, in paying their dues, paid for the liquor. If they do not drink, then they are paying for others' liquor. Goldsen *et al.* (1960, p. 63) quote fraternity pledges' accounts of the biting criticisms by their "pledge-masters" concerning the amount of activity and time spent at the house, seriousness of attitude toward the fraternity, table manners, personal appearance, etc. It seems quite clear that these "shaping-up sessions" have punitive aspects and are explicitly designed to eliminate undesired responses.

Although it is desirable to discover the formal penalties of a group whose normative behavior is being studied, individual measures have the advantages of insuring comparable data and being applicable to informal peer groups as well as formal ones. Such measures should be directed at the expectations of the student concerning the reactions of his peers to a violation of group rules. Questions could involve either the respondent himself as a rule violator or a hypothetical group member with whom he can identify. For each infraction the student would be asked whether he had experienced, been threatened with, had a friend who experienced or heard of someone who experienced the punishment that he has mentioned.

After student judges had rated the severity of the types of punishment mentioned, the responses could be scaled in terms of their severity, and hypotheses tested that relate attitude change as a dependent variable to severity of punishment experienced, heard of, or anticipated. This could be done both for specific aspects of behavior and for overall socialization.

For example, one could find out whether those students who reported being criticized or abused (or that they had heard of someone so treated) by their peers for playing classical music on their phonographs had changed their attitude toward such music. Summing severity scores across different types of infractions, one could find out whether students or groups of students who experienced or anticipated more severe punishments became more effectively socialized to group rules.

INTERNATIONALIZATION VERSUS SHORT-RUN CONFORMITY

Throughout this chapter the dependent variable has been the acquisition of habits positively valued by the group. When an individual changes markedly, so that some of his habits are more in line with those of the group, he is said to have been socialized by the group. There is question, however, about how long the change will last and under what conditions. One of the imperfections involved in applying the principles of habit acquisition to non-laboratory situations is the difficulty of finding conditions which approximate those of extinction trials. In these, the experimenter can test the permanence of a habit by repeatedly eliciting the response under non-reinforcing conditions and recording the number of trials before the cue stimuli fail to elicit the responses. The student of human socialization, however, usually deals with individuals whose later environment reinforces the habits, making it difficult to tell whether the behavior of the individual is due to earlier learning or contemporary pressures.

This difficulty is inherent in studies of college experience as a socialization process, and it is inevitable in any society in which educational institutions are at all integrated with the adult role system.

In terms of research, the investigator may choose to concentrate on measurable change in behavior in college and not concern himself with its permanence or depth, or he may conduct a study of "internalization" in which the aim will be to find those independent variables that leave the deepest and most enduring mark. In the first case, the procedure would be to take measures of the behavior of the same individuals at college entrance (or shortly after), at graduation (or shortly before), and perhaps at several intermediate stages. The degree of change over the four years or some fraction of it would be tested for its correlation with the aspects of peer environments discussed above. In the second case, the same design would be supplemented by research on the endurance and intensity of the change. The endurance of the change in behavior after college graduation can be charted by using seniors as a panel whose behavior is measured during the five, ten, or twenty-five years after they leave college.

Under some conditions it might be possible to find two groups of students whose behavior had changed in the same direction during college, one of which is exposed mainly to postcollege environments favorable to the maintenance of the senior-year value or attitude, and one group exposed to environments the investigator judges to be unfavorable to its maintenance. He would then be able to see if there is differential retention in the two groups.

For example, suppose that among a group of students attending a college with a strong intellectual-aesthetic atmosphere, one found that the magazines they read regularly changed from mass-circulation weeklies in their freshman year to "little" magazines in their senior year. He could then compare the reading habits of alumni who chose artistic or academic careers with ones who entered the business and professional world, to see if the senior-year habits of the latter fall off relative to the former group. A third group, one of business-professional people who were alumni of a different type of college, could be compared to the business-professional alumni of the intellectual-aesthetic college to find out if the latter college left a permanent mark on its alumni. The example is hypothetical but illustrates a design that can be used if one is investigating a variable that is comparable in college and postcollege life.

Research can also be conducted into the intensity or "depth" of a change in behavior found in college. Various techniques, experimental and psychometric, are available for assessing the degree to which the adoption of an attitude is superficial or genuine. Though these techniques are suitable for use in studies of college students, their evaluation is not within the scope of this article.

SUMMARY

The college experiences of American youth are varied and complex; they do not fit neatly into any single theory of social recruitment or personality development. No unqualified answer to the question of how much college peer groups affect student values is likely to hold for even a majority of institutions or students. Indeed, even contradictory views on the effect of college life on student behavior may be equally valid, but in different colleges and for different students. However, if there is any empirical justification for viewing college experience as a socialization process, then general principles of social learning, developed in other contexts, should apply to it.

I have attempted to show the pertinence of these principles to the study of behavior-modifying processes in college peer groups. Since selective recruitment and self-selection operate to obscure the effects of such processes in many American college environments, it was necessary to devote some attention to unusual educational experiences in which change in behavior and its probable causes were more obvious. These unusual institutional settings more closely approximate optimal conditions for behavior-modification than does the average American college, and it was possible to extract their common features that promote social learning and formulate them as dimensions that might also be found at varying strengths in college peer groups.

Suggestions were made for research on these variables and their effects on college students. These suggestions serve only to illustrate the tactics of theoretically oriented research on socialization in college settings. Recognizing that future studies on college peer groups will be dictated by the interests of the investigators undertaking them, I nevertheless venture to urge that such efforts be informed by and related to extant theories of social learning and social organization.

Part II

Problems of Empirical Inquiry

5

Field
Experiments
in the Study of
Peer Groups

BEN WILLERMAN

This chapter examines the use of experimental methods in the study of college peer groups.[1] I shall discuss the advantages and difficulties of this approach, the opportunities for using it on a college campus, and the kinds of experiments which may be and have been done. These fall into two classes: experiments manipulating the composition of peer groups and experiments that study peer group influence more directly by manipulating the opinion environment and factors affecting communication. In the course of this discussion I shall describe the methods and some of the substantive findings of relevant experiments but I do not intend a comprehensive exposition of experimental methods.[2] Although many laboratory experiments on peer effects have been done, I will refer to them only occasionally. This discussion will concentrate on field experiments.

Many studies of peer group effects on college students have been done, but they have been mostly surveys and field studies.

[1] In addition to the editors and other seminar members I wish to thank Professors R. F. Berdie, R. L. Hall, and H. H. Kelley for their helpful comments on this chapter.

[2] For more extensive discussions of field and laboratory experiments, see French, Jr. (1953) and Festinger (1953). The present discussion has borrowed heavily from these two chapters.

Field studies and surveys can be valuable and are often the only methods by which certain problems can be studied, but these procedures have some inherent limitations that the experiment does not have.[3] When the investigator wishes to avoid these limitations in testing a hypothesis about certain peer group influences, or in evaluating their effects, he might well consider performing an experiment in the laboratory or in the "natural" setting of the college.

A GENERAL COMPARISON OF FIELD EXPERIMENTS, LABORATORY EXPERIMENTS, AND FIELD STUDIES

In the following discussion the term "field study" refers to studies of individuals or groups in their "natural" settings in which no attempt is made to manipulate any of the conditions that affect the variables to be measured. The investigator simply measures the existing variations in the conditions and uses statistical procedures to determine whether the variables are related. He attempts by logic, theory, and experience to make a convincing case that one of the variables is a cause of the other and tries to eliminate alternative explanations by proper analysis of his data.[4]

The "field experiment" also refers to a study in a "natural" setting, but certain conditions are intentionally manipulated in order to determine whether they have certain effects. The manipulated conditions are commonly called independent variables, and the measured consequences of these conditions are called the dependent variables. Frequently, everything else in a situation is left unchanged in order to evaluate the importance of an independent variable in comparison with the multitude of other factors affecting the subject's behavior.

The laboratory experiment is distinguished from the field experiment, as Festinger (1953, p. 137) points out, by two features: "whether or not there was an attempt to create a specially suited situation, and the degree of precision in the con-

---

[3]For a comprehensive discussion of the advantages and problems of field studies, see Katz (1953).

[4]For a discussion and an example of this approach see Chapter 6, by Hanan Selvin and Warren Hagstrom, in this volume.

trol and manipulation of variables." The main purpose of a laboratory experiment is to test a hypothesis under the purest conditions possible. Hence, it makes no attempt to duplicate the "real life" setting, in all its complexity, but creates a situation which permits the investigator to examine the relevant phenomena under uncomplicated conditions.

The laboratory experiment is thus preferred to the field experiment when a theoretical hypothesis is to be tested under the most favorable conditions possible—provided that the necessary conditions can be created. The field experiment is preferred to the laboratory experiment when the investigator wants to determine if, in a particular setting, the independent variable is important in determining the outcomes that interest him.

Advantages of Experiments over Field Studies

Ideally, an experiment studies the effect of one variable upon another in such a way that changes in the magnitude of the dependent variable can be attributed only to the influence of the independent variable. All the other factors which might affect the dependent variable are controlled by matching, equating, randomization, or elimination (such as studying only one age group). Hence, if the experiment is done well, a statistically significant difference in the dependent variable between the experimental and control groups can be attributed only to the effect of the experimental treatment.

In the field study, on the other hand, one variable can never be said to cause another no matter how strong their association. Some other variable may be responsible for the covariation. Even when these other variables have been controlled by statistical or analytic means, the possibility still remains that some unmeasured variable was the effective independent variable.

Another closely related advantage of the experiment is the ease of determining the direction of cause and effect. For example, a finding that students who are close friends are more similar in attitudes than students who are acquaintances can be interpreted as showing that similarity of attitudes determines choice of friends or that friendship results in more similar attitudes.

The experiment has another advantage, which is not inherent in the method but which in practice is more apparent there than in the field study. This concerns the specificity with which the variables are defined and measured. In principle, there is no reason why the definition and measurement of a variable in the field cannot be as precise as it is in an experiment, but it seems that the process of designing an experimental condition forces the investigator to define more clearly the variables he wishes to study.

These things being so, it is apparent that one of the chief reasons for experimenting in a field setting, rather than studying it without creating experimental conditions, is the greater possibility of obtaining reasonably conclusive results. Another reason for experimenting in a field setting is to study the effects of conditions which may not occur conveniently in that setting. Thus an entirely new scheme of grouping students in a dormitory may be required to meet the definition of the independent variable that the investigator is interested in studying.

These comments are not intended to oversell field experimentation. The approach may not be appropriate for studying certain problems. Indeed, before conducting an experiment, we need advance information about the particular setting in which it is to take place. We can get this information through preliminary surveys or field studies. Unless the investigator has a good grasp of the relevant variables in that particular situation, he may discover too late that he has overlooked some variables which he should have controlled and manipulated others that were not important.

Disadvantages of Field Experiments

Many types of field experiments are more difficult to execute than field studies. The difficulties increase with the duration of the experimental manipulation and with the time between it and the collection of data, since, as the duration increases, more time is available for undesirable events to occur, including loss of subjects.

To collect the necessary data, a field study requires the co-operation of administrators or leaders of groups as well as of the subjects. The field experiment not only requires this but may also require changes in organization or routines or whatnot. Even after resistance to such changes has been overcome, the problem of maintaining consistent adherence to the experimental conditions remains. This problem may be caused less by reluctance on the part of administrators or group leaders than by an insufficient appreciation of the requirements of the experiment. These problems include maintaining constant conditions between the experimental and control groups except for the experimental treatment and conforming in day-to-day practices with the experimental treatment.

Although the field experiment is designed to overcome the limitations of field studies, in practice it rarely has complete control over the subjects and the chain of events. When complete control is lacking, the investigator often resorts to the same methods of analyzing his data that are used in field studies, and he is not much better off than if he had conducted a field study in the first place. Also, the manipulations are often so complex that it is difficult to determine what the independent variable was. Specific examples of such problems will be mentioned in later sections.

The laboratory experiment is sometimes a desirable alternative to the field experiment. Uncontrolled variables are held to a minimum, as are many of the other problems of field experimentation. The use of laboratory experiments for the study of college peer group effects has focused primarily on the processes of interpersonal and group influence over very short spans of time.

The theories of social influence developed to explain the laboratory phenomena are doubtless also useful in accounting for the effects college peers have on one another. But for the purposes of identifying the specific effects and the means by which students influence one another over the long time span of a college education, it will still be necessary to conduct research in the field setting. For example, a laboratory experiment might show that students can influence one another's evaluation of the desirability of certain occupations. If one were interested in learning whether students do affect one another's actual occupational choice, a study of the interactions of students over a fairly long period of time would be required.

A field experiment, then, should be done when the investigator wants to test a hypothesis about the effects of a particular independent variable in a moderately rigorous way and when he wishes to determine whether the independent variables to be manipulated are important in the particular setting of the experiment.

OPPORTUNITIES FOR EXPERIMENTS ON PEER EFFECTS IN COLLEGE SETTINGS

Opportunities for such studies range from experiments designed to study the effects of programs already existing on the campus, to exposing the students to especially contrived situations in either a "natural" or a laboratory setting. Simply by using a control group, many existing programs could be evaluated to determine their effects.[5] If it is not possible to have a control group in which no treatment at all is given, the effects of an existing program can be compared with those of some alternative program. Existing practices that are too complex or unclear to be studied scientifically can also be modified so that the experimental manipulation may more closely fit the definition of the independent variable.

The rest of this chapter will discuss several types of experiments to illustrate the possibilities of and problems in using the experimental approach to study college peer influence. From the point of view of their purposes, the experiments can be classified under two broad headings: (1) experiments to determine the effect on students' attitudes and behavior of associating, over a fairly long period of time, with students having certain characteristics; and (2) experiments to determine how the immediate behavior of a student is affected by the presence of his peers or by the occurrence of certain events.

In the first type of study, which is referred to as the experi-

[5] For a discussion of the use of various types of control groups in social experiments, see Campbell (1956).

mental study of selective association, the manipulation consists of organizing students with certain characteristics into a relatively stable group so that the reciprocal impact of these characteristics on the students can be evaluated. Having composed these groups, the investigator leaves the students free to behave as they will. After a period of time, he obtains measures of the dependent variable and compares them for the various groups.

Since the focus of the research in the second type of study is usually on the immediate impact of peers, measures of the dependent variable follow closely upon the onset of the experimental manipulation. Indeed, the dependent variable may be the behavior immediately stimulated by the experimental situation. Frequently, the purpose of such studies is to study the actual process of peer influence or to test more specific hypotheses than is possible in experiments on selective association. The experiments I shall discuss under this heading deal principally with communication and social influence.

The discussion will focus on the experimental manipulations performed in the two types of experiments. These manipulations have been selected because they seem important in determining peer effects and because most of the field experiments done in college settings have used such manipulations. It is also desirable to have concrete illustrations for discussion. Though other types of manipulations — style of classroom teaching or of student leadership, organization of student groups — would doubtless have effects on peer influence and would be feasible, I shall not discuss them here.[6]

EXPERIMENTAL STUDIES OF SELECTIVE ASSOCIATION

The experimental manipulation of the kinds of students with whom one has contact makes it possible to assess the differential effects of selective association. Control over those with whom a student interacts can be achieved by increasing the physical proximity between individuals and groups or by requiring or inducing interaction. The first method of control is illustrated by assigning some students to one section of a dormi-

[6] For a discussion of a research program of experiments in college classrooms, see McKeachie (1958).

tory and other students to another section, in the expectation that those students living closer to one another will interact more often than they will with students living farther away. The second type of control is illustrated by assigning some students to a common task or committee or classroom and other students to other comparable situations in the expectation that engaging in a common activity will result in differential contact. I shall present only examples of the first type of control. Such manipulations avoid the strong likelihood of self-selection, a critical defect of correlational studies of the relation between contact and attitude formation.

The few studies predetermining contact among certain students in their natural settings have been done in student residences. Since students spend much time there, it is reasonable to suppose that the effects of peers in these settings should be at least as strong as in other college settings. The manipulations in these studies consist for the most part of exposing some students to others who are similar to them in certain attributes and exposing a comparable group to students different from them on these attributes. Homogeneity and heterogeneity need not, of course, be the only basis of group composition — a point which will be developed later.

Manipulating Similarity and Difference in Attitudes and Personality

One of the simplest studies of selective association to perform (although not necessarily the simplest to interpret) is one in which the investigator does not actually create any conditions but takes advantage of known differences in existing conditions. The subjects are randomly assigned to two or more existing conditions which differ in some important respect, thereby avoiding the problem of self-selection. This is illustrated by a study made by Siegel and Siegel (1957) on the relative effect of two types of residence groups on changes in E-F (authoritarianism) scores, one type having residents who were higher in authoritarianism than the other.

All female freshmen at the university studied were required for their sophomore year to move from a large freshman dormitory to other housing. Among the several types of housing available were some former sorority houses located on Fraternity Row. The fact that residents of Row houses had higher E-F scores than non-Row residents had been established in an earlier study.

Toward the end of the year, following a customary annual procedure, the freshmen ranked the several types of housing in order of preference. Those students who ranked Row housing as their first choice were the subjects of this study. A "drawing" was then held that served as a device to determine a random assignment of subjects to the experimental conditions — Row housing versus non-Row housing.

At the end of the sophomore year these students, along with others involved in a large-scale testing program, took the E-F test for the second time, the first having been taken during their freshman year. The housing preferences of students who wanted to change their residences were also obtained at the annual drawing. The investigators were thus able to compare changes in E-F scale scores of three groups, all of whom had shared at the end of their freshman year a common membership group (freshman dorm) and a common reference group (aspiring to live in the Row houses). Group A consisted of those who drew low enough numbers as freshmen to live in a Row house during their sophomore year and who did not indicate a desire to leave after having lived there almost one year. Group B was made up of those who lived in non-Row housing during the sophomore year but preferred to live in the Row house. In Group C were those who lived in non-Row housing during the sophomore year and did not desire to leave. Since the authors do not mention a fourth group, we might assume that there were no occupants of Row houses who wanted to leave.

The investigators predicted from membership and reference-group theory that Group A would show the least reduction in authoritarianism, since they had been exposed to norms similar to the ones they carried into the residences. Group C was expected to change the most, since not only were the norms of their membership group less authoritarian than their own, but, in addition, they had indicated by no longer wanting to live in a Row house that their reference group had changed. The amount of change in Group B was expected to be intermediate since the less authoritarian norms of their imposed membership group conflicted with the norms of their reference group (Row houses).

The data were consistent with these predictions. In addition to statistical tests measuring the extent of change, two other tests were made: a test of the influence of membership groups (Group A versus B and C combined) and a test of the influence of reference groups (Groups A and B versus C). Both tests were also significant in the expected direction. This study thus provides experimental evidence that college residence groups do affect attitudes. It should be noted that although the experiment apparently demonstrates that the authoritarianism of students relatively high on that trait can be reduced by association with students relatively low on authoritarianism, it does not demonstrate the converse.

It should also be noted that of the three comparisons made, only the one on membership-group influence is truly experimental. To study experimentally the influence of reference group changes on attitude change, we would have to change the reference group for some subjects, and their changes in attitude would have to be compared with those of a control group. It should be noted further that the accuracy of the conclusions depends upon an unbiased loss of subjects. The investigators report that of the thirty-nine original subjects, twenty-eight remained for study. If the eleven unavailable subjects had actually lived in one of the two types of housing and were lost for reasons correlated with their change scores, the experimental conclusions might be invalid.

An example of an experiment within one student residence is that of Newcomb (1956) who studied the development of interpersonal attraction over a full semester in a seventeen-man student house at a large university. He had complete control over the selection and room assignments of the residents who were required to provide information about themselves and to take certain attitude scales before and immediately after their arrival. One of the criteria for selection was that residents had to be previously unacquainted. The conditions necessary for an experiment with his objectives were thus met.

In the first of two projects in this setting, roommate assignments were made at random. Thus the data pertaining to roommate relationships as a function of previous measures of the individuals can be regarded as experimentally derived. The comparison of the degree of interpersonal attraction between roommates, floormates, and persons on different floors can also be regarded as experimental.

In the second project, roommates were assigned by experimental criteria including scores on attitude measures. "Half of the roommate combinations were . . . assigned in such manner as to insure (as we thought) that *minimal* attraction would result, and *maximal* attraction in the other half of the combinations. (Our assignments were based upon data provided by mail some weeks before the men arrived)" (Newcomb, 1956, p. 580). No difference in roommate attraction between these two conditions was observed, but the level of roommate attraction as a whole was higher than that of non-roommate pairs.

The fact that this latter finding was only weakly present in the first study led Newcomb to a re-examination of the hypothesis that propinquity increases the likelihood of attraction. After further analysis of his data, he concludes (Newcomb, 1956, p. 584) that "propinquity is a facilitating but not a sufficient condition for the development of attraction."

Manipulating Similarity and Difference in College Major

The effect of similar or different major fields of study was the focus in a study by Willerman (1951). Male freshmen who applied to a dormitory at a large university and who had not selected roommates were assigned to rooms and floors according to a design intended to assess the effects of similar and different majors on congeniality and other aspects of social interaction. Where possible, students were assigned at random to a similar or different roommate, although in order to obtain a large enough number of homogeneous floors, strict randomization could not be employed in floor assignments.

Toward the end of the first quarter, a questionnaire was given. One finding was that roommates with the same major helped one another in their studies more than did roommates with different majors. Roommates with the same major presumably have more courses in common and thus are in a better position to help one another. Congeniality between roommates was not affected by similarity of major.

It should be mentioned that the independent variable of similar or dissimilar majors was not selected on the basis of data gathered in a field study. Had such a prior study been made, a correlational analysis might have shown other factors to be potentially more powerful determinants of congeniality and social interaction among freshmen. This study in fact served as a preliminary field and correlational study. The particular experimental manipulation was performed because it seemed better than collecting data based on a haphazard method of room assignments.

Manipulating Similarity and Difference in Academic Ability

Hall and Willerman (1963) examined the educational effects on students at a large university of having roommates who were similar or different in predicted academic achievement. They were interested in the effects on college grades, out-of-class activities, discussion, study practices, and congeniality.

The dormitory directors gave the investigators complete freedom to make room assignments of any students who had not requested either a roommate or a particular room. Since most students who had previously attended the university had already selected their roommates, the experimental groups consisted primarily of freshmen and a small number of transfer students. The high-school percentile rank (HSR) of the students was used as the index of predicted academic achievement.

The design resulted in three types of roommate pairings: both relatively high in HSR (high similars); both relatively low in HSR (low similars); and one relatively high and one relatively low (dissimilars). Each student in a similar pair was matched on HSR with a corresponding student in a dissimilar pair. The data consisted of responses to a questionnaire administered to the subjects toward the end of the first quarter, ratings of the students by their dormitory counselors, and grades for the full academic year.

The major hypothesis for experimental test was that students living with high roommates would study more and obtain better grades than students matched with low roommates. Full analysis of the data gave results more intricate than originally hypothesized, however. The "high-achieving" students did not have an overall differential effect upon their roommates, although the manipulation did affect the congeniality of the roommates and the extent to which the roommates disturbed one another during studying. The high similars were the most congenial and the low similars the least congenial of the three types of pairings. The high similars least frequently complained that their roommates interfered with their studying.

The initial hypothesis was evidently too simple (Hall and Willerman, 1963):

Apparently two variables that were not experimentally controlled had considerably more effect than expected. These were the extent of course overlap between RM's, and the birth order of subjects and RM's. In general, experimentally assigned pairs of RM's who shared many courses did better than those who did not share courses. Furthermore, among males the beneficial effect of sharing courses was especially strong for *first-born* males.[7]

The unexpected effect of these two variables suggests that, despite every effort to examine alternatives, it is still possible that some correlated variable that could not be controlled by the study is responsible for the effects. In this respect, the conclusions suffer from the same defects as those derived from field studies.

In experiments on selective association, as in all fieldwork, restrictions on the manipulation of subjects and variables are encountered. In this case because many upperclassmen have already selected their roommates, only freshmen and transfer

[7] This study appears to reinforce the findings of Schacter (1959) that suggest that important differences exist between the socialization of first-born and later-born children. Research in this area would be useful for understanding susceptibility to social influence.

students can be freely assigned to rooms in large numbers. Therefore, a research design which depends upon the deliberate or random assignment of individual upperclassmen will be difficult to execute. Although the experimental study of roommate effects is not feasible under such circumstances, it is feasible to study problems such as the effect of homogeneous-heterogeneous composition of larger units in the residence if the roommate pairs can be experimentally assigned in the residence. Such a design was used in Willerman's (1951) study to include freshmen who had selected their roommates. Again, major field of study was used as the basis of group composition of floors. Many variations of this basic design are possible to answer such questions as whether the presence of a large number of mutually chosen roommates on the same floor results in low cohesiveness on that floor and, consequently, less influence from floormates than from roommates.

In the event that the assignment of neither individuals nor pairs of roommates can be controlled, strict experiments of the foregoing kind will, of course, be impossible. The type of experiment on selective association that is possible when the investigator is forced to study intact groups hinges on placing a small number of individuals, perhaps only one, in strategic positions in the group. The assumption is that one individual, on the basis of his personal characteristics or role in the group, could influence a large number of individuals. Thus, in dormitories that employ graduate student residence counselors, the counselors themselves, on the basis of certain personal criteria, could be assigned to living units at random in order to assess their effects on students. It is well to note that in such designs the total number of cases for certain statistical tests of significance will be the number of counselors; hence, no matter how many students are involved in the study, the investigator will need a minimum number of counselors (say, at least six of each of two types) to stand much chance of demonstrating significant differences between counselor conditions.

In studying intact groups it is probable that the groups will differ from one another in significant ways. To control the effect of initial group differences on the dependent variable, two procedures can be used. First, a pre-post design enables the investigator to measure directly the effect of the experimental treatment, taking into account the initial differences between groups. Second, the use of analysis of covariance, a technique for statistically controlling initial differences, is possible when measures correlated with the dependent variable are available.[8]

Other Opportunities for Experiments on the Effects of Selective Association

In addition to student housing, other out-of-class situations exist which have effects and in which group composition can be manipulated. Orientation groups and freshman camps are examples. I have noticed that friendships are formed, or at least acquaintances are made, in these settings. How lasting these are I do not know. At some universities new students are oriented in relatively small groups. It would be a fairly simple matter to form these groups according to certain criteria to study the effects on such matters as attitudes toward college education or the formation of friendships.

The Adequacy of Manipulations Based on Propinquity

The specific purposes of the research will determine whether manipulations relying on the proposition that propinquity increases the likelihood of association are adequate. That propinquity does not insure more than a minimum of contact is not at all disturbing if, as in Newcomb's (1956) study, the focus of the research is the development of interpersonal attraction. In fact, the amount of contact between roommates may be regarded as an important consequence of the experimental manipulations and thus one of the dependent variables. The manipulation is also adequate for testing hypotheses about other kinds of effects of roommate assignment per se. If certain experimental combinations of roommates result in less roommate contact, and hence weaker roommate effects than other

---

[8] See, for example, McNemar (1955) for a discussion of this technique.

combinations, this fact may be precisely what the investigator wants to know.

However, if the purpose of the research is to study the effects of differential association, a manipulation based entirely on propinquity is risky, because roommates are free to associate differentially with individuals other than those required experimentally. For instance, if the research question in the Hall and Willerman (1963) study had been, "How does the HSR level of one's associates (rather than one's roommate) affect one's academic performance?" it could not have been experimentally answered by their procedure, because the amount of contact between roommates was different for the experimental groups.

Such manipulations can be bolstered by creating inducements to interaction, increasing the number of individuals experimentally eligible for association, and increasing the difference in physical proximity between the "eligible" and "non-eligible" students. The apparent success of the Siegel and Siegel (1957) study was probably based on the presence of these factors. The experimental environment of the students in their study included a relatively large number of other students living in the same residential unit. The experimental groups probably engaged in intraresident activities of a group type. The functional distance between students of the same housing unit was probably much less than the distance from their unit to other units.

Some Comments on Attributes Used for Grouping

Almost an infinite number of student attributes[9] could be used for assembling roommates or larger groups. The purposes of the study, of course, will determine which attributes are used in a given study. Dromitory directors and educators have raised questions concerning the advisability of mixing freshmen and upperclassmen in a given unit. Should assignment to units strive for homogeneity or heterogeneity? Such questions are too broad for research purposes, and even when they are narrowed down,

[9] See Chapter 3, by E. K. Wilson, in this volume for an extensive discussion of attributes of students which might be used in experiments on selective association.

the variables are so complex that the investigator should be prepared for complex relations. For example, a moderate degree of homogeneity may lead to the greatest change in attitudes, while extreme homogeneity and extreme heterogeneity may result in little change. Homogeneity may not provide enough difference in opinion and information to afford opportunities for frequent communication and change. Extreme heterogeneity may result in a minimum of communication or in mutual rejection of students as adequate reference groups or individuals.

When gross attributes such as high school percentile rank, academic aptitude scores, socio-economic level, or major field of study are used for grouping, it is well to recognize that they are strongly correlated with other important characteristics of the individual or his situation. For example, the different colleges in a university may have different requirements for admission. If such requirements include the level of academic aptitude, and if this attribute is used for grouping, the results of such a study may be misleading; instead of aptitude's determining differential effects, similarity of major field or college may be the effective independent variable. Foreknowledge of such correlations makes it possible to design the study to randomize or hold them constant or to build in measures which may be used for statistical control.

When the purpose of the study is theoretical rather than practical, we can turn to current social psychological theory and research findings for help in selecting those attributes to be used in composing our peer groups.[10] A good place to start is with the variables which affect social influence. One of these that has been shown to influence cognition and behavior in laboratory and field situations is the attractiveness of the group (Festinger, 1950; Newcomb, 1953). Thus any attribute which increases the attractiveness that groups have for an individual may be presumed to affect the degree to which he will be influenced by the group. These attributes include the prestige of individuals, their potential for providing satisfactions of needs, and common

[10] See, for example, Thibaut and Kelley (1959) for an analysis of dyadic relations suggesting a variety of theoretical attributes to use in group composition.

interests and activities. The combining of individuals to form groups on the basis of their attractions to the various attributes should be done by considering the particular relevance of each attribute to the individuals concerned. Thus, if students differ in the criteria they use in evaluating the prestige of other students, one would first have to learn which of these criteria — academic versus athletic ability, for example — were important to the potential subjects of the study. Then the subjects could be combined in a way that would insure that some experimental conditions include students who mutually regard one another as having prestige or, if not mutually, at least unidirectionally.[11]

Some new developments in interpersonal need theory are at the point at which relevant measuring instruments are ready for use in field experimentation (Schutz, 1958). The approach of Schutz is that the prediction of interpersonal compatibility is a function of the correspondence between the individuals' needs to express certain types of behavior toward others and their needs to receive these types of behavior from others. Schutz believes the needs for affection, inclusion, and control are sufficient to account for most interpersonal behavior. He describes a field study in a fraternity in which measures of these needs were used successfully to predict a variety of sociometric choices. These measures could be used for the experimental study of roommate relations in dormitories, as in the second of the two Newcomb (1956) studies.

An important aspect of homogeneity-heterogeneity that could be manipulated is the degree to which the students are placed in overlapping group memberships or in which the norms of the immediate group differ from those of their home group or other groups to which they belong.[12] It is apparent that new norms and points of view are adopted in situations in which the norms differ from those one imports into the situation. Hence, this type of study should be most fruitful for the study of the effects of peers. Some students could be assigned to groups having norms consistent with those of their other group memberships; some could

[11] For a review of the relation between attributes and sociometric choices, see Lindzey and Borgatta (1954).

[12] See Chapter 4, by R. LeVine, in this volume, for a discussion of this topic.

be assigned to groups whose norms are incompatible with their other group memberships. The effects of overlapping group membership on cognition, attitudes, and behavior could prove very important.

In a field study of these effects Watson and Lippitt (1955) observed four different ways in which foreign students coped with the problems of adjusting in this country and their problems of readjustment after returning home. Some students were dominated by whichever group they were in at the time; for some, their native membership remained dominant in this country; some not only identified strongly with the group in this country but rejected some of the standards of their native group; and a few individuals tried to maintain a balanced point of view between the two groups.

Checking on the Behavior Presumed To Reflect the Experimental Attribute

In laboratory experiments the investigator frequently determines whether his experimental conditions actually had the intended impact on his subjects. This check is made by means independent of the experiment's effect on the dependent variable. The same sort of check should be made in the field experiment to determine whether the behavior which the investigator expected from the subjects' attributes actually did occur. If the experimental conditions produce no difference, this check will enable the investigator to decide whether his hypothesis was wrong or whether the experimental treatment per se was a failure.

For example, in the Hall and Willerman (1963) study of the effect of roommates on one another, ratings of the subjects' interest in cultural activities were obtained. The high HSR students were only slightly higher on these ratings than the low HSR students. Knowing this, the investigators were not surprised that the experimental manipulation produced no differential effect on the roommates' participation in cultural activities.

Another related type of check is often necessary in field experiments. This is a check on the conditions which are necessary but not sufficient for a given relationship to hold. For example, if the hypothesis being tested concerns the extent to which attitudes will change as a function of the attitude distribution in the group, it will be important to determine whether communication on the issues related to the attitude occurred. This problem will be present in any experiment in which the behavior reflecting the dependent variable is contingent on some condition not in itself experimentally produced. Unfortunately, the objectives of many studies of the effects of peers require such contingent conditions.

EXPERIMENTAL STUDIES OF SOCIAL INFLUENCE AND COMMUNICATION

It is clear that when group composition is manipulated, other factors such as the content and type of interaction are also varied. The criteria that are used in manipulating group composition are often differences in the attributes of persons that are correlated with their communication behavior. In studying the effects of selective association, it is not at all certain that these attributes will be sufficiently realized in behavior to provide the experimentally intended conditions for the subjects. Nor can we be certain that the attribute used in composing the groups was the effective independent variable.

In this section, I shall discuss approaches to the study of social influence and communication which usually insure that the manipulations produce the independent variable. For example, rather than composing groups that are homogeneous and heterogeneous on certain opinions and hoping that relevant opinions may be expressed within these groups, the experimenter provides the subjects with information showing that their opinions are either similar to or different from others in their group. As another example, some of the experiments to be described hold conditions constant that in selective association experiments are free to vary. For example, in order to study the effect on a subject's communication produced by variations in the social identification of the recipient of his communication, stimulus-persons differing in group membership are trained to behave in similar ways toward the subject.

The experiments discussed below are primarily studies of the determinants of the opinion environment of the student. On the one hand, they can be seen as studies of how the opinion environment affects the student's opinions, and on the other, of determinants of the contribution he makes to the opinion environment of other students. Since the opinion environment of a student is an important factor in peer effects, experimental manipulations of this environment should have strong effects. The opportunities for manipulating the factors which affect communication and opinions are many, but only a few types of manipulations will be described.

Manipulating Knowledge of Group Opinions

One phenomenon of social psychology which can be reproduced in a variety of settings is the shift in the opinions of members toward the modal position of the group when the group's opinions are made known to them. Whether this phenomenon is explained in terms of pressures toward uniformity arising from a need for social reality (Festinger, 1950) or in terms of a strain toward symmetry among persons who are co-oriented (Newcomb, 1953) or in reward-punishment terms for conformity and deviation, the empirical conditions necessary for its occurrence are fairly well known.

Lau (1954) conducted a large-scale study in which changes in opinions concerning admitting minority group members were produced among the members of thirty fraternities by means of providing them with information about the distribution of opinion within their own fraternity and among all campus fraternities. Survey data on this topic were collected before the experiment and then presented to the members during a meeting. Charts, informal lectures, and group discussions were used to present the information. Actually, the experiment proper had to do with an evaluation of the relative effectiveness of two techniques of feedback—directive and non-directive. However, the intended differences between the two techniques were not sufficiently realized, partly because the conduct of some members of fraternities in the non-directive condition was not well controlled. This is an example of one type of uncontrolled factor which plagues field experiments. Such problems can be avoided by selecting experimental manipulations that permit only a minimum of uncontrolled variance or by the pretesting of manipulations to gain skill in dealing with uncontrolled events.

Lau's hypothesis that members who held deviant opinions would shift toward the modal position of their houses seemed to be supported by the data. It is interesting to note that when the survey data were tested for the existence of group standards about attitudes toward admission policies, the results were negative (Ross, 1955). The fact that opinions shifted toward the modal position may have meant that the manipulation created a group standard.

The approach used in this study, that of providing the members of groups with information about the entire group's opinion, seems to be very effective for changing opinions, especially if the opinions are such that for one reason or another they do not ordinarily get expressed.

Other kinds of studies which could be done might be those in which the opinions of certain individuals or other groups on campus are made known to the subjects.[13] Such manipulations could provide information concerning which sources on campus are most influential with respect to what issues. In Lau's study, for example, it seemed that knowledge of the opinions of fraternity members as a whole was less important in creating the shifts in opinion than knowledge of the opinions of one's own fraternity.

Manipulating the Situation in Which Opinion Is Expressed: Public vs. Private Expression

It is well known that the opinions a person will express in public do not necessarily reflect those he will reveal in private. On what do such discrepancies depend? Gordon (1952) performed an experiment to answer this question, using a cooperative living project made up only partly of students. He had each individual first record his private opinions on Russia and then asked him to express his opinion in the presence of his fellow members. The students were later also asked to make an esti-

---

[13] For an example of a laboratory experiment on a closely related topic see Kelley & Woodruff (1956).

mate of group opinion. Gordon (1952, p. 58) found the follow-ing.

In general, the individuals tended to conform to their concep-tion of the group norms when giving their public opinion. The typical pattern is for the individual to compromise between his private opinion and his conception of the group opinion when expressing his public opinion.

Manipulating the Subject's Relationship to His Listener

The manner in which expressed opinions are affected by the subject's relationship to the listener can be studied in a variety of ways. For example, in one social psychology class the students acted as the interviewers in a survey in which the relationship of the respondent to the interviewer was varied (Willerman, 1959). The purpose of the research was to determine whether respondents expressed different opinions and gave different information about themselves to interviewers who were their friends than to interviewers who were strangers. Each student in the class was asked to name his two closest student friends outside of the members of the class. He was then given the names of two persons to interview. One of the persons was one of his close friends; the other was a close friend of another student, assigned at random. The interview schedule consisted of ques-tions concerning certain opinions and personal behavior. Each subject was interviewed only once, but since each student interviewed one of his close friends, and his other close friend was interviewed by some other student, the responses of the two sets of close friends could be compared.

The results show that the respondent's relationship to the interviewer does make a difference in his expressed opinions. For example, students interviewed by their friends expressed more extreme opposition to certain groups (fraternities and the Catholic church) than students interviewed by strangers, if neither the students nor their interviewer-friend were affiliated with these groups. Some other differences seem to depend on the degree of closeness of friendship, but these results were obtained by correlational analysis and were not experimentally derived.

Many variations on this design can be made to study the effects of friendships or other relationships on opinion and attitude change, as well as on content and style of communication. Such experiments can be designed so that they approximate the precision of laboratory experiments.

Other factors in interpersonal relationships which affect the expression of opinions are discussed by Kelman (1956), who has developed a theory of the conditions under which behavior that is influenced by others will be manifested. He tested some hypotheses from this theory in a combined field and laboratory setting. The experiment consisted of the exposure of Negro students to tape-recorded interviews on a given topic in which variations in these recordings reflected variations in "the source and degree of the communicator's power, while keeping the message of the communication constant." For example, in one of the three variations the speaker was introduced as a wealthy benefactor who might withdraw his support from the college if he learned that the students disagreed with his views. As far as the subjects knew, these communications were real and were important to the welfare of their college.

Manipulating the Social Attributes of the Listener

In determining the effect on expressed opinions, it is not always easy to make the distinction between the subject's relationship to the recipient of the communication and his social attributes. For example, a friendship with someone implies that one knows his various social identifications and many of his opinions. Thus, in the previous study (Willerman, 1959) students expressed more opposition to certain groups when interviewed by their friends than by strangers only if the friends were not affiliated with those groups. Apparently, this difference in expressed opposition was caused by the knowledge that friends have of one another's group affiliation rather than by other aspects of their relationship. To separate the effect of the relationship from the effect of social attributes, it is necessary to hold one of these factors constant while varying the other. The two studies described below have held constant the subject's relationship to the recipient.

Robinson and Rohde (1946) studied the effect of the group identification of the interviewer on the opinions expressed by the respondent. Questions concerning attitudes toward Jews were asked by four different types of interviewers: "Jewish appearing" persons who used Jewish names in introducing themselves to the respondent; "Jewish appearing" persons who did not mention their names; "non-Jewish appearing" persons who used non-Jewish names; and "non-Jewish appearing" persons who did not mention their names.

By means of this design the investigators were able to separate the effect of appearance from the effect of the name as well as the interaction between the two variables.

The study was not done on a college campus, but the approach used is easily adapted to the campus. Student interviewers could introduce themselves to other students according to a wide range of experimental variables. For example, opinions about fraternities could be obtained by interviewers who introduce themselves as fraternity members to some respondents and as non-fraternity members to others.

Another experiment that varied the social identification of the recipient of communication is one by French and Zajonc (1957). What are the consequences, they asked, of being placed in a situation of cross-cultural norm conflict? The specific hypothesis tested (French and Zajonc, 1957, p. 224) was that "the resolution of intergroup norm conflict favors the norm of the group whose situational potency is increased." The term "situational potency" refers, in this instance, to the heightening of one's awareness of his membership in a particular group. The particular norms studied were the amount of deference a student displayed toward a professor.

Using an approach which brought into the laboratory a "real" situation from the field, students from India attending a university in the United States were placed in two situations in which they discussed some controversial items, presumably with an Indian professor in one case and an American professor in the other. The students were instructed to behave toward the Indian professor as they would in India and to behave toward the American professor as they normally did. The behavior of the "professors," who were actually confederates of the experimenter, was standardized. The main dependent variable was measured by observations of the students' deference behavior in the two situations. Because the instructions to the subjects were not particularly effective, the results could not clearly be taken as supporting the hypothesis.

This particular study is described because its general approach is useful in transferring peer group field situations to laboratory settings. A hypothetical example of such a problem, sticking fairly close to the objectives of the above research, would be a study of how college women resolve norm conflicts about how one should behave toward college men and toward college women in a given situation.

Manipulating Tendencies To Communicate and Seek Information

As in any community or organization, information of various types is communicated among students by word of mouth. The study of the determinants of types of content transmitted, and of who communicates with whom, is important for an understanding of student culture. Many laboratory but few field experiments on this problem have been done.[14] Among the independent variables of the laboratory experiments were differences in opinion and status among group members, differences in the relevance of the content to the individuals and the group, being in the majority or minority on the issue, and confidence in one's opinions. For purposes of experimenting in the field some of the manipulations used to create these independent variables could be taken over with little modification.

An example of a field experiment on the transmission of rumors is one by Schachter and Burdick (1955). The study was not done in a college setting, but in a girls' school. Nevertheless, it is an excellent illustration of a type of field experiment which could

[14] See Cartwright and Zander (1960) for reports of a number of these studies.

be done in college settings and which puts a laboratory-based hypothesis to test with a consequent revision of the hypothesis.

The hypothesis concerns the extent of rumor transmission and the degree to which distortion takes place in rumor transmission. The investigators planted rumors in the school with the help of student confederates under several conditions and traced the spread of the rumor by interviews. One of the conditions created was that of "cognitive unclarity." This was accomplished by staging an incident in a classroom involving the principal of the school and a student.

The conclusion drawn from this study could be useful to investigators who desire to study rumor transmission by means of planting rumors that have a good chance of being spread (Schachter and Burdick, 1955, p. 371): "Under conditions of wide-spread cognitive unclarity there is far more transmission of a planted rumor and far more speculation involving new rumors when the issue is important than when it is relatively unimportant." Contrary to certain laboratory based findings, little distortion of the planted rumor was found.

The college campus provides a wide variety of opportunities for the experimental study of how students affect one another's attitudes, opinions, skills, and social behavior. The experimental approach should be used whenever the investigator wants to draw conclusions that do not have to be greatly qualified by the possibility that the determining factor was some variable other than the one he labels "independent," whenever he cannot tolerate ambiguity about the direction of causation, and whenever he wants to evaluate the importance of an independent variable in a real-life setting.

Some of the field experiments described in this chapter may be rigorously carried out. One of the distinguishing characteristics of such studies is the short duration of the manipulation and the short time interval between the manipulation and the collection of data. However, many types of field experiments are difficult to carry out rigorously because of the difficulty of preventing uncontrolled events from affecting the results. Sometimes a desirable alternative to the field experiment is a field study and sometimes a laboratory experiment that can control more variables. Before conducting a field experiment, the investigator should become thoroughly familiar with the setting in which it is to take place. Frequently this will be done by means of a field study.

Manipulating the composition of groups on campus is a feasible means of studying peer group formation and influence. Several experiments of this type have been done in student residences with some success. As we gain more knowledge about significant individual difference variables, and as better measures of these variables are used, the manipulation of group composition variables will be more successful.

Other types of manipulations which affect the opinion environment and the communication behavior of students have had some success in the field and more especially in the laboratory. Some of these manipulations consisted of providing the subjects with information about other students' opinions, obtaining the opinions under public and private conditions, varying the subject's relationship to and social identification of the recipient of this communication, and staging an incident to create motivation to communicate with others.

6

The Empirical
Classification of
Formal Groups

HANAN C. SELVIN
and
WARREN O. HAGSTROM

It is easier to find variations in behavior among the members of different groups than to isolate the factors that produce these variations.[1] Part of the difficulty, of course, is theoretical. A century and a half elapsed between Suessmilch's compilation of suicide rates in 1741 and Durkheim's sociological theory of suicide in 1897,[2] and sociologists are still grappling with the problems that Durkheim posed in the study of groups (see Durkheim, 1951). Another part of the difficulty is methodological. An adequate explanation of the group effects presupposes an adequate description of the groups, but neither Durkheim nor his modern followers have adequate tools for describing the groups they study.

[1] The major portion of this paper first appeared in *The American Sociological Review* (Selvin and Hagstrom, 1963) and is reprinted here with the permission of the American Sociological Association. The final section, "Criticisms and Afterthoughts," has been added for this volume. The study used as an example in this chapter was supported by the Institute of Social Sciences of the University of California, Berkeley. We are grateful to O. Andrew Collver for helping in this study.

[2] Durkheim's student, Maurice Halbwachs (1912), credits Suessmilch with being the first to discover the constancy of suicide rates.

Durkheim's methodological difficulty appears near the beginning of his chapter on anomic suicide, where he examines the alleged causal relation between poverty and suicide rates. Far from there being a positive relation, he argues, poverty "tends rather to produce the opposite effect. There is very little suicide in Ireland, where the peasantry leads so wretched a life. Poverty-stricken Calabria has almost no suicides; Spain has a tenth as many as France." But these countries are not only poor; as Durkheim himself notes elsewhere, they also have high proportions of Catholics and low levels of education. The low suicide rates in these countries are not simply the product of poverty — or of Catholicism or lack of education; they result from the combination of all three of these variables and of other important variables that Durkheim does not study, such as low levels of urbanization and industrialization.

The same formal problem appears in the work of Blau (1957) and Davis (1961) on "structural" or "compositional" effects. Like Durkheim, these authors ignore the fact that their group variables are related. In three successive tables Davis classifies his discussion groups according to the proportion of members who are new to the group, the proportion who have contact with other members outside the group, and the proportion who are active in the discussions. It seems obvious that these three characteristics are "confounded" — that just as individuals who are new to the groups are likely to have few outside contacts and to be inactive in discussions, so the group characteristics formed from these individual variables are probably associated. If so, the effects that are attributed to one of these variables are really the effects of all three variables.

There are two essentially different solutions to this problem of describing groups adequately in a causal analysis. One is to make the univariate description adequate by getting rid of the unwanted variables experimentally or statistically. The other solution is to abandon entirely the effort to describe the groups according to a single characteristic and to construct a multivariate description. After discussing the conditions under which the first solution is applicable, we shall examine the logic of the second procedure and describe its steps in detail.

EXPERIMENTS AND SURVEYS IN THE STUDY OF GROUP PROPERTIES

The problem of classification or multivariate description does not arise in most laboratory studies of groups. The experimenter constructs sets of groups that differ in prescribed ways, so that he can study the effects of variation in any one group property or combination of properties on the behavior of the members. He can vary the composition of the group, the kind of leadership, the nature of the group task, the perception members have of each other, and even the channels of information within the group. The formal groups that are found in field studies obviously cannot be manipulated in this way except in special circumstances, but when there is a large enough number of formal groups—of the order of two hundred or more—it is often possible to select sets of groups that are alike on most variables other than the one whose influence is being measured. For example, in assessing the effect of the size of a college residence group on the members' behavior one would compare large and small dormitories, large and small sororities, large and small boarding houses, and so on. This would make it possible to separate the effects of size from the effects of the legal organization of the group.

The experimenter can make causal statements about the effects of important group properties with many fewer cases than the survey investigator because he can eliminate unimportant independent variables by proper experimental design. He can set up as many large and small groups with specified patterns of other characteristics as he thinks necessary or as his resources will allow. And, finally, by randomizing the assignment of subjects to groups he can turn constant differences between groups into random variables whose effects can be estimated statistically.

Field or survey research is ordinarily limited to statistical manipulation after the data have been gathered. In trying to "hold constant" a large number of variables the survey investigator always "runs out of cases." This is why a well-designed survey that seeks to test or explore causal hypotheses has hundreds of individual respondents. To deal with group variables in this way would similarly require hundreds of groups.

Few studies can afford the expense of gathering data on several hundred groups and on the thousands of members that would be required if even a small sample of each group were taken.[3] Sometimes the necessary data cannot be obtained: even when all available groups are included in the sample, the number may be insufficient for this kind of cross-tabulation, and the groups may not be different enough to remove the unwanted variables. If, for example, there are only two cooperative houses on a college campus, one large and the other small, it would be impossible to study the effect of group size on the behavior of co-op members. Differences in behavior between the two groups might as well be attributed to the personalities of the house mothers as to size—or any other characteristic of the two groups.

Some method of classifying groups into meaningful types is necessary when the number of groups is too small for cross-tabulation of group characteristics. The procedure to be presented here is especially useful in situations with from fifteen to two hundred groups (both figures are approximate).[4] This procedure derives in part from three earlier schemes for classifying group properties, but it also differs significantly from them.

TYPES OF GROUP CHARACTERISTICS

After reviewing earlier attempts to classify group properties, Merton (1957) selected twenty-six that promised to be significant. His list begins with "clarity or vagueness of social definition of membership in the group," "degree of engagement of members in the group," and "actual" and "expected" duration

[3] Lazarsfeld and Thielens, Jr. (1958) reported data on 165 colleges and universities, but they did not attempt to disentangle their confounded group variables analytically, nor did they construct a systematic typology of colleges along the lines to be presented here. The only example we know of in which group and individual characteristics have been manipulated analytically in the same study is still in progress: Natalie Rogoff's re-analysis at the Columbia University Bureau of Applied Social Research of data collected by the Educational Testing Service from a sample of some 25,000 seniors in 500 high schools. Murdock (1949) did cross-classify characteristics of total societies, but he had too few societies to carry his analysis very far: most of his relations are between one independent variable and one dependent variable, with nothing held constant.

[4] Larger numbers of groups may be described in the same way, but in such cases the alternative of cross-tabulation is simpler and possibly more effective. With fewer than fifteen cases, neither procedure works.

of individual membership. The problem confronting any user of this list is that twenty-six is too many. The list cannot help to classify groups empirically without the additional step of deciding whether *conceptually* distinct properties are *empirically* distinct, so that the variables used in the classification can be reduced to a manageable number.

Hemphill and Westie (1950) were both theoretical and empirical. Much like Merton, they began with a list of fourteen dimensions based on previous theory and research. Their list included such variables as autonomy ("the degree to which a group functions independently of other groups"), control ("the degree to which a group regulates the behavior of individuals"), and polarization ("the degree to which the group is oriented and works toward a single goal which is clear and specific to all members"). A sample of two hundred people was then asked about the characteristics of forty-five groups to which they had belonged, ranging from a women's church club to an entire university. The aim of this empirical study was not, however, to test the adequacy of the theoretically derived dimensions, but to develop scales for measuring each of these variables.

The Merton and Hemphill-Westie lists of group properties are valuable primarily for a general theory of group structure. They apply to groups of any kind in any context. By way of contrast, Cattell (Guetzkow, 1951) began with a far larger number of variables, many of them applicable only to restricted classes of groups. His 150 variables included such items as "accuracy of conclusion in committee-like debate on given data," "frequency of change of formal leader at periodic voting," and "reduction of strength of pull when tug-of-war rope is electrified." Through factor analysis of these variables, Cattell (1953) attempted to find dimensions presumably applicable to all groups.

On a more general level Cattell also provides a threefold classification of group variables. *Syntality variables* "describe the performance of the group acting as a whole." An example is the kind of social program that the group undertakes. *Structure variables* are "based on particulars of internal structure and interaction," such as the average number of friends chosen from within the group. *Population variables* are characteristics of the distribution of personality, status, and attitude-interest variables among the members of the group—for example, the proportion interested in campus politics. Cattell hopes to find relations between particular variables in each of these classes and eventually to explain variations in syntality as functions of population and structure variables. His classification covers *all* group variables and thereby helps to reveal the limitations of other lists of group properties (e.g., with one or two possible exceptions, the Hemphill-Westie list of group properties has no population variables).

Theories of group structure are still in a primitive stage of development, as indicated by the lack of agreement among the various lists of group properties and by their failure to indicate which properties are conceptually, experimentally, or statistically independent. This hampers the design of experiments and the construction of instruments for field studies. In our opinion the strategic direction for work on group structure is the empirical reduction of the theoretically derived lists of properties to a few underlying dimensions, which can then be the ingredients of different theories of group structure.

RELATIONS BETWEEN INDIVIDUAL AND GROUP PROPERTIES

One of the reasons why our procedure for group classification works well is that it is based on *aggregative* group variables, characteristics of groups that are derived entirely from characteristics of their component individuals and smaller groups. The logic of the relations between individual and group properties was first set forth in two papers by Lazarsfeld and his associates (Kendall and Lazarsfeld, 1950; Lazarsfeld and Menzel, 1961). It is presented here in a somewhat more general and more concise form.

There are only two types of group properties in this formalization: *aggregative properties*, which are based on characteristics of smaller units within the group being described, and *integral properties*, which are not based on smaller units.[5] An example of

---

[5] Lazarsfeld and his associates have used the terms "analytic" and "global" in place of "aggregative" and "integral." The only justification for our use of new terms is that they convey the underlying distinction more clearly. "Global" falsely suggests an overall description of the group, which is not what was intended, and "analytic" emphasizes the decomposition of group properties into individual data rather than the combination of individual data into group properties—the more common procedure in empirical research.

an aggregative property of a group is the mean length of membership, which is obviously derived from the behavior of the individual members. Whether or not the group has a written constitution is an integral characteristic: it is not derived from the behavior of the individual members or of any subgroup. This simple distinction between integral and aggregative properties is the basis of the classification of group properties in Table 6.1.

Across the top of the table are collectivities on five levels — individuals, pairs of individuals, primary groups, secondary groups, and total societies (this is an arbitrary list; additional categories might be included, or some of these might be combined). The principle of the table is most easily seen by reading across any row. In the cell at the left of each row is an integral characteristic of the unit listed at the top of the corresponding column. As one moves from left to right, this integral characteristic becomes the basis for aggregative characteristics of successively higher-level groups. For example, the first row begins with an integral characteristic of an individual, such as his age, sex, or response to some attitude question. Moving to the right, the members of any larger collectivity will display a distribution of each of these integral characteristics; any parameter of the distribution at some level is an aggregative property at that level. Thus the proportion of males or the mean age can be taken as a property of pairs, primary groups, secondary groups, or the total society — all aggregative characteristics built from an integral characteristic of individuals. Similarly, the second row shows the ways in which properties of pairs of individuals can be used to make aggregative properties of high-level groups. In addition to means and proportions, other statistical parameters fit into the scheme equally well. The dispersion of ages in a group is a measure of social heterogeneity, and the skewness of the distribution of ages tells something about the relative balance of old and young.

Finally, the table can also be used to generate "contextual properties" — properties of an individual or group that stem from its being included in a higher-level group (Lazarsfeld and Menzel, 1961). One can describe an individual by saying that he is a member of a cohesive group or that he is a student at a college

Table 6.1 Integral and Aggregative Characteristics of Groups

Source of Data	Unit Being Described				
	I. Individual	II. Pair	III. Primary Group	IV. Secondary Group	V. Total Society
Individual	Integral characteristic of individual (e.g., age, sex, attitude)	Parameter of distribution of individual integral characteristic over pair (e.g., whether sexes are same, numerical difference in age)	Same as in II but distribution over members of primary group (e.g., proportion male, mean and dispersion of age)	Same as in III, but over secondary group	Same as in IV, but over total society
Pair	—	Integral characteristic of pair (length of friendship)	Parameter of distribution of pair characteristic over primary group (mean length of pair friendships)	Same as in III, but over secondary group	Same as in IV, but over total society
Primary group	—	—	Integral characteristic of primary group (whether formal leader is sociometric "star")	Parameter of distribution of primary group characteristic over secondary group (proportion of primary groups in which leader is "star")	Same as in IV, but over total society
Secondary group	—	—	—	Integral characteristic of secondary group (presence of written rules)	Parameter of distribution of secondary group characteristic over total society (proportion of organizations with written rules)
Total society	—	—	—	—	Integral characteristic of total society (number of languages)

where most students come from families of high socio-economic status. No new principle of constructing group properties is involved; an individual or a group at any level below the total society can be described "contextually" by the characteristics of larger groups to which it belongs. One should be careful, however, not to confuse an attribute of an individual's context with an attribute of the individual himself: being a member of a wealthy sorority is not the same as being wealthy.

THE ILLUSTRATIVE DATA

To see how well this method works, we applied it to data from a study of 809 members of twenty women's residence groups on the Berkeley campus of the University of California — dormitories, sororities, boarding houses, and two kinds of cooperative houses — non-selective cooperatives, which admit women in the order of their application, and selective cooperatives, which take into account such criteria as grades and participation in campus activities. The smallest number of respondents in any group was sixteen, and the median rate of response was 82 per cent. In every group, then, the respondents are a large sample of the total membership — an important fact for a procedure that rests on describing groups through the aggregated responses of their members.

In all, sixty-one aggregative characteristics were computed for each group. Most of them were based on attributes of individual members — for example, the mean length of membership in the group and the proportion reporting themselves "highly satisfied" with the opportunities for meeting men. Not all, however, were simple means or proportions; thus the standard deviation of the ages of the members was included as a measure of social heterogeneity. These sixty-one characteristics were selected either because they were mentioned in discussions of group structure as theoretically interesting or because they reflected what was believed to be the operation of important group norms.

REDUCING THE NUMBER OF VARIABLES

Along with the use of aggregative group variables, our procedure rests on the possibility of reducing the large number of group variables. Do the sixty-one variables represent sixty-one essentially different aspects of group structure, or can they be considered manifestations of a smaller number of more basic dimensions? The answer to this question lies in the ways in which the sixty-one variables are related to each other. At one extreme, if all of the intercorrelations are zero, there will be no "basic dimensions": the set of observed characteristics will be irreducible. At the other extreme, there are patterns of intercorrelations such that all the variables can be considered as manifestations of a single underlying dimension. The usual case is between these extremes, with the correlations indicating the presence of several important dimensions.

Even with a small number of variables it is dificult to see what is going on by inspection of the correlation matrix. With sixty-one variables (1830 independent correlation coefficients) only the systematic computations of factor analysis can show how many underlying dimensions or "factors" are present.[6] A centroid factor analysis isolated seven factors, the first five of which have clear and meaningful interpretations (Table 6.2).

[6] Robert F. Winch (1947, pp. 58–75) was apparently the first to suggest using factor analysis to classify groups into empirical types as an alternative to what he called "heuristic types." However, Winch himself did not use factor analysis in empirical research at that time.

Table 6.2 Factor Analysis of Student Characteristics

Factor	Working Title	Groups That Score High on Given Factor Have High Proportions of Members Who
I	Social satisfaction	Are satisfied with many aspects of their group and with social life on campus
II	Sociometric cohesion	Spend much time in group activities; choose their friends and advisers on personal problems within the group; have a long average length of membership
III	Political conservatism	Call themselves Republican; supported Eisenhower in 1956
IV	Economic status and lack of achievement orientation	Do not come from low status families; are largely supported by their parents; get low grades, think grades are unimportant, and do not plan to work long after graduation; have little interest in national affairs.
V	School spirit sentiment	Attend many football games; feel that there should be more school spirit at Berkeley

SOME STATISTICAL DETAILS OF THE STUDY OF GROUP STRUCTURE BY FACTOR ANALYSIS

This factor analysis was based on sixty-one characteristics of twenty women's living groups at the Berkeley campus of the University of California. Computations of correlations, a centroid factor extraction, and a rotation to orthogonal simple structure were all carried out on the IBM 701 at the university's Computer Center. Time for this study was made available through a grant to the Computer Center from the National Science Foundation, whose help is gratefully acknowledged.

Items with loadings of more than 0.50 are listed in Table 6.3,

Table 6.3 Factor Loadings

Group Characteristic	Factor Loading
Factor I. "Social satisfaction"	
Proportion dating more than five hours per week	+.62
Proportion very satisfied with opportunities to meet women	+.84
Proportion very satisfied with women friends	+.72
Proportion very satisfied with opportunities to meet men	+.84
Proportion very satisfied with living group	+.64
Proportion personally acquainted with student government leader	+.63
Proportion voting in student government elections	+.61
Proportion of group feeling their families have incomes equal to that of most others in the group	+.75
Proportion of group feeling their families are wealthier than those of most others in the group	−.68
Standard deviation of estimates of the proportion of members of the group who are Republican	−.64
Size of group	+.13
Proportion of three best friends who are group members	+.26
Proportion for Eisenhower	+.15
Proportion with fathers of low occupational status	−.29
Factor II. "Sociometric cohesion"	
Proportion spending two hours or more weekly in organized living-group activities	+.64
Proportion of three best friends who are group members	+.68
Proportion who feel the person whose political opinions they respect most highly is a group member	+.56
Proportion who are most likely to seek personal advice from a person who is a group member	+.72
Average length of membership in the group	+.81
Degree to which leadership in opinion formation on political subjects is concentrated in a few individuals	
Standard deviation of ages of members	−.55
Proportion from the San Francisco metropolitan area	+.56
Proportion who have transferred from another college	−.63

(Table 6.3 continued)

Table 6.3 *Continued*

Proportion for whom all or nearly all college expenses are provided by parents	+.55
Size of group	+.47
Proportion for Eisenhower	+.25
Proportion very satisfied with living group	+.24
Proportion with fathers of low occupational status	−.17
Factor III. "Political conservatism"	
Proportion for Eisenhower	+.81
Proportion favorable to Nixon	+.87
Proportion sympathetic to unions	−.64
Proportion correctly informed about recent events in Republican party politics	+.66
Proportion greatly or moderately interested in student government	+.61
Interquartile range of estimate of the proportion of the group in favor of more school spirit at the University	−.81
Mean error in estimate of the proportion of the group who are Republican	+.87
Size of group	+.20
Proportion of three best friends who are group members	+.28
Proportion very satisfied with living group	+.21
Proportion of fathers with low occupational status	−.27
Factor IV. "Economic status and lack of achievement orientation"	
Proportion with fathers of low occupational status	−.74
Proportion who expect to be housewives five years after graduation	+.56
Proportion for whom all or nearly all of college expenses are provided by parents	+.58
Proportion spending five hours or more weekly in part-time work	−.56
Proportion feeling that most members of their group feel grades in courses to be very important	−.57
Mean grade-point average	−.60
Mean number of elected leadership positions members hold in other groups	−.69
Proportion highly interested in national and world affairs	−.72
Proportion Jewish	+.65
Proportion spending some time weekly at religious services	−.54
Size of group	+.33
Proportion of three best friends who are group members	+.05
Proportion very satisfied with living group	+.00
Factor V. "School spirit sentiment"	
Proportion feeling that greater efforts should be made to increase school spirit at the University	+.66
Proportion greatly or moderately interested in student government	+.51
Mean number of football games attended	+.76
Proportion personally acquainted with student government leaders	+.52
Proportion satisfied with class lectures	+.55
Proportion whose major subject is education	+.56
Proportion who are "independent" in national politics	−.80
Size of group	+.05
Proportion of three best friends who are group members	−.07
Proportion with fathers of low occupational status	+.23
Proportion very satisfied with living group	−.17

along with a few items of general interest. These factor loadings, which potentially vary from -1.0 to $+1.0$, are the correlations of the items with the factors under which they are listed. Factors VI and VII have no ready interpretation and are not described here.

A precise measure of the extent to which the factors represent the original items is provided by the "communalities" (h^2), which can be interpreted as the proportion of the variation in each of the original items that is explained by the seven factors (alternatively, the square of the multiple correlation of the item with the seven factors). The distribution of communalities is presented in Table 6.4. The figures are impressive: 86 per cent of the sixty-one original items have communalities over 0.50, and 31 per cent are over 0.80, figures far in excess of those usually achieved with so many items and so few factors in individual data.

The importance of having at least eight or ten members per group is revealed by comparing these results with those of Borgatta and Cottrell (1955). The behavior of 166 three-man laboratory groups in two types of situations was recorded in Robert F. Bales's twelve categories of interaction; additional data included such variables as sociometric measures of consensus and expansiveness, and the mean age and mean IQ of the group. All these variables are in the form of group rates or group

Table 6.4 Distribution of Communalities

h^2	Per Cent of 61 Items
.90 – 1.00	5
.80 – .89	26
.70 – .79	21
.60 – .69	21
.50 – .59	13
.40 – .49	7
.30 – .39	7
.00 – .29	0
Total	100

means—i.e., aggregative group characteristics. Seven factors were obtained from the original thirty-four variables. However, aggregative variables computed over only three individuals, even if they are based on many observations during the life of the group, apparently do not lead to patterns of correlations and factors as clearcut as do those based on larger numbers. Compared to the results of many psychological factor analyses, Borgatta and Cottrell's communalities are high—44 per cent are above 0.50 and 9 per cent above 0.80; but these figures are about one-half of those found in the Berkeley study. The difference may well be due to the lower reliability of the items.

The size of the group does not matter as much as the number of members about whom individual data are obtained. If sociometric data are to be used, it is necessary to obtain responses from almost all members (see Chap. 7, on this subject, by Peter H. Rossi). As reported above, Hemphill and Westie used one or a few informants from each group to measure fourteen basic group variables. When Borgatta, Cottrell, and Meyer (1956) performed a factor analysis of the Hemphill-Westie correlation matrix, they obtained four factors, which, incidentally, casts some doubt on the conceptual independence claimed for the original fourteen variables. The communalities were much lower than those obtained in the Berkeley study; 57 per cent of the items have communalities above 0.50, and only 14 per cent are above 0.80.

Even more striking results have been achieved when the items were not as diverse as in the Berkeley study. In a study of leadership (Selvin, 1960) three factors accounted for almost all the variation in fifteen items. An analysis of economic and social conditions in underdeveloped countries (Schnore, 1959) showed that only one factor was needed to explain the variation in twelve items ranging from the number of physicians per capita to the rate of electric power production. Both studies were based on aggregative characteristics.

The first two factors (Table 6.3), which are statistically the most important, apparently refer to "social cohesion," particularly as this concept has been used in research on small groups.

Aggregative variables that are important in factor I include the proportion satisfied with their residence group, the proportion satisfied with the opportunities to meet men and women (in many cases these opportunities are provided by the group), and the average time spent per week in dating. A high score on this factor thus denotes a group in which most of the members are satisfied with the social aspects of campus life, including their own house. This seems to be close to what investigators in the group dynamics tradition have called the "attractiveness of the group." The items important in factor II include the proportion of the closest friends chosen from the group, the mean time spent in group activities, the mean length of membership, and the proportion seeking advice on personal problems from other members of the group. Common to all these items is the extent to which friendship relations and social activities are centered in the group. This factor has therefore been called "sociometric cohesion."

There are, then, two relatively distinct dimensions of social cohesion, the first based on the social satisfaction of group members and the second on their interaction. In other words, social cohesion does not appear to be a unitary concept — a result of some theoretical interest in view of the prolonged controversy over this term.[7]

Factor III represents the average political conservatism of group members. Prominent among the items associated with

[7] Other studies have found similar results. Working with thirteen women's cooperative houses at the University of Minnesota, Gross and Martin (1952a) found indicators of "cohesiveness" which were that different, as well as low intercorrelations. A study of fourteen student groups at the University of Colorado yielded similar results (Eisman, 1959). Schachter (1952), in replying to Gross and Martin, argued that cohesiveness is essentially undimensional, that the different indicators need not be highly intercorrelated in order for cohesiveness to be considered a "unitary concept" (see also Gross and Martin, 1952b). In an effort to resolve the controversy, Hofstaetter (1952) did a factor analysis of the Gross-Martin data and found that, despite the low intercorrelations, the different indicators of cohesiveness could be represented adequately by a single factor. Because of the small number of groups and items, Hofstaetter's results were, as he pointed out, only suggestive; they were presented primarily to illustrate the potential utility of the method of factor analysis. We have considered these theoretical implications at length in our paper, "Two Dimensions of Cohesiveness in Small Groups" (Selvin and Hagstrom, 1965).

this factor are the proportion approving of President Eisenhower and Vice-President Nixon (the study was conducted in the spring of 1957) and the proportion unsympathetic to unions. The interpretation of this factor underscores the importance of distinguishing associations between characteristics of individuals from associations between characteristics of groups. In our data and in most other studies *individuals* who are politically conservative usually have high economic status. Among the *groups* we studied, however, there is only a small positive relation between the average conservatism of the members and the average economic position of their families, which is measured by factor IV.

Along with items indicating a high average economic status of the group members, such as a high proportion with fathers in professional and managerial positions and low proportion working part time, factor IV includes some items representing a lack of "achievement orientation." Groups with high average economic status usually have low grade-point averages, few members who think grades are important, and few who are leaders in other organizations. That is, residence groups in which very wealthy girls predominate apparently did not attract or select a high proportion of ambitious or studious members.

The fifth factor measures the extent to which the members support and participate in the political and social activities of the campus. Houses with high scores on this factor have many members who feel that more efforts should be made to increase school spirit, who take an interest in the student government, and who attend home football games often.

These five factors can be viewed as dimensions in a "space" of group properties (Barton, 1955). Considering only the first two factors for the moment, every group can be located at a point in the two-dimensional space determined by its scores on factors I and II. Adding the third factor makes it possible to locate each group in a three-dimensional space. Geometrical representation is no longer useful for spaces of four and five dimensions, but the idea that each of the twenty groups corresponds to a point in a five-dimensional "property space" can be readily grasped.

LOCATING TYPES OF GROUPS IN A PROPERTY SPACE

This five-dimensional picture can be simplified by recognizing that the goal of this procedure is to classify the twenty residence groups into a small number of broad types, not to locate them precisely along these five dimensions.[8] Even the crudest possible "measurement" — the classification of each group as "high" or "low" on each dimension — is adequate for this purpose. The complicated five-dimensional space therefore reduces to 32 discrete classes, ranging from the class that is high on all five dimensions to the one that is low on all five.

The data are even simpler than this classification indicates, however, since the twenty groups cluster together into a small number of types. For example, five of the eight sororities fall into the class that is high on all five dimensions, and two of the three remaining sororities differ only slightly on one of the five dimensions. Despite this clustering of the sororities, the error committed by classifying groups according to their common labels — "sorority," "dormitory," "cooperative house," and so on — shows up clearly here. No one of these labels corresponds precisely to one of the empirically determined classes.

A closer inspection of the data simplifies the classification even more. The major axes of differentiation turn out to be factor II (sociometric cohesion) and factor IV (economic status and lack of achievement orientation). The four classes formed by dichotomizing scores on these factors into "high" and "low" make it possible to locate nineteen of the twenty houses unambiguously. (The twentieth, a large university dormitory,

---

[8]To say that crude classification suffices here is not to condone sloppiness, but rather to emphasize the methodological differences between the theoretically oriented study of groups or individuals, as in sociology, and the diagnostic study of individuals, as in personality testing and educational measurement. In the latter, where the end-product is a decision about a person, the social and individual costs of error are high. In the former, where the end product is a decision about a relation between variables, the consequences of a moderate amount of random error are some attenuation of the measure of relationship. The costs of this are indeterminate and probably small; reducing a correlation coefficient from .48 to .38 seems a small price to pay if the labor that would have gone into the construction of elaborate measuring instruments for individual variables can be devoted to considering new hypotheses. The arguments here are adapted from Cronbach and Gleser (1957), an iconoclastic inquiry into the logical bases of psychological testing and, by implication, of all measurement procedures in the social sciences.

appears to be an intermediate type lying almost equidistant from the four principal types when they are plotted on a graph.) The four types, with illustrative labels, are the following.

Typical sororities. — Relatively high in satisfaction, cohesion, conservatism, wealth, and school spirit; includes six of the eight sororities.

Self-supporting houses. — Close to average on all factors except factor IV (economic status and lack of achievement orientation), on which they are extremely low; includes a small, low-status sorority, a small dormitory, a selective cooperative house, and a large, church-sponsored boarding house.

Wealthy houses. — Low on school spirit, high on economic status and lack of achievement orientation; includes a Jewish sorority, a largely Jewish boarding house, and one other boarding house.

Amorphous houses. — Generally low on satisfaction, cohesion, conservatism, wealth, and school spirit; includes the two non-selective cooperatives, a selective cooperative, and three boarding houses.

THE EFFECTS OF GROUP TYPES

To assess our procedure for classifying formal groups we shall present a brief analysis of some of the Berkeley data, first without the group types and later with them. An important kind of behavior on a college campus is indicated by "school spirit," a commitment to the distinctively non-academic aspects of the school culture. In the Berkeley study those women who agreed that "more efforts should be made to increase school spirit" were more likely than those who disagreed to go to many football games and to vote in the student government elections (Wenkert and Selvin, 1962). Another study of Berkeley students showed that they were much less likely to give broad support to the civil liberties guaranteed by the Bill of Rights.

The behavior of those who advocate more school spirit in part reflects a more basic value, the belief that the most important thing one can get out of a college is training for a specific career. Among students with this kind of "vocational" orientation, 49 per cent strongly supported efforts to increase school spirit, as compared with 36 per cent of the less vocationally oriented. Rejection of the humanistic goals of the university's undergraduate liberal arts program is associated with the support of the student culture.

The most effective means of transmitting and sustaining the student culture is the residence group, with its close interaction and relatively long duration of membership. But, as Table 6.5 shows, the various types of residence groups have different effects on the values of their members.

In the "typical sororities" in the first row of the table, the association between vocationalism and school spirit is small: 51 per cent of the vocationally oriented girls agree strongly that more efforts should be made to increase school spirit, as compared with 45 per cent of the girls without a vocational orientation, a difference of six percentage points. Similarly, only six percentage points separate the vocationally oriented and the non-vocationally oriented in the "self-supporting" groups. In the "wealthy" groups the difference between the two orientations rises to seventeen percentage points, and in the "amorphous" groups it reaches twenty-six percentage points, more than four times the difference in the first two types of groups. The relation between vocationalism and school spirit thus depends significantly on the nature of the group.

This differential impact of the group context on the relation

Table 6.5 Support for School Spirit, by Type of Group and Vocational Orientation

Type of Group	Per Cent Strongly Supporting Efforts To Increase School Spirit, among Girls with A		
	Vocational Orientation*	Non-vocational Orientation*	Total
"Typical sorority"	51 (162)	45 (179)	47 (341)
"Self-supporting"	42 (62)	36 (64)	38 (126)
"Wealthy"	53 (55)	36 (59)	44 (114)
"Amorphous"	48 (110)	22 (110)	35 (220)
Total	49 (389)	36 (412)	42 (801)

*A vocational orientation means agreement with the statement, "The most important thing one can get out of college is training for a specific career." The numbers in parentheses are the bases of the percentages. The one "intermediate" group mentioned in the text has been classified with the "amorphous" groups in this table.

between vocationalism and school spirit stems from the nature of the four types of groups. The two types in which the relation is small have high sociometric cohesion: the members choose to spend much of their time together. This high level of satisfying interaction leads in turn to a high level of consensus on issues like school spirit that are important to the members of the group (Homans, 1950). The influences of a cohesive group on individual attitudes thus reduce the influence of such pre-existing values as vocationalism. On the other hand, in groups with low sociometric cohesion there is little or no pressure toward consensus, and each member's vocational outlook can play a greater part in determining her school spirit.

The same data can be looked at fruitfully from another direction. Among women to whom college means primarily vocational training (in the first column of the table) the various types of groups have almost the same effect on school spirit: the maximum difference is only eleven percentage points, between the 53 per cent in the wealthy groups and the 42 per cent in the self-supporting groups. But among the women who reject this view the group context has a strong effect on support for school spirit; there is a difference of twenty-three percentage points between the 45 per cent in the typical sororities and the 22 per cent in the amorphous groups. Here the theoretical explanation shifts from the properties of groups to those characteristics of the members that make them more or less sensitive to differences in group structure. The first kind of analysis emphasizes the "differential impact" of the group context on the relations between individual characteristics and individual behavior; the second looks at the "differential sensitivity" of various kinds of people to differences in group context (Selvin, 1957).

THE BASIC STEPS AND SOME METHODOLOGICAL ISSUES

Our procedure for classifying groups has five distinct steps, most of which have several parts. Although all these steps are made up of routine statistical operations, the overall procedure is rather elaborate. It may therefore be helpful to outline the procedure briefly and, at the same time, to take up some important methodological and statistical issues that should be understood by users of the procedure.

1. *Choose a set of formal (delimitable) groups in which the same kinds of data are gathered from each individual.* As the word "delimitable" suggests, the point of having formal groups is that the investigator be able to identify all of the members so that he can select an adequate sample (in small groups, a 100 per cent sample). Actually, the procedure will work equally well for relatively long-lasting informal groups, such as street gangs. The information gathered from each individual may treat him as a *respondent*, as an *informant*, or both. Our examples in this paper have all been of "respondent data": information about the individual's own attitudes, social characteristics, and experiences. It is also possible to ask the individual to describe other people, such as his friends or the leader of the group (Selvin, 1957) and groups (his own group or even other groups to which he does not belong).[9]

2. *Compute aggregative characteristics for each group.* The larger the number of observations in each group, the less the means, proportions, and other parameters are influenced by random or idiosyncratic errors of response. How large a number is enough depends, of course, on the visibility and uniformity of the phenomena being studied. Our smallest group had 16 respondents out of 19 members, and this seemed to yield meaningful group parameters, judging by what we knew of the group from other sources. However, Halpin reports satisfactory results with only three independent judges describing the behavior

[9] In their work on describing "college environments," Pace and Stern (1958) have relied entirely on the ways in which the members of their samples perceived their colleges. This seems satisfactory when the questions deal with integral characteristics of the college, such as its rules, the conduct of courses, and the nature of extracurricular activities. But many of their questions ask for the students' perceptions of aggregative characteristics of the student body—for example, whether "the big college events draw a lot of student enthusiasm and support." Whether it would be better to ask students about their own enthusiasm than about the enthusiasm of other students can be determined only by a study that systematically includes both types of questions; as far as we know, no study has done this yet (Stern, 1962). The Pace-Stern procedure also raises a question of interpretation. Is a college where 80 per cent of the sample say that there is a lot of enthusiasm at big college events more enthusiastic than one where 50 per cent give the same answer? It probably is, but the intrinsic difference between the two sets of responses is one of consensus rather than enthusiasm (cf. Leonard, 1959).

of school superintendents (Halpin, 1956; see also Borgatta and Cottrell, Jr. 1955). Another question that arises here is which statistical parameters to compute: is the mean age enough, or should one also compute the standard deviation and the skewness of ages? In a narrow, statistical sense, means (and proportions) convey more information than the higher-order parameters and they are more stable, but the decision on which to include is primarily theoretical and substantive: what does each parameter tell about the way that the group functions?

The most important fact about the use of aggregative group variables is that they lead to more accurate descriptions of the groups on the dimensions studied than is possible with a single observer, no matter how careful he is. One reason for this is the sharp reduction in random errors when many independent observations are aggregated. Another reason is the reduction in "perspectivistic distortion": no observer can see as much of a group or reflect its behavior as adequately as a large sample of its own members. And even the occasional facetious answer has virtually no effect on these aggregative variables.

3. *Compute the correlation of each pair of aggregative variables over the entire set of groups.* Just as the number of individuals sampled from each group affects the statistical stability of the aggregative group variables, so the number of groups affects the stability of the correlation coefficients. Our figure of fifteen groups is arbitrary; smaller numbers may be adequate if the regressions are linear. The importance of correlating aggregative variables rather than single observations appears here in the magnitude of the correlations: they are much higher than those obtained from the report of a single observer.[10]

4. *Factor the correlation matrix, rotate the factors, and compute factor scores.* Since our intention has been to set forth

[10]A number of students of groups, working in the tradition of psychological testing, have manipulated their data in such a way as not to realize these advantages fully. For example, Hemphill and Westie (1950) computed scores for individual observers rather than groups, and they correlated the judgments made by observers rather than the average judgments given to groups. The resulting lower reliability of their measures doubtless contributed to the low intercorrelations of their group variables.

the logic of our procedure, we have not considered the technical operations of factor analysis, nor have we presented the detailed data on our own factor analysis. All that is necessary here is to understand that factor analysis can take a large number of correlated variables and transform them into a small number of uncorrelated variables—in effect, a multivariate scaling procedure. And the newest generation of computers does this so cheaply that any other scaling procedure—even the construction of arbitrary scales on a counter-sorter—becomes unreasonably expensive. The ability of these machines to handle large numbers of variables also makes it unnecessary to combine individual variables into scales and then to aggregate the individual scale scores, as has been done in the studies of college environments by Pace and Stern.[11]

5. *Examine the joint distribution of factor scores for all groups in order to classify the groups into a small number of types.* The groups may fall naturally into a small number of types. This happened in the Berkeley study, where nineteen of the twenty groups fell into only four of the thirty-two possible types. Had these groups been more diverse, their scores on the five dimensions might have led to fifteen or twenty types—too many to be useful in analysis. If this happens when a classification is based on several factors, the solution is to use fewer factors. In the Berkeley study, for example, limiting the construction of the typology to three factors would have led to eight possible types. Such a typology, which is a compromise between completeness of description and simplicity of analysis, does have the virtue that the types are based on the three most important axes of differentiation between the groups. No other combina-

---

[11]Pace and Stern first combined the responses of each individual to ten different questions to get an individual score on each of the thirty scales; these scores were then averaged over the sample to give thirty scale scores for each college. Only then were correlations between these scores subjected to factor analysis. The procedure in our study was almost the reverse: the responses to each question were averaged separately in each group, and the different questions were combined only after the individual data had been thus transformed into group data. Pace and Stern scaled individual data; in effect, we scaled group data. Since both studies are describing groups (residence groups and whole colleges), it seems preferable to form the scales from group data.

tion of the data that went into this factor analysis would separate the groups as clearly.

A CONCLUDING NOTE

The availability of fast computer programs makes the procedure reported here cheap and easy to use in the comparative study of groups.[12] This may be both an asset and a liability. The psychologists who invented factor analysis expected it to help them uncover the basic dimensions of personality. (Thurstone's first book on his method of multiple factor analysis was called *The Vectors of Mind.*) But this did not happen; instead, it was almost as if each psychologist who applied the new technique produced a new set of factors that he hoped would supersede those of his predecessors.

This fate need not befall factor analysis in the study of groups. For one thing, factor analysis is better adapted to the study of groups than it is to the study of individuals, since the use of aggregative group variables reduces errors of response and perception much more effectively than is possible with individual data. The result is that fewer factors are needed to describe a set of groups. Furthermore, sociology can benefit from the experience of psychology by making a stronger effort toward a set of group types that are both theoretically relevant and empirically derived.

CRITICISMS AND AFTERTHOUGHTS

In the two years since the paper from which this chapter is taken first appeared, several investigators have commented on it in the pages of the *American Sociological Review;* the method has been applied to a larger set of data than was used in the original example, and we have had some further thoughts on the virtues and defects of the method. As a guide to the reader who may want to apply the method in his own work, we present here a brief account of these developments.

[12]In a study of eighty characteristics of one hundred groups, now in progress at the Center for the Study of Higher Education of the University of California, Berkeley, the correlations, factor extraction, rotation, and factor scoring (steps 3 and 4) took six minutes on the IBM 7090 and cost thirty dollars. The program was written by Alan B. Wilson.

Criticisms

Davis (1962) has objected to our saying, in the second and third paragraphs above, that he, Blau, and Durkheim all "ignore" the associations between their group variables. Our reply (Selvin and Hagstrom, 1962)[13] admits that "ignore" was too strong, since all three authors do consider some combinations of group variables; it goes on to explain, however, that, unlike the method described here, cross-classification cannot ordinarily treat combinations of more than four or five variables *simultaneously*, even when the investigator's analysis requires such treatment.

In a report on multiple discriminant analysis Rettig (1964) has asserted that it is a better method for classifying groups than either latent structure analysis or factor-analysis methods such as the one we used. Rettig's discussion does not make clear the distinction between *classification* and *discrimination,* in the sense in which systematic taxonomists now use these terms (Sokal and Sneath, 1963). *Classification* is the construction of categories into which units may be sorted; *discrimination* is the process of deciding on the category to which a particular unit belongs.[14] One procedure makes the pigeonholes, the other uses them. Multiple discriminant analysis is clearly the right technique when conventional categories make sense, as in Rettig's example of sex, and when the investigator wants to show how the members of these categories differ on many variables. If there are no good conventional categories, then classification must precede discrimination. Although we were not aware of this distinction at the time, the method we used is classification, up to the rotation of the factors. Beginning with the computation of factor scores it is discrimination, and in this situation the computation of factor scores closely resembles multiple discriminant analysis.

[13]This reply also treats the problem that stems from having more variables than cases (groups). This same problem also appears when one tries to include all values of a polytomy in a factor analysis (e.g., including "yes," "no," and "all other responses" as distinct variables; at least one category must be omitted, *not* combined with another).

[14]Statisticians have generally restricted their attention to "discrimination," but, as Sokal (1963) has noted, their use of this term interchangeably with "classification" and "taxonomy" has caused some confusion.

Gold (1964) has criticized at some length two interpretive passages in our illustrative example. His first criticism deals with the sentence on page 181 in which we refer to Homans (1950). Gold notes, correctly, that the data in Table 2 disagree with the point made in this sentence. He then goes on to speculate on why we made this error. Our reply (Selvin and Hagstrom, 1964) offers a different diagnosis; in any case, neither the error nor its diagnosis bears on the value of the procedure we used. Gold's second criticism attacks our interpretation of the first two group dimensions as "social satisfaction" and "sociometric cohesion." The substantive issues that Gold raises are treated at length, along with several others, in another paper (Gold, 1965).

Finally, Gold recommends several procedures for factor analysts to follow in presenting and interpreting their data. It seems to us that these recommendations apply to the precomputer era of factor analysis; with the large numbers of variables used today they would be impossibly expensive, and they would not achieve the ends Gold has in mind. Our reply concludes with a call for a reconsideration of standards of presentation in factor analysis.

Afterthoughts

Application of this method to a much larger sample of student groups at Berkeley[15] has revealed many important problems that were not apparent in our earlier and smaller sample. A report on this study is in preparation, but we should like to present some of these problems and results here in order that potential users of the method may benefit from our experience.

Perhaps the most encouraging result is that the factorially derived dimensions again made a great deal of empirical sense. A factor essentially the same as "sociometric cohesion" appeared in all of our analyses. And since more attitude and value questions were included than in the example in this paper, there was always at least one clear "climate of values" dimension. An

[15]This study is supported by a grant from the National Institute of Mental Health to the Center for the Study of Higher Education, University of California, Berkeley. David Nasatir, Travis Hirschi, Ian Currie, and Henry Finney collaborated in various phases of this study, which was directed by Selvin.

especially interesting value dimension turned up in one of our samples of women's residence groups; it combined expressions of interest and activity in political, cultural, and social affairs, leading us to call it a "League of Women Voters" factor.[16]

One disappointment in our new study was the failure of the groups to cluster as compactly as did the twenty groups in the earlier study. In part this results simply from having more groups — a minimum of forty in our women's sample. Another reason is probably the absence of sororities from our new data (for reasons beyond our control, the sororities refused to participate). Since there are more sororities than any other kind of women's group, and since they have been shown to be relatively similar to each other and to differ considerably from most other groups, their absence contributes to the greater fuzziness of the factorial types.

Because this problem of a large number of types — more than can be conveniently handled by cross-classification — may well occur in other studies, we have given some thought to alternative procedures for taking group dimensions into account as independent variables. One possibility is not to construct types at all but to use the group factor scores as independent or "contextual" variables, perhaps in some form of multiple regression.[17]

The major disappointment of the larger study is the failure of our factorially derived dimensions to account for individual behavior as well as does the conventional typology of "fraternity," "dormitory," and so on. The factorial dimensions did account for a great deal of individual behavior, but in every case

[16]Those who accuse sociologists of discovering the obvious may be pleased to learn of our having demonstrated factorially the importance of sex: our first factor analysis in this study included both men's and women's residences, and the first factor extracted was made up of activities like intercollegiate athletics and activity groups that are not coeducational.

[17]This simple suggestion involves many problems that we cannot consider here — e.g., the likelihood that the effects of the group variables will not be additive, so that linear multiple regression will not be adequate. Some of these problems are considered in a report by Selvin (1954).

the multiple correlation was slightly greater for the conventional typology. Our first impulse was to blame the method, but we are inclined to reject this explanation for two reasons: first, there is another plausible explanation for the (relatively) poor correlations, and second, we have since learned that methods similar to this one have been used successfully in many different fields of study.

In our judgment, the main reason for the low multiple correlations was our poor choice of group variables. Too many of our aggregative variables had little to do with the aspects of group life in which we were interested, and we did not try hard enough to find operational measures of theoretically important group properties like those of Merton or of Hemphill and Westie. In short, bemused by the elegance of the method, we paid too little attention to the nature of our data.

Despite this disappointment, the factorial dimensions do illuminate the distinctive character of the conventional types. For example, as with the sororities in the earlier study, the fraternities have the highest scores on "cohesiveness," and one can distinguish more cohesive from less cohesive groups within each conventional type.

Finally, in the light of these results, we take some comfort in reporting that what we had considered a slightly new combination of established techniques now appears as only one of a large family of numerical methods applied to classificatory problems. Sokal and Sneath (1963) present a detailed and illuminating account of numerical taxonomic methods in biology; despite the large differences between biology and the study of groups (notably the absence of genetic mechanisms in the formation of groups), those who wish to study large numbers of groups empirically will find much of value in this book—for example, the reasons why general-purpose sets of categories must always be basically multivariate. If it is comforting to see similar methods firmly established in other fields, it is also chastening to find our work anticipated to such an extent—a phenomenon that one of us has studied as it happens to other people (Hagstrom, 1965).

7

Research Strategies in Measuring Peer Group Influence

PETER H. ROSSI

.

Although in common discourse the terms "peer group" or "crowd" or "clique" cause no great difficulty, in empirical research outside the laboratory, it is not readily apparent what such concepts or their equivalents imply in the way of research operations. One of the central methodological problems in the study of peer group influences arises directly from this difficulty in defining for research purposes precisely what a peer group is and how it might be isolated for study.

The purposes of this chapter are to review some of the major attempts to give clarity to the concept of the peer group and to propose a new approach, which I have labeled "interpersonal environment." I will not deal in any great detail with the experimental study of group effects or with studies of formally constituted groups, such as fraternities or clubs. Such groups have been dealt with more extensively in other chapters.

My primary concern here is with the "natural, informal group," loosely defined for our purposes as a set of individuals who interact with each other on a face-to-face basis, who do so relatively frequently, and who have formed themselves into such a group without the intervention of outside directives. Such an informal group may also be organized within or into a formal association with rules of membership, clearly defined division of labor and authority, and other essential characteristics of formal associations. But for our present purposes we shall consider primarily informal association.

PROBLEMS IN THE STUDY OF PEER GROUPS

In studying the effects of peers upon individuals, there are two major research problems. The first problem concerns defining the group whose effects are to be studied and includes questions such as the following. What is a peer group? Should one try to define peer groups and then place individuals within the group structures which emerge? Or should one define groups of peers, each of which may be different for every individual involved? The second problem concerns characterizing peer groups. In order to study effects, it is necessary somehow to characterize the direction and strength of the presumed influence. Here we are concerned with the problem of measuring what influence a peer group or group of peers is exerting.

Defining the Group

There have been two broad types of strategies employed in the definition of groups: one concerned with "peer groups" and the other with "sets of peers." The first approach—a group-centered strategy—starts with the identification of groups through interconnections among individuals typically employing some variant of the sociometric test. Once groups are identified, individuals are placed as members within such groups. The second approach—the individual-centered strategy—prefers to define for each individual the set of persons who are his peers without too much attention to the interconnections among such peers. The typical research device here is also a variant of the sociometric test, although the data obtained are handled quite differently. The choice between one strategy or the other is a choice between an approach which defines peer groups and an approach which defines sets of peers. I will discuss each approach in some detail.

Peer Groups

Obviously, in dealing with formal groups such as fraternities, ·clubs, classes, and the like, the problem of determining who is a member is not serious. The constitution of formal groups provides a relatively unambiguous criterion of membership even though formal membership often may be only an indirect or attenuated index of the potential influence of a formal group on an individual member. Yet such formal memberships have been useful in some research. For example, in some presidential elections the mere fact of union membership has marked off individuals with somewhat different voting habits from other individuals of comparable socio-economic status (Lipset *et al.*, 1954).

Similarly, church members have been shown to be different from non-members in a variety of ways (Stouffer, 1955; Rossi and Rossi, 1957). We will not be concerned here with the knotty problem of determining what is cause and what is effect in such findings, except to point out that the mere fact of membership in some sort of formal organization is often a personal characteristic of considerable utility in social research.

In any event, in dealing with formal groups mere membership is not much of a research problem. Rather, the problem centers on identifying different degrees and kinds of membership and of distinguishing between different kinds of formal groups.

We can expect that the central members of formal organizations, e.g., officers and persons who attend meetings regularly, are in a better position to be influenced by membership than those whose membership is merely nominal. Similarly, we can expect that organizations which encompass more of the total lives of their members are more important sources of influence on their members than organizations which do not. Thus, on a liberal arts college campus we can expect that fraternities and sororities and other living groups which form the basis for much of the on-campus lives of their members typically would be of much more importance than special-interest clubs.

The problems of measuring variability among formal organizations and measuring variations in the intensity of membership are mentioned here primarily because they highlight similar problems for informal groups. Informal groups can be expected to vary in their importance in their members' lives and the amount and kind of memberships in such groups can also be expected to vary widely among individuals.

Perhaps the most serious problem in the study of informal groups is how to detect them in a clear and unequivocal way. By definition, informal groups are without clear-cut membership criteria, locations, and structures. Furthermore, as groups they are more ephemeral, shifting over a period of time in their compositions and in their activities, since they consist in empirical patterns of behavior rather than as normative patterns embodied in a formal constitution.

The non-random associative behavior which characterizes all human behavior is familiar to all observers and familiar to the participants themselves. For example, studies of small local communities by Warner *et al.* (1949) indicate the extent to which the natives thought of their communities as composed of networks of small "cliques" and "crowds." There is no doubt about the reality of informal groupings within closed communities such as colleges or within open communities such as cities or neighborhoods. The only problems arise over how to define and isolate objectively such informal groupings clearly and unequivocally.

The research device which has been used most frequently to discern the patterns of such groupings is the sociometric test.[1] The sociometric test essentially consists in asking each individual in a population to designate the other individuals in his population with whom he is either in some kind of interaction or would like to be. Thus some tests ask the individuals to name their best friends, others to name persons with whom they would like to be friends, and so on.

An informal group is then defined usually as a subset of individuals each of whom names the other members of the subset in response to a sociometric test. For example, Gordon (1957) in

---

[1] Other devices have also been employed. In the famous observations of the bank wiring room described by Roethlisberger and Dickson (1940) the pattern of association among workers was observed directly by an observer who sat in the back of the room and recorded every instance of interaction among the workers.

his study of a small high school, asked each student to designate the three persons he would prefer as best friends, the persons with whom he spent most of his time, with whom he would prefer to attend a party or share a locker, whom he would prefer to represent him in the student assembly, and whom to date. Each of the questionnaire protocols for Gordon's population would consist of a maximum of eighteen designations, three for each of the six sociometric tests. Presumably these answers reveal or reflect the patterns of association among the individuals in the population in question and from the data it may therefore be possible to detect the group structure.

The total set of answers to a sociometric test for a population of any appreciable size presents a monumental task of analysis. Although a number of analytical procedures have been employed, each has yet to demonstrate that it clearly and unambiguously depicts the pattern of informal association within the population studied.

The earliest analytical scheme devised was the sociogram,[2] a chart in which points representing individuals are joined by directed lines representing choices. By arranging points so that persons who choose each other are located closer than persons who do not, clusters of points appear that represent informal groups. Clear directives on how to arrive at this end result have not yet been formulated. As a consequence, different research workers can arrive at different sets of informal groups, especially when the population is large and when the group structure is somewhat ambiguous. Furthermore, the sheer labor involved is considerable, especially when the population is large. When the population is as large as eighty, as in Gordon's work, sociograms are far from masterpieces of clarity.

More sophisticated analytical schemes have been devised which rest on more clearly formulated rules for discerning groupings within a population. Forsyth and Katz (1946) suggested arranging sociometric data in matrix form, columns and rows representing choosers and chosen, respectively, with cell entries indicating the choice relationship between the persons whose rows

---

[2] The sociogram was named and first used by Moreno (1934), the originator of sociometry.

and columns intersected in each cell. Rearranging rows and columns so that adjacent ones contained persons who chose each other reveals the group pattern as a pattern of cell entries in the matrix, Luce and Perry (1949) suggested more complicated matrix manipulations showing that if the matrix of choices were raised to higher powers through matrix multiplications, the cell entries in the resulting matrices would indicate the number of steps in chains of choices between the individuals involved, the length of the chains to be discerned being a function of the power to which the original choice matrix was raised.

As originally formulated by Luce and Perry, a group could be identified by the matrix multiplication method only if all members of the group chose each other. A later formulation by Luce (1950) relaxed this restriction somewhat, and further steps in this direction have recently been taken by Harrison C. White of Harvard University.

Working in a somewhat different direction, Coleman and MacRae[3] devised a "cascading" criterion for rearranging choice matrices through the use of high speed computers in which, by iterative procedures, persons choosing one another were brought closer and closer together in a choice matrix. Coleman[4] applied this method to the analysis of sociometric data from high schools, but without notable success in producing clear-cut subgroupings within his population.

Further work with high speed computers is now being undertaken by MacRae[5] employing factor analysis models. This method classifies in groups persons with similar choice patterns with subgroupings emerging as factors in the resulting factor matrix.

The directions which have been taken by recent work on the analysis of sociometric data all point to the complexity of the problem and indicate that the eventual solution will have a corresponding complexity. Part of the difficulty with the analysis of sociometric data lies in the nature of informal groups themselves, and part of the difficulty lies in the nature of the sociometric

[3] Unpublished research.
[4] Unpublished research.
[5] Unpublished research.

test. By definition, informal groups have vague boundaries and fluctuating memberships. Furthermore, sociometric tests are fallible instruments and their use to discern group structures accentuates their fallibility. We will consider these two points in some detail.

Clear and unambiguous patterns of social relationships are unlikely to define the limits of informal groups. As Coleman has indicated in his study of Illinois high schools, cliques of girls or boys which are characterized by intense and frequent interaction and with clearly defined boundaries are likely to be characteristic primarily of the few high status pupils in each school. The remainder of the school population—close to two-thirds—are involved in much looser and less intense informal groups or in no groups at all.

We may expect very much the same phenomenon in colleges. A few groups encompassing a relatively small part of the student body will be easy to define, but the majority of the population will not be easy to place within an informally organized group structure. But this does not mean that they are not influenced by their peers. It only means that the set of peers to which they are reacting is not a peer group. The implication of this patterning for the study of peer influences on individual students is clear: for a large portion of the students, it will not be possible to place them within a clearly definable peer group.

The second point concerns the fallibility of sociometric tests. It must be taken for granted that a sociometric test is subject to the usual errors of measurement. However, when used to discern groups, sociometric data accentuate considerably the measure-

Table 7.1 Mutual Designation Probabilities in a Three-Man Group

Probability of One Person's Designating Another	Probability of All Three Designating Each Other
.92	.61
.95	.70
.98	.87
.99	.90

ment errors which exist in the instrument. For example, let us assume that if a social relationship exists between two individuals, each will identify the other, in response to a sociometric test, 90 per cent of the times he is asked. If we have three persons characterized by this degree of reliability, then each and every individual in that three-man group will designate each and every other person some 53 per cent of the time.[6] A probability of .90 does not seem to be terribly low: many items on the typical attitude test have much lower reliabilities. Even greater probabilities do not yield much higher chances of complete consistency among members of a three-man group, as the computations in Table 7.1 indicate.

If we add more persons to the group the chances of mutual choices fully defining such larger groups would drop still further. It would be quite rare that informal groups of six persons would all designate each other even when the probability of each person's designating each other person is very high. As an example, Table 7.2 shows the corresponding figures for a four-man group.

To some degree these calculations are misleading, because one would not ordinarily apply the criterion that all persons in a three-man group should designate each other to define a three-man group. The set of probabilities for different numbers of unreciprocated choices among members of a three-man group, given the probability of an individual to designate any other as .90, is shown on the following page.

[6] Since there are six designations involved, $N(N - 1)$, then the probability of the joint occurrence of the six designations is p^6.

Table 7.2 Mutual Designation Probabilities in a Four-Man Group

Probability of One Person's Designating Another	Probability of All Four Designating Each Other
.90	.28
.92	.37
.95	.51
.98	.78
.99	.82

All choices reciprocated	.5314
One unreciprocated choice	.3546
Two unreciprocated choices	.0990
Three unreciprocated choices	.0140
Four unreciprocated choices	.0012
Five or six unreciprocated	.0006

If we were to insist, given the above set of probabilities, that a three-man group be defined as any set of three persons among whom at least five choices are given, then we would include "real" three-man groups almost 90 per cent of the time — certainly an acceptable level of error.

The main point that I want to bring out here is that sociometric tests must have reliability much greater than that ordinarily demanded in questionnaire work in order to be useful in determining group structures of any appreciable size. We must keep in mind, however, that our general interest is not in group structure per se but in group structure as it usefully illuminates the working of peer influences on individuals. We shall now turn to a set of methods which accomplishes this goal but bypasses the problem of the identification of group structures. These are the techniques which earlier I labeled "individual centered."

Sets of Peers

The starting point of the individual-centered techniques is the individual or individuals on whose behavior the influence of peers is supposed to play. In studying peer influences on academic achievement, for example, we are concerned with measuring how a student's peers affect his grades, perhaps seen in relation to his ability. In the college environment his peers are his fellow students and particularly those students with whom he is in contact and whom he values in some way, even negatively. If there were some way of getting at this interpersonal environment directly without necessarily being concerned with its organization, the purpose of discerning peer group influence could be accomplished with relative ease.

Many studies have followed along these lines and studied some aspect of the interpersonal environments of individuals.

Dyadic analysis which studies the relationship between pairs of individuals (for example, best friends or dormitory companions) are part of this tradition. Similarly, studies which seek to answer the question whether spouses choose each other because of their similarity or because of the complementarity of their needs are studies which start with an individual — in this case a spouse — and then find the person with whom that individual is in some defined relationship.

More complex interpersonal environments have been studied in recent research on voting behavior. A study of the 1948 presidential election (Berelson *et al.*, 1954) asked respondents to name their three best friends and three co-workers and then asked questions about the voting preference of the persons so designated. An earlier study reported by Katz and Lazarsfeld (1955) first asked housewives from whom they would accept advice on political matters; then the investigators interviewed the persons designated by the original sample.

In such studies the individuals designated and their characteristics are used to describe the interpersonal environments of individual respondents. For example, it was shown by Berelson *et al.* (1954) that when all three of the respondent's friends preferred the same candidate, the respondent was likely to prefer that candidate, but when the friends were divided, the respondent was more likely to take a longer time than usual to make up his mind and was more likely not to vote on election day.

Note that this technique in comparison to the sociometric minimizes measurement errors. For example, if we assume that the probability of an individual's designating a "real" friend as a friend is .90, then the probability of his designating both of two "real" friends is $.90^2$, or .81. The chance that, of a group of three friends, all will designate each other under these conditions, however, is only .53. In other words, it is easier to determine an individual's peers reliably than to determine his peer group.

The advantages of the individual-centered strategy in research on peer influences has led us to develop a new research approach to which I have given the term "interpersonal environment" (or IE). A detailed description of this proposed approach is given below.

THE CONCEPT OF INTERPERSONAL ENVIRONMENT AND ITS MEASUREMENT

The "interpersonal environment" of an individual is defined most broadly as the set of stimuli presented to the individual by those persons with whom he is in contact on a direct and un-mediated basis. This is a conception of each individual as being on the receiving end of communications from a limited and specific set of others with whom he is in face-to-face contact. Obviously, this concept does not cover all the stimuli impinging on the individual. It deliberately excludes those which have origins outside the face-to-face range, such as mass media, stimuli from teachers in a classroom, speakers at a political rally, and the like.

Note that there are two critical features of this concept. First, it is centered around individuals rather than around groups. It does not attempt to define the world of other persons in terms of the structure of that world but only in terms of aggregates of individuals who may or may not be structured into patterned relationships among themselves. This is not to deny that the degree and kind of patterning among the individuals in a person's interpersonal environment has some relevance but only to exclude this patterning from consideration primarily for reasons of research expediency. Second, the concept of interpersonal environment uses the criterion of face-to-face interaction as a boundary-setting device. Persons with whom an individual is not in direct interaction are outside his interpersonal environment. While there is no doubt that the kinds of potential influences excluded are of considerable importance, we are not presenting a general model of behavior but only a model which considers elements arising from face-to-face interaction.

This broad definition of interpersonal environment allows us to construct a variety of specific hypotheses relating such environments to the behavior of individuals. The Appendix to this chapter presents one such hypothesis in detail, primarily as an illustration of the utility of the general concept, and also because we believe the particular hypothesis to be of some value per se.

In order to generate propositions concerning the influence of interpersonal environments on individuals, we must distinguish aspects of such environments presumably related to such influences. Although the literature on interpersonal influence covers a wide variety of variables each distinguishing some aspect of the relationships among individuals, we have chosen only a very small subset. There are two reasons behind this restriction of choice. First, we believe that these are among the most important aspects. Second, we believe that they are variables which lend themselves easily to operational translation.

Assuming for the moment that it is feasible to collect the data appropriate to the indices suggested in the Appendix, there are several features of these indices worthy of attention. First, they are psychologically meaningful. It does make sense to think of influence as affected by the variables which are the components of the indices. Second, they lead to simple data-handling tasks. An index is computed for each individual as either a simple sum or as a weighted sum of his responses to a small series of questions to which are then added the responses of the other persons involved. For large populations the computations may be considerable in scale but, nevertheless, would be easily accomplished using modern electronic computers.

Many additional indices may be generated by considering different combinations of variables and different principles of combination. However, for our purposes of determining how an individual's interpersonal world presses upon him in one or another direction, the indices of most interest are those represented by the prototype "net climate" (E). This index produces a value for each individual representing the way in which his interpersonal environment presents to him a particular climate of opinion, values, attitudes, behavior, or performance. If the current conceptions are correct concerning the importance of peers in determining the behavior and dispositions of individuals, then some index along these lines should have predictive power in indicating the direction and extent of change in an individual. We can expect that individuals tend to change their behavior in the direction of reducing the differences between themselves and their interpersonal environments or of changing their interpersonal environments to achieve the same end result.

Whether the specific features of the particular approach suggested above have any merit must be decided by empirical evidence, some of which my associates and I are now collecting and analyzing.

THE MEASUREMENT OF CHARACTERISTICS OF
IDENTIFIABLE GROUPS

We now turn to a problem which is closely related to the ones considered in the earlier sections of this chapter. For many purposes, the social scientist is not concerned with characterizing individuals by their group environments but in measuring characteristics of existing and identifiable groups. In studying undergraduate colleges one may wish to compare their value climates. Or, within a college, dormitories or fraternities may be contrasted according to some characteristics of their memberships.

In research in which this problem has come up, it has been met by forming simple summary measures reporting central tendencies in opinions, values, attitudes, or the like. Several ways of forming these summary measures have been employed. For example, in a work of Lipset *et al.* (1956), printing plants were characterized according to the predominant political climate of opinion by classifying shops according to how much of a majority the union members in each shop gave to one or the other political party. Similar procedures were followed by Selvin and his collaborators in research on University of California living groups reported elsewhere in this volume.

A much more elaborate approach along the same lines is represented by the College Characteristics Index (CCI) devised by Pace and Stern (1958), and discussed by Pace in Chapter 8 of this volume. Summary measures taken over a sample of college students are used to characterize a school according to a number of social psychological dimensions. Note that in the Pace and Stern approach the respondent is used as a reporter whose perceptions define the characteristics of their colleges. The CCI has been used with considerable success to measure differences among colleges. For example, in a study by Thistlethwaite (1959), it was shown that National Merit Scholarship holders did best in colleges whose characteristics rewarded intellectual achievement and were unhappy in other types of colleges. More recently Pace has devised a modification of the CCI for use on subgroupings within colleges, e.g., fraternities, dormitories, departments, and the like.

In his study of Illinois high schools, Coleman characterized each of the high schools according to their "social climates" (i.e., essentially average responses to a series of questions ascertaining the students' occupational aspirations, what they considered to be most important in getting ahead, and so on).

Although devised primarily as a social psychological instrument, the concept of interpersonal environment and derivative indices have applications in the study of identifiable groups. We believe that this will be an important type of application of the measures suggested here.[7]

For groups whose membership boundaries are known or arbitrarily set by an investigator, a very suggestive set of indices may be constructed by summations of the indices suggested earlier over the members of the group. We have in mind such groups as fraternities, college classes, neighborhoods, and clubs or associations, whose membership limits are well known. Obviously the point in using such indices is to characterize the group according to the way in which it serves as an interpersonal environment for its members.

It should be noted that the group indices suggested in the Appendix are particularly useful within such institutional contexts as colleges and high schools, which have many organizationally determined ways of defining groups (dormitories, classrooms, seminars, etc.). If one wishes to determine the effects of alternative arrangements of students, the indices shown might be able to provide ways of contrasting alternative arrangements and of indicating ways to maximize or minimize particularly desirable or undesirable outcomes.

[7] Obviously, the data collected for use in the measurement of interpersonal environments may also be analyzed along the lines of other types of sociometric data (e.g., choices), since they are quite similar in basic ways. For example, it may be feasible to analyze the group structure of a college or dormitory using either mutual interaction or attraction as a criterion for setting the boundaries of cliques or friendship groups. But I do not see any special advantage in using the technique in this way, especially when the data will undoubtedly be more complex than that obtained in the more traditional sociometric test.

SOME OPERATIONAL PROBLEMS IN THE USE OF INTERPERSONAL ENVIRONMENTS

There can be scarcely any doubt that the utility of the concept of interpersonal environment depends heavily on whether it is possible to collect appropriate empirical data. The criteria for evaluating such data are the usual ones: the data should be reliable, valid, and relatively inexpensive.

The problems of data collection center around the three central variables: interaction, attraction, and content. We need to find some reliable and inexpensive way of determining with whom, how frequently, and with what attraction individuals interact with other persons in a given population. The magnitude of the task obviously varies with the size of the population in question as well as the ability of individuals to provide such information about themselves.

Interaction and attraction present the greatest difficulties in data collection. Obviously, it would be best to make direct observational measures of interaction, but such observations are feasible only under very limited conditions, such as experimentally constituted small groups. The attraction of members of a population for each other can only be obtained from subjective accounts. Of course, there is good precedent for such measures in the sociometric test tradition.

The content variable presents much the same difficulties encountered in conventional attitude testing. An attitude questionnaire distributed to each member of a population to be studied can constitute, providing the questionnaire satisfies the usual canons of measurement, an adequate measure of the content of the interaction.

The data collection problem boils down to this: How can we obtain from an individual a list of persons with whom he is in contact and the frequency of such contact? Drawing on the experiences of the sociometric tradition, several devices can be suggested: population listings, use of context reminders to aid recall, and open-ended recall.

Population Listings

If the population to be studied is "small" enough, perhaps a thousand or fewer in size, a likely technique would be to present each respondent with a complete listing of every individual in that population, asking him to designate the ones with whom he is in contact and how frequently the contact occurs. A listing has the advantage of aiding recall of those relationships which might be frequent but not salient. Individuals so designated by respondents may then be rated by the respondent according to their attractiveness to the latter. This technique was employed with considerable success in a recently published study by Wallace (1966).

Recall Aided by Context Reminders

For larger populations with fairly well-structured contact modes, it might be feasible to ask respondents to list persons whom they see and talk to, specifying clearly a number of contexts in which such contacts typically occur. Thus, in a college, one might refer to dormitory or fraternity mates, classmates, dates, laboratory benchmates and the like, attempting to make a fairly extensive coverage of contact contexts.

Open-ended Recall

While this is the least attractive of the techniques suggested here, it is probably the one which can be employed with least cost. Essentially, it consists of asking each individual to designate those others with whom he has some contact and to specify the frequency of such contacts. The dangers of the employment of such a device reside in defects in individual recall. We can expect that subjects will underenumerate the persons with whom they interact, particularly when the relationship in question is neutral.

Assuming that the data collection problems listed above can be solved, there still remain other operational problems which are worth mentioning. To begin with, for any population of appreciable size, a complete survey of individuals becomes both costly and unwieldy. Is there a sampling design which might be employed in this connection?

"Snowball sampling" may be the answer to the study of very large populations. Essentially, a "snowball" sample is an ordinary probability sample supplemented by interviews with persons designated by the members of the original sample. Thus, a sample of college students may be drawn by the usual methods, and those persons designated by the sample as constituting their interpersonal environments interviewed in a follow-up.

Another problem needs some attention. The interpersonal environment of an individual can only be measured with some degree of reliability if his environment is relatively large. For example, if an individual has only two other persons with whom he interacts with any frequency, then many of the measures suggested earlier will be of doubtful reliability. While at present we do not know the typical sizes of subjects' interpersonal environments, if such turn out to be relatively small — say fewer than ten persons — many of the indices which we have suggested will be too elaborate to be employed. There is some evidence from the Wallace study that interpersonal environments, at least within the context of the small liberal arts college, are large enough to justify considering elaborate indices.

Similarly, a prime focus of the analysis of measures of the interpersonal environment will be differences between individuals and their environments. The measures on individuals will be less reliable than the measures based on environments. Hence, differences between individuals and environments will be confounded by measurement errors and hounded by the regression effect.

In the actual computation of the indices proposed, we also encounter a problem in scale. If the three variables of interaction, affect, and content are seen as multiplicative, then the scale on which each variable is placed can act as a weighting device. Thus, if interaction is on a scale from 0 to 100 and affect is on a scale from 0 to 5, interaction will count twenty times more than affect in a final score which multiplies the two together. It will probably be the best procedure at first to place the variables on the same scale, perhaps as standard scores, and hence give them equal weight.[8] However, it might make more sense eventually to weight some variables more than others. For example, we might conceive that affect may be more important than interaction and hence give affect a heavier weighting than the others.

---

[8] Another procedure would be to transform the variables into logarithms and perform multiple regression analysis. The resulting beta weights would yield the best-predicting weighting system.

THE "MIDWEST COLLEGE" STUDY OF INTERPERSONAL ENVIRONMENTS

Shortly after the initial formulation of the concept of interpersonal environments in the summer of 1959, there was an opportunity to try out the concept in a field research. Walter L. Wallace, then a graduate student and Research Associate at the University of Chicago, and I received a grant from the College Entrance Examination Board and started to conduct a small-scale study on the relationship between peer group influences and academic achievement at a small liberal arts college, which we shall call "Midwest College."

The design of the study contained the following important features. (1) Measures of interpersonal environments were made on each of the 1,050 undergraduates. (2) Freshman students were given the interpersonal environment measures twice, once early in their freshman year and again toward the end of their freshman year. (3) Interpersonal environments were measured by presenting to the student a list of every student in the college. The student was asked to check every name which he was able to recognize and, if he checked a name, how many hours a week he spent with that person and how much he liked or disliked him. (4) Background data on the student plus an inventory of his values were also collected. The background data include grades, high-school rank, grade received on college selection tests, such as the Scholastic Aptitude Test or the American Council on Education psychological examination.

Despite the obvious length of a questionnaire which contains the names of every student in the college, it was possible for the field team to collect completed questionnaires from 95 per cent of the student body.

The interpersonal environments of the Midwest College students show a considerable range. Some students have apparently checked off at least one-half of the student body as known to them, while others merely checked off a handful. On the average, students appear to spend a great deal of time — more than five hours a week — with about twenty other students. Note that this number is much larger than we would find in any one sociometrically defined clique and probably represents individuals with whom the student is in contact in a wide range of activities.

At the present time, none of the data are available in the form of findings which bear on anything but the feasibility of the concept as a research tool. We can say definitely that it is possible to collect interpersonal environment data of apparent validity, but it is still too early to say whether the model of personal influence posited here is a useful formulation.[9]

This chapter presented a brief summary of techniques employed in the measurement of peer groups and proposed a new and as yet untried approach to the measurement of interpersonal influence.

In the review of research strategies we made a distinction between approaches which attempt to define peer groups and approaches which try to isolate groups of peers. The first approach was judged as involving problems of great complexity in measurement and as not exhausting the possibilities inherent in the notion of peer group influence. As a consequence, our primary emphasis has been given to ways of measuring the influence of the group of peers which surrounds individuals. A new way of approaching the problem was presented, one which is a logical extension of previous attempts at the measurement of the influence of peers. The new approach, interpersonal environment, attempts to construct around each individual the group of other individuals with whom he is in enduring and meaningful interaction. Pilot research is already under way to test the utility of this approach, and a more precise evaluation can be made when the results are finally analyzed.

APPENDIX: MEASUREMENT OF INTERPERSONAL ENVIRONMENT

We will distinguish three important dimensions of the relationship between an individual, *i*, and another individual, *j*.

---

[9] Since the time of this writing (1960), further analysis has shown that the interpersonal environment concept used in the Midwest College study serves an explanatory as well as a descriptive function in accounting for college student grade achievement. See Wallace (1966).

1. The interaction between i and j may vary in frequency, f, with positive values from zero to some maximum defined by the specific scale employed.

Definition. The frequency of interaction, f, between individuals i and $j - f_{ij}$ - is a function of the number of times i and j interact in a given time period.

2. A measure of the quality of the interaction between i and j is the value of the relationship attributed to it by i, here given the name of "attractiveness," a.

Definition. The "attractiveness" of j for $i - a_{ij}$ - is the value which i places on the relationship with j. Presumably this is a measure which would take on both positive and negative values.

3. The interaction between i and j has a component determined by j, which we shall designate as "content," c, the raw material of the communications sent by j to i. Such communications might cover a wide range of attitudes, values, directives, etc. In practice one would ordinarily be interested in one type of content, a particular value orientation, attitude, opinion, political preference, and the like. The actual values taken by c_{ij} would therefore be some combination of the scores obtained by j on an attitude scale, an intelligence test, or whatever happened to be the appropriate instrument for the measurement of the content under study.

Definition. The "content," c, of the interaction between i and $j - c_{ij}$ - is defined as the things which j communicates to i in interaction, as measured by some standard test administered to j.

The rationale for distinguishing these components of the interpersonal environment is as follows. (1) Frequency of interaction measures the opportunity for influence. Presumably the more frequent the interaction between individuals the more likely are opportunities that they will influence each other, independently of other aspects of the interaction in question. (2) The more an individual values, positively or negatively, the other person involved in interaction, the more likely he is to be influenced by that person. (3) Finally, the stimuli (attitudes, gestures, behavior, etc.) which are communicated in interaction indicate the direction in which influence is exerted.

Up to this point we have been discussing primarily the relationships between hypothetical pairs of individuals i and j. The concept of interpersonal environment, however, is defined as the "set" of such relationships; hence we need now to specify the ways in which the paired relationships can be aggregated into measures characteristic of entire sets. We will consider only the simplest forms of aggregation, hoping that in practice these forms will prove sufficient.

Using these three variables, summed over the set M (consisting of individuals j to m) and with whom the individual i is in contact, we have been able to suggest the following indices along with some intuitive notion of their meaning.

Gross interaction (GI_i) *for individual* i.

$$GI_i = \sum_j^m f_{ij}$$

This is a measure of the sheer quantity of interaction engaged in by individual i in the context under study. Presumably this is a measure of what has also been called "sociability," "expansiveness," etc.

Note that an individual, i, can get a high score by either having many individuals with whom he is in relatively infrequent contact or having a few individuals with whom he is in very frequent contact. For some purposes it may be useful to form an index which removes the influence of the size of the set, M, as, for example, the following.

1. Gross interaction intensity (GII_i).

$$GII_i = \sum_j^m \frac{f_{ij}}{m}$$

A measure of the average frequency of interaction of i with other members of his environment.

2. Gross interaction dispersion (GID_i).

$$GID_i = \sigma^2_{f_{ij}}$$

A measure of the extent to which individual i distributes his interaction uniformly among the persons with whom he is in contact or concentrates it on a few.

Gross environmental affectivity (GEF_i).

$$GEF_i = \sum_j^m a_{ij}$$

A measure of the attractiveness in gross of i's interpersonal environment. It can take positive or negative values.

1. Gross affective intensity (GAF_i).

$$GAF_i = \frac{GEF_i}{m} = \sum_j^m \frac{a_{ij}}{m}$$

Average affectivity of environment eliminating effect of interaction range.

2. Partisanship.

$$P_i = \sigma^2_{a_{ij}}$$

A measure of the degree to which i spreads his affect over his environment or concentrates on some portion.

Gross climate (GC_i).

$$GC_i = \sum_j^m c_{ij}$$

A measure of the content of the interpersonal environment with which the individual, i, is in contact.

1. Average climate.

$$AC_i = \frac{GC_i}{m} = \sum_j^m \frac{c_{ij}}{m}$$

A measure of climate free from the range of contact.

2. Climate consensus.

$$CC_i = \sigma^2_{c_{ij}}$$

A measure of the dispersion of content (values, attitudes, etc.) among the individuals in i's environment.

The indices considered so far were formed by considering each of the major variables separately. A more interesting set of indices can be formed by considering the variables jointly. In forming such compound indices, the primary consideration is how the variables should be considered. Should the attractiveness of a relationship between *i* and *j* be added to the frequency of interaction, or should the two measures be multiplied to obtain the joint effect? We have chosen to regard the relationship as multiplicative, recognizing that empirical research may indicate more fruitful forms of combinations.

Some suggested joint variable indices are shown below.

Net interaction affectivity.

$$NIA_i = \sum_{j}^{m} f_{ij}a_{ij}$$

This measures the interaction of the individual weighted by the attractiveness of the individuals involved in the interaction. As in the case of the single measures discussed earlier, this measure may also be considered as an average by dividing through by *m* or considered as a measure of dispersion by taking the variance of *NIA*.

1. Average net interaction affectivity.

$$ANIA_i = \frac{NIA_i}{m}$$

2. Interaction affectivity dispersion.

$$IAD_i = \sigma^2_{f_{ij}a_{ij}}$$

An intuitive interpretation of this last measure is somewhat obscure. A high measure of dispersion indicates an individual discriminating elements of his environment in terms of affect and frequency of interaction.

Net climate.

$$NC_i = \sum_{j}^{m} f_{ij}a_{ij}c_{ij}$$

This is a measure of the content of the interaction of *i* weighted by the frequency of contact and the attractiveness of the source of the contact. It weighs heavily those contents which are backed more heavily by frequent contacts and by the attractiveness of the source. Presumably this is a measure of the pressures on the individual from his interpersonal environment. Additional measures derived from this index may also be formed along the lines indicated above. For example, the following.

1. Average net climate.

$$ANC_i = \frac{NC_i}{m}$$

2. Net climate consensus.

$$NCC = \sigma^2_{f_{ij}a_{ij}c_{ij}}$$

Some of the indices which suggest themselves as being of particular interest for groups whose membership boundaries are known are those indices characterizing a group, x, composed of N individuals, i through v.

Gross interaction level (GIL_x).

$$GIL_x = \sum_i^v GI_i = \sum_i^v \sum_i^v f_{ij}$$

(Note that summation limits are over the members of the group x.) This measures the extent to which members of the group are in interaction with each other. Presumably groups will vary in this respect, and the index provides a means of making group comparisons.

Group cohesion (GC_x).

$$GC_x = \sum_i^v GEF_i = \sum_i^v \sum_j^v a_{ij}$$

Group integration (GI_x).

$$GI_x = \sum_i^v NIA_i = \sum_i^v \sum_j^v f_{ij}a_{ij}$$

A measure of group cohesion weighted by the frequency of interaction of members of the group.

Social climate (SC_x).

$$SC_x = \sum_i^v GC_i = \sum_i^v \sum_j^v c_{ij}$$

Net social pressures (NSP_x).

$$NSP_x = \sum_i^v NC_i = \sum_i^v \sum_j^v f_{ij}a_{ij}c_{ij}$$

A measure of the social climate of the group weighting heavily the opinions of frequent interactors and highly liked individuals.

Additional indices easily suggest themselves as logical extensions of those listed above. For example, another set of group indices may be built around measures of dispersion indicating cleavage within the group along associational or opinion (content) lines.

8

Attainment Patterns in the Environmental Press of College Subcultures

C. ROBERT PACE
and
LEONARD BAIRD

The "multiversity" is not a monolithic institution.[1] It is not a single mass but rather an assortment of parts and pieces loosely held together by people and programs having roughly similar, but by no means common goals. The impact of such an institution upon the attainments of students may well be a differential one, depending on the characteristics of different programs and the people in them. Even in smaller liberal arts colleges the attainments of students may be more closely related to the impact of a major field—sociology or physics, for example—than to the impact of the college as a whole. On the other hand, despite the existence of clear differences between the atmosphere of one part of the institution and another—between the School of Business and the School of Engineering, for example—all students are part of the total college environment and experience

[1]The research reported herein was performed under a contract with the Office of Education, United States Department of Health, Education, and Welfare (Grant No. 1083).

in common many of its overall characteristics, such as general rules and regulations, required courses, athletic events, concerts and special lectures, the library, the student union and the various living centers, and other common facilities. It may be that the perception of these pervasive characteristics has a greater impact on the attainments of students than the impact of more homogeneous segments within the total environment. The research described in this chapter attempts to throw some light on these alternative speculations.

The problem can be stated more formally as hypotheses to be tested.

1. In colleges of varying size and complexity there are subcultures which differ significantly from the college as a whole in their environmental press, in the personality characteristics of their members, and in their members' attainment of various outcomes.

2. The attainment of various outcomes will be related both to the environmental press of subgroups and to the personality characteristics of subgroup members.

3. When the environmental characteristics of subgroups and the personality characteristics of their members are congruent, the combined influence on relevant attainment measures will be greater than the influence of either factor alone.

4. The pattern of attainment of similar students in contrasting subcultures will be related to the press of the subculture. The same will be true of contrasting students in similar subcultures. In short, attainment will be more frequently consistent with environmental emphases than with personality characteristics.

5. Attainment will be more strongly related to the environmental press of subcultures within the college than to the press of the total college environment.

The testing of these hypotheses requires information about the college environment, information about the students, and information about students' attainment.

Information about the college environment was obtained from an instrument called the College Characteristics Analysis (CCA). This instrument measures the degree of environmental press in each of four main directions which had previously been identified from a study of the College Characteristics Index (CCI) by factor analysis (Pace, 1960). These main directions of emphasis, or press, reflecting ways in which college environments differed from one another, are (1) an intellectual, humanistic, aesthetic emphasis (IHA); (2) a friendly, group welfare emphasis (W); (3) a scientific, independent emphasis (SI); and (4) a practical, status-oriented emphasis (PS). Data bearing on the validity of these factors have been reported by Best (1961). These four variables, or directions of press, represent a consolidation into larger patterns of the thirty press variables which had been included in the initial development of the CCI (see Pace and Stern, 1958). In addition to this consolidation, the CCA differs from the CCI in two other crucial respects: it identifies the sources of press as well as the direction of press, and it measures the press of specific academic and student subcultures as well as the press of the environment as a whole.

Structurally, the CCA consists of four scales of forty-five items each, corresponding to the four environmental emphases noted above. Each of these total press scales in turn consists of three subscales of fifteen items each, corresponding to three different sources of press: administrative, academic, and student. Items classified as reflecting administrative sources of press are ones describing conditions (rules and procedures, facilities, and overall features) which exist primarily or probably because of the actions or decisions or attitudes of administrators. Items considered to reflect academic sources of press are ones describing conditions (curricula, classroom procedures and expectations, etc.) which exist primarily or probably because of the characteristics, actions, and attitudes of faculty members. Items classified as student sources of press refer to extracurricular programs, informal activities, and the characteristics and attitudes of students.

The instructions for responding to the test (to mark each statement as generally true or not true) are diagnostic in specifying the parts of the college or university to which the student's replies should refer. The set of items classified as administrative sources of press are answered with reference to the college or university as a whole. For statements related to academic sources of press, the student's answers refer to the specific academic part of the institution with which he is identified, that is, his major department or school (engineering, business, literature, music, physics, etc.). For statements related to student sources of press, his replies refer specifically to the circle of friends and associates he knows best and to the extracurricular and informal activities he specifically knows about. The idea back of these diagnostic instructions is that a student is probably more clearly aware of, and perhaps more strongly influenced by, the characteristics of the particular parts of the total environment with which he identifies — his major field or division, and his own circle of student friends — than by the academic program in general or by the students in general.

Because the CCA is not a published instrument (it is reproduced, however, in the Appendix of a recent report; see Pace, 1964) the organization of the items and the nature of the scales are further illustrated by Table 8.1.

Information about the characteristics of students came from various aptitude and personality measures. The same tests were not used in all colleges. Among the tests used, at one college or another, were the Allport-Vernon-Lindzey Study of Values, the Heston Personal Adjustment Inventory, sections of Gough's California Psychological Inventory, and the Stern Activities Index. In some instances, students' scores on these tests were available from college records; but in most instances the tests were given as part of the present research study. At some colleges, scores on the Scholastic Aptitude Test or the American Council on Education Psychological Examination were also available from college records.

Information about students' attainment was obtained from a questionnaire printed on the back of the CCA answer sheet. We use the word attainment here as meaning the criterion measures employed in this research project. There were three criteria of attainment: students' sense of progress toward the achievement of various educational objectives, their satisfaction with college life, and their grades. A list of eleven objectives was preceded by the statement, "For each objective described below, check the degree of progress you feel you have made

Table 8.1 Illustrative CCA Items

Sources of Emphasis	Direction of Emphasis			
	Intellectual, Humanistic, Aesthetic	Friendly, Group Welfare	Independent, Scientific	Practical, Status-oriented
Administrative				
Rules and protocol	Students are allowed to help themselves to books in the library stacks	The student government has a responsible role in regulating student behavior	Students who don't make passing grades are quickly dropped from school	Student organizations must get administrative approval to take a stand on controversial issues
Facilities	There is a theater on or near the campus specializing in foreign films	Dormitories are nicely arranged for small informal gatherings	Laboratory facilities in the natural sciences are excellent	Athletic facilities are modern and well equipped
Overall features	The school has an excellent reputation for academic freedom	The school helps everyone get acquainted	Students here are encouraged to be independent and individualistic	There is a lot of fanfare and pageantry in many of the college events
Academic				
Faculty	Many of the professors are actively engaged in writing	Many faculty members are active in community work—churches, charities, schools, service clubs, etc.	Many of the professors are actively engaged in research	Faculty members always wear coats and ties on the campus
Curricula	There are good opportunities for students to study and criticize important works in art, music, and drama	Many courses are designed to prepare students for well-informed citizenship	Accelerated or honors programs are available for qualified students	Many courses stress the concrete and tangible rather than the speculative or abstract

(Table 8.1 continued)

Table 8.1 *Continued*

Sources of Emphasis	Direction of Emphasis			
	Intellectual, Humanistic, Aesthetic	Friendly, Group Welfare	Independent, Scientific	Practical, Status-oriented
Instruction	Class discussions are typically vigorous and intense	Students who are having difficulty with a course are encouraged to talk with the professor about it	Frequent tests are [not] given in most courses	Students almost always wait to be called on before speaking in class
Student Student characteristics	Students set high standards of achievement for themselves	Students have a lot of group spirit	Many students are planning careers in science	Students are more interested in specialization than in general liberal education
Extracurricular programs	Many students belong to departmental clubs; e.g., French Club, Philosophy Club, Math Club, etc.	Many upperclassmen play an active role in helping new students adjust to campus life	Receptions, teas, or formal dances are seldom attended	Student elections generate a lot of intense campaigning and strong feeling
Informal activities	Many students are attracted to concerts and art exhibits	Students often have small parties to celebrate pleasant events	Most students [do not] dress and act pretty much alike	There is very little studying here over the weekends

toward its attainment," with progress being classified as "very much, quite a bit, some, not very much." The objectives listed were (1) acquiring a broad cultural and literary education; (2) vocational training—skills and techniques directly applicable to a job; (3) background and specialization for further education in some professional, scientific, or scholarly field; (4) understanding different philosophies, cultures, and ways of life; (5) social development—gaining experience and skill in relating to other people; (6) personal development—understanding one's abilities and limitations, interests, and standards of behavior; (7) knowing how to participate effectively as a citizen in one's community and in wider areas; (8) developing an ability to think critically and an understanding of the origin, nature, and limitations of knowledge; (9) developing an ability to write, speak, and communicate clearly, correctly, and effectively; (10) developing an appreciation and enjoyment of art, music, and literature; and (11) developing an understanding and appreciation of science and technology.

Three questions were addressed to the second criterion, satisfaction with college life: "How well do you like your college?" "How much of the time do you feel satisfied with your college?" "To what extent have you found groups in the

Table 8.2 Cross-Section of Upperclassmen in Nine Colleges Taking CCA

Institution	Number of Students Taking CCA	Number of Academic Subgroups Analyzed
Bennington	38	3
Swarthmore	85	6
Antioch	119	10
St. Olaf	95	7
DePauw	134	9
Eastern Washington	115	9
Mississippi	248	6
Florida	205	7
San Jose	306	11
Total	1,345	68

college which were really congenial and with which you felt happy?" Four alternative responses were listed after each of these questions. The last criterion question was, "What grades have you made in college?" to which the alternative responses listed were "mostly A," "about half A and half B," "mostly B," "about half B and half C," and "mostly C."

A cross-section of upperclassmen in nine colleges was studied. Three of the institutions were small liberal arts colleges, where few, if any, deviant subcultures were expected. Two were larger liberal arts colleges and four were much larger and more complex institutions, presumably having various subcultures which differ from one another. Although some personality data were obtained at all but one of the colleges, it was only in the last five colleges listed in Table 8.2 that such data were available for all, or nearly all, the students who responded to the CCA and to the criterion questions on the back of the CCA answer sheet.

METHODS OF ANALYSIS

In each college the students were classified into appropriate academic subgroups, such as majors in English, psychology, business, engineering, etc. For each subgroup the mean scores on all the CCA scales and subscales were computed, together with the mean ratings of progress toward each of the eleven objectives, the mean ratings on each of the three satisfaction items, the mean report of grades, and, as available, the mean scores of the subgroup members on various personality measures.

For each of these variables the deviation of each subgroup mean from the mean of the college as a whole, plus or minus, was computed, and *t*-tests were made to identify all scores of subgroups which differed significantly from the composite. This procedure meant that the *t*-tests were somewhat conservative, since each subgroup was included in the composite with which it was compared. In addition, two-tailed tests were used in all comparisons, and all cases of "borderline significance" were not considered.

Next, relationships were considered between environment and attainment and between personality and attainment. To make these analyses, decisions had to be made about which objectives, environmental emphases, and personality characteristics were relevant to one another. Some of these decisions were fairly obvious and easily defended; for example, the aesthetic emphasis of the environment, the aesthetic score on the Allport-Vernon-Lindzey Scale of Values, and the enjoyment of art, music, and literature are clearly relevant to one another. In the case of less obvious relationships, the writers looked at reported validity and correlational data in various test manuals and inspected test items before deciding how the variables would be classified. The assumed patterns of relevance listed in Table 8.3

Table 8.3 Assumed Patterns of Relevance

Environmental Press	Supportive Personality Measures	Objectives Relevant to These Press and Personality Characteristics[a]
Intellectual, humanistic, aesthetic (IHA)	Analytical thinking (Heston) Theoretical values (A-V-L) Aesthetic values (A-V-L) Reflectiveness (AI)[b] Achievement via independence (Gough) Intellectual efficiency (Gough)	(1) Acquiring a broad cultural and literary education (4) Understanding different philosophies and ways of life (10) Developing an enjoyment and appreciation of art, music, and literature
Group welfare (W)	Sociability (Heston) Personal relations (Heston) Social values (A-V-L) Religious values (A-V-L) Welfare (AI) Responsibility (Gough) Sociability (Gough)	(5) Social development, getting along with others (7) Effective citizenship
Scientific, independent (SI)	Analytical thinking (Heston) Theoretical values (A-V-L) Determination (AI) Dominance (AI) Achievement via independence (Gough) Intellectual efficiency (Gough)	(3) Specialization for further professional, scientific, or scholarly work (8) Critical thinking (11) Understanding science and technology
Practical, status-oriented (PS)	Economic values (A-V-L) Political values (A-V-L) Deference (AI) Exhibitionism (AI) Sociability (Gough)	(2) Vocational training

[a]From numbered list presented to students.
[b]AI scores are composites of several related scales (see Pace, 1964).

are the ones used in this study. In a sense, they can also be regarded as a set of predicted relationships. The weakest part of
the set is in relation to the objective of vocational training.
There should be another objective in this category which reflects
the gaining of status and personal advantage, because vocational
training is relevant to only a part of the PS environmental press.

Two analyses were performed with these data. The first examined all significant deviations of a subgroup, whether they
occurred on a press scale, a personality scale, or the sense of
progress toward an objective. Is a significantly high press accompanied by a significantly high sense of progress? Or is the
result at least consistent? And correspondingly, is a significantly
high personality score accompanied by a significantly high, or
at least consistent, sense of progress? An examination of the
consistency or inconsistency of these two sets of associations
provided some estimation of the degree and influence of each
press and personality variable. A more inclusive but less rigorous
analysis was performed by simply noting whether a subgroup
was above or below the college average on a press scale or on
a personality scale and then observing whether or not that subgroup's mean score on each of the relevant attainments was
above or below the college mean. Here, rather than examining
significantly deviant cases, we examined consistency across all
cases by a sign test. All of the various patterns and relationships were summarized, and the total number and relative proportions of consistent and inconsistent associations were
examined in each college.

The next set of analyses considered for each subgroup the
congruence between environment and personality in relation
to relevant attainment scores. "Congruence" was defined simply
as meaning that the average score of the subgroup on both
measures was either higher or lower than the corresponding
average score for the college as a whole. "Consistent" refers
to the relationships between environment and personality mean
scores, on the one hand, and mean rating of progress toward a
relevant objective, on the other. This allowed a comparison of
the consistency of attainment, subgroup by subgroup, when
press and personality were congruent and when they were in-

congruent. When compared with the separate analyses of personality and press with attainment, it provided some indication of the cumulative influence of these two factors.

The relative influence of environment and personality on attainment was also looked at for the college as a whole, as well as cumulatively by subgroups. This was done by combining all groups that were alike in certain respects. All subgroups which had a mean score above the composite college mean on a particular CCA dimension were considered together as a "high press" group, and all subgroups whose mean was below the college mean on that CCA dimension were formed into a "low press" group. Second, within each of these groups the students were divided into two categories: those who scored above the college average on a particular personality test and those who scored below the college average. And third, in each of the four groups thus produced, the mean attainment rating on all relevant objectives was computed and classified as above or below the college average. This mode of analysis was performed for all the relevant combinations of environment, personality, and attainment. The results provide a general answer to two questions. What happens to similar students in different environments? And what happens to different students in similar environments? When all these patterns of high and low scores are combined, the results indicate the total relative influence of environment and personality on the relevant attainment variables.

Finally, an analysis was made to identify the frequency with which any totally consistent pattern of relationships occurred. The method is similar to that described in the preceding paragraph, in that the students are divided into four groups, and the attainment ratings of these four groups are classified as above or below the college average. But then it proceeds beyond this point to identify only those patterns that are totally consistent with a press influence, or a personality influence, or totally the opposite of either. The initial successive sorting process yields the combinations shown in Chart 8.1. A totally consistent press influence is illustrated in Table 8.4. In short, for all the four possible combinations between environment and personality, the attainment is always consistent with the environment. This exact combination must exist before the relationship is defined as totally consistent.

There can also be three other totally consistent combinations: one that is completely consistent with a personality influence, one that is completely the opposite of a personality influence, and one that is completely the opposite of an environmental influence. None of the ten other combinations which could be formed would be a totally consistent one. By examining the theoretical probability of the frequency of each of these combinations or patterns, we can assign exact probabilities to their actual occurrence, thus providing a test of the non-chance nature of the result. Since there are fourteen possible combinations, the theoretical probability for any one combination is one in fourteen. Since there are four totally consistent patterns, the theoretical probability of obtaining patterns as opposed to non-patterns in the total matrix is four in fourteen, or 29 per cent.

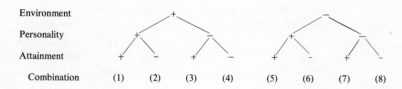

Chart 8.1 Combinations Resulting from Successive Sorting Process

Table 8.4 Relationship between Attainment and Press Influence

| Environment | + | + | − | − |
Personality	+	−	+	−
Attainment	+	+	−	−
Combination	(1)	(3)	(6)	(8)

RESULTS

In the full report of this research, each of the nine institutions was considered a case study. In the present chapter we shall give only the main results summarized over all the colleges in which they were performed.

The extent to which subgroups differed from the college composite on the various environmental, personality, and criterion measures is shown in Table 8.5. For all nine colleges combined there were sixty-eight subgroups, with each subgroup having sixteen CCA scores (three subscores and a total score on each of four press dimensions) making a total of 1,088 possible comparisons between subgroup scores and the corresponding composites. Of these, 11 per cent were statistically significant.

With respect to environmental press, then, the number of significant differences was certainly not large, but in many cases no differences were expected because of the presumably homogeneous nature of certain colleges selected for the study and because not all the CCA scores referred explicitly to the characteristics of subgroups. The administrative subscores on the CCA, for example, refer to the college as a whole, not to the

Table 8.5 Number and Per Cent of Instances in Which Any Subgroup Differed Significantly from the College Composite on Environment, Personality, and Attainment Scores

Type of Score	All Nine Colleges		Last Five Colleges Only		Four Largest and Most Complex Colleges Only	
	N	Per Cent	N	Per Cent	N	Per Cent
On all environment scores	121/1,088	11	88/672	13	78/528	15
On environment scores with administrative subscores omitted	104/816	13	74/504	15	68/396	18
On all personality scores	–	–	46/203	23	40/176	23
On ratings of nine relevant objectives	124/603	21	93/378	25	81/297	27
On ratings of three satisfaction items	12/201	6	8/126	6	5/99	5
On grades	9/68	13	7/42	17	7/33	21

specific subgroup. If we consider only the number of significant differences between subgroups and the composite when the administrative subscores of the CCA are omitted, 13 per cent of the possible number of differences are significant. Considering only the four largest and most complex institutions, where the greatest number of differences would be expected, the proportion is 18 per cent.

In the five colleges in which personality test data were available for analysis, there were significant differences between the subgroup means and the college composite in 23 per cent of the comparisons. In all colleges and subgroups, the ratings of progress toward nine relevant objectives were significantly deviant in 21 per cent of the comparisons, and in the four largest institutions the figure was 27 per cent. Subgroup ratings of satisfaction with college life did not differ from the college composite with any more than chance frequency. With respect to grades, there were some subgroup differences, but the number of comparisons is so small that the corresponding percentages cannot be regarded as very reliable.

Over all, most measures of environment, personality, attainment, and satisfaction for subgroups are not significantly different from the average of the college. The importance of the total college atmosphere is highlighted by this fact. At the same time, the number of significant differences obtained in the present studies is a very conservative number. With more reliable measures, with a larger number of students, and with more refined statistical treatments, the number of significant differences would be greater. But the atmosphere of the college as a whole, even in the case of the largest or most complex colleges, is dominant.

The importance of such differences as were found, however, gains added strength and meaning when we look at the specific location of these differences, for they tend to be concentrated in certain areas and in a certain direction. To make these analyses we combined various subgroups into larger categories. For example, chemistry, biology, physics, mathematics, etc., were combined into a category we called "sciences." Altogether, nine such categories were formed: sciences, social sciences, humanities, arts, engineering, education, business, nursing, and other vocational groups. The groups most often divergent from their college in environmental press were nursing, business, sciences, and education.

In mean personality scores on various measures the most frequently divergent groups were nursing, business, social sciences, humanities, and sciences. The objectives having the most divergent attainment ratings were understanding science and technology, vocational training, preparation for further scholarly work, and developing an appreciation of art, music, and literature. In the composite of the nine colleges there seem to be three cultures: a science culture, a humanities – social science culture, and a vocational culture. The science culture is typically high on SI press, on personality characteristics relevant to that press, and on the attainment of science-related objectives. The humanities – social science culture is typically high on personality characteristics relevant to the IHA press and the attainment of IHA-related objectives. The assorted vocational cultures are typically high in both PS and W press and have personality scores typically below average on IHA-related measures and attainment ratings typically above average for the objective concerned with vocational training. Consistent patterns such as these accounted for between one-half and two-thirds of all the significant differences reported.

In general, the statement of the first hypothesis is confirmed by the results given in Table 8.5. There are deviant subcultures — at least in the large complex colleges — although not in the small liberal arts colleges. In the large complex institutions between 20 and 30 per cent of all the t-tests were significant. The fact that a majority of the t-tests were not significant suggests that most subgroups have characteristics which vary only moderately from the total college of which they are a part. But the concentration of significant t-test results into a few fairly well-defined patterns suggests the prevalence of three cultures that are most often divergent: scientific, social science and humanistic, and vocational.

In testing the second hypothesis we examined separately, for all subgroups in all colleges, the frequency with which environment scores and relevant attainment ratings both deviated from the college composite in the same direction—i.e., a consistent rather than an inconsistent association—and then the frequency with which personality scores and relevant attainment ratings both deviated in a consistent rather than an inconsistent way. This is a simple "sign test." For example, if the total IHA press score of a subgroup is above average (+) and if the mean rating of attainment for each of the three IHA-related objectives is also above average (+++), then the association is classified as fully consistent. If the attainment ratings showed two pluses and one minus, the relationship was classified as mainly consistent. Table 8.6 summarizes all these directional relationships. The results show that both environmental characteristics and personality characteristics are consistent, rather than inconsistent, with the attainment of relevant objectives in a ratio of two to one.

A sharper picture emerged when we summarized only those relationships in which one or both of the related variables differed significantly from the college average (environment and attainment or personality and attainment). These data are shown in Table 8.7. Over all nine colleges, the association between environment and attainment scores was consistent (rather than

Table 8.6 Directional Relationships between Environment and Attainment and between Personality and Attainment in All Subgroup Comparisons

Relationship	Environment and Attainment (All Colleges)	Environment and Attainment (Five Colleges)	Personality and Attainment (Five Colleges)
Fully consistent	113 ⎫ 164	78 ⎫ 106	127 ⎫ 148
Mainly consistent	51 ⎭	28 ⎭	21 ⎭
Neutral	26	16	24
Mainly inconsistent	20 ⎫ 78	7 ⎫ 46	25 ⎫ 89
Fully inconsistent	58 ⎭	39 ⎭	64 ⎭
Total	268	168	261
Ratio: consistent to inconsistent	2:1	2½:1	1⅝:1
Ratio: fully consistent to fully inconsistent	2:1	2:1	2:1

Table 8.7 Significant Relationships between Environment and Attainment and between Personality and Attainment in All Subgroup Comparisons

Relationships	Environment and Attainment (All Colleges)	Environment and Attainment (Five Colleges)	Personality and Attainment (Five Colleges)
Both significant and consistent	35 ⎫	26 ⎫	23 ⎫
Environment or personality significant and attainment consistent	18 ⎬ 95	12 ⎬ 66	18 ⎬ 90
Attainment significant and environment or personality consistent	42 ⎭	28 ⎭	49 ⎭
Neutral	5	3	1
Environment or personality significant and attainment inconsistent	11 ⎫	9 ⎫	9 ⎫
Attainment significant and environment or personality inconsistent	16 ⎬ 31	12 ⎬ 25	29 ⎬ 47
Both significant but inconsistent	4 ⎭	4 ⎭	9 ⎭
Total	131	94	138
Ratio: consistent to inconsistent	3:1	2½:1	2:1
Ratio: both significant and consistent to both significant and inconsistent	9:1	6½:1	2½:1

inconsistent) in a ratio of three to one, but when both measures differed significantly from the college average, the corresponding ratio of consistency was nine to one. The results are also shown for the five colleges in which we had both environmental and personality data. In these comparisons the consistency of association between environment scores and attainment ratings is greater than the consistency of association between personality scores and attainment ratings. The second hypothesis is confirmed by these data.

In order to test the hypothesis about the effects of congruity and incongruity, we summarized, for the five colleges in which both personality and environmental data were available, the relationships to attainment when these two potential influences were mutually supportive and when they were in conflict. Congruence between relevant personality and environment scores exists when, on both measures, the subgroup means are both above average or both below average in relation to the college composite. "Consistent" means that the subgroup attainment ratings of relevant objectives are either above the college average or below the college average in the direction to be expected from the environmental and personality characteristics of the group. From the data in Table 8.8 it is evident that personality and environmental characteristics of a subgroup are more likely to be congruent than non-congruent — 60 per cent to 40 per cent. When they are congruent, attainment is consistent, rather than inconsistent, with their combined influence in a ratio of three and one-third to one. When they are not congruent, attainment is consistent with the environmental emphasis, rather than with the personality characteristic, in a ratio of one and one-third to one. Since the consistency ratios from the sign test analysis previously reported for environmental and personality factors separately were two to one, and since the consistency ratio is three and one-third to one when these factors are mutually supportive, we can conclude that the third hypothesis is confirmed by these results.

In testing the fourth hypothesis the method of successive sorting described in the previous section was followed. We illustrate this, with examples drawn from two of the colleges, in Table 8.9. In College X, the mean attainment ratings for objectives 1, 4, and 10 were all above average when the students were in above-average IHA press groups, even though their scores on the A-V-L scale of aesthetic values were below average. In College Y, the mean attainment ratings for objectives 1, 4, and 10 were all below average when the students were below average on the A-V-L aesthetic scale, despite their being

Table 8.8 Summary of Relationships to Relevant Attainment when Environment and Personality Variables Are Congruent and when They Are Different—for All Subgroups in Five Colleges

Relationship	Number of Examples	Per Cent
When environment and personality are congruent, the relationships to relevant attainment are:		
Fully consistent	92 ⎱ 110	35 ⎱ 42
Mainly consistent	18 ⎰	7 ⎰
Neutral	14	5
Mainly inconsistent	6 ⎱ 33	3 ⎱ 13
Fully inconsistent	27 ⎰	10 ⎰
Total	157	60
When environment and personality are different, the relationships to relevant attainment are:		
Fully consistent with environment	37 ⎱ 53	14 ⎱ 20
Mainly consistent with environment	16 ⎰	6 ⎰
Neutral	12	5
Mainly consistent with personality	6 ⎱ 39	2 ⎱ 15
Fully consistent with personality	33 ⎰	13 ⎰
Total	104	40
Grand total	261	100

Table 8.9 Successive Sorting as Applied to Two Colleges

College	Environment (IHA)	Personality (Aesthetic Score)	Relevant Objectives		
			1	4	10
X	+	−	+	+	+
Y	+	−	−	−	−

members of groups with above-average IHA press. Within each of the five colleges, all combinations of relevant press, personality, and attainment ratings were tabulated in this fashion. These data were then summarized across all colleges, with the results shown in Table 8.10. Students who were in an above-average press situation, and whose relevant personality scores were also above average, reported mean achievement ratings on relevant objectives that were also above the college average in sixty-six out of seventy comparisons, or 94 per cent. Under consistently below-average conditions (double minuses), achievement ratings were also below average in sixty-two out of the seventy comparisons, or 89 per cent. Where below-average students were in above-average environments, their achievement was below average in thirty-seven out of the seventy comparisons, or 53 per cent. When above-average students were in below-average environments, their achievement was also below average in thirty-seven out of the seventy comparisons, or 53 per cent. There is, apparently, a slight tendency for above-average students to be pulled down by below-average environments. At the same time, and by the same slight tendency, below-average students are not pulled up by above-average environments.

Table 8.11, which is really a set of tables, shows the results summarized for all colleges when the same successive sorting procedure is carried a step further to produce what we have previously called "totally consistent" patterns. Each column of

---

Table 8.10 Combinations of Attainment, Environment, and Personality for Five Colleges

Environment	Personality	Relevant Attainment		
		+	−	o
+	+	66	4	−
+	−	32	37	1
−	+	32	37	1
−	−	7	62	1

Table 8.11 Summary of Totally Consistent Patterns of Influence on the Criterion Variables of Attainment, Satisfactions, and Grades — Five Colleges

Environment*	Patterns of Influence Organized around Press Scores†												Patterns of Influence Organized around Personality Scales												
	A On Attainment of Relevant Objectives				B On Satisfactions with College Life				C On Grades				D				E				F			
	+	−	N	O	+	−	N	O	+	−	N	O	+	−	N	O	+	−	N	O	+	−	N	O
IHA	32	−	14	6	9	10	27	6	9	4	2	−	15	7	33	1	14	10	22	10	4	4	10	1
W	27	−	9	1	30	−	23	6	1	11	6	−	15	4	27	1	14	5	51	2	9	5	3	1
SI	50	−	9	2	1	20	29	9	10	1	2	1	14	19	31	−	13	11	16	9	2	4	10	1
PS	11	11	−	1	16	1	24	8	−	5	9	2	10	6	2	5	11	6	20	16	6	8	−	1
Total	120	11	32	10	56	31	103	29	20	21	19	2	54	36	93	7	52	32	109	37	21	21	23	3
No. of patterns	173 (66%)				219 (63%)				63 (54%)				190 (68%)				230 (62%)				68 (55%)			
Non-patterns	88				129				53				90				142				56			
Total	261				348				116				280				372				124			

*Personality counterparts of "Environment" scales in "Patterns of Influence Organized around Personality Scales" columns.

†+, totally consistent with press; −, totally anti-press; N, totally consistent with personality; O, totally anti-personality.

the table is identified by a letter. In the first half of the table (sections A, B, and C) the data are organized around press variables; in the second half (sections D, E, and F) the data are organized around personality variables.

Section A is interpreted as follows: when IHA press is compared with the attainment of relevant objectives, one finds thirty-two instances in which the association is totally consistent with press, regardless of students' scores on any of the personality measures. At the same time, there are fourteen instances in which the attainment is totally consistent with some personality dimension. In order to see the effect of particular personality dimensions, we must look at the N column of results in section D of the table. There, the number of totally consistent patterns associating each category of personality needs and relevant objectives is given. Also, under the plus (+) column, the number of patterns indicating the effect of some press categories is given, although these may be any of the four press dimensions. Thus, the relative size of the relations must be considered to interpret the strength of the relation, and the incidence of combinations of patterns which are in the opposite direction may be taken as an indication of the reliability of the relation.

In section A of the table, then, the predicted relations between press and attainment occur quite consistently and reliably in all cases except for PS, in which the results are as often in a direction opposite to the press as they are in the same direction. The personality dimensions, as seen in column N of section D, are also consistently related to the attainment of relevant objectives, except for the PS dimensions. However, as seen in the relative number of plus and minus patterns, environmental influence also plays a considerable role. When we compare the two sections, we see that the proportion of patterns which are related with each set of relevant objectives is greater for the environmental comparisons than for the personality comparisons.

In section A, 120 of 173 patterns are totally consistent press patterns, or 69 per cent; in section D, 93 out of 190, or 49 per cent, are totally consistent personality patterns. This provides an indication of the relative strengths of the relationships.

Thus, for the sense of progress toward objectives, the relation is somewhat more consistently stronger with the environmental press of the subgroup than with the personality characteristics of its members. The relationship seems to be especially strong between the attainment of goals relevant to the scientific independent orientation and the SI press of the subgroup. This general conclusion of the relative strength of personality and press is supported by an examination of the data within each set of results. Thus, while there are 120 press patterns compared to 32 "personality" combinations in section A, there are 93 personality patterns compared to 54 "press" patterns in section D, or a ratio of four to one compared with two to one.

A different picture emerges when one takes satisfaction with college life as the criterion. Applying the same logic, we see that 56 of 219 (26 per cent) of the patterns are press patterns in section B, while 109 of 230 patterns (47 per cent) in section E are personality patterns. Over all, satisfaction with college life is more strongly related to students' personality characteristics than to the characteristics of the college environment. However, two modifications of this conclusion need to be made. First, of the 109 patterns just mentioned, 51 are patterns referring to the "welfare" or sociable, outgoing, friendly aspects of personality. Second, there are weaker, but still quite significant, results in section B of the table which show that satisfaction is related to the degree of the subgroups' welfare press, and to the opposite of a scientific, independent press. Thus the extent to which students like their college experience seems to depend rather clearly on their finding conditions in the college environment which reward their own needs for friendship and communal experience.

Although the total number of patterns related to grades is small, the data in sections C and F of the table at least suggest that the same two elements discussed above also play a differential role here. The scientific, independent press of the environment tends to be related to grades, regardless of students' personal characteristics; and student characteristics of independence and scientism tend to be related to grades regardless of the environmental press of the college—a complementary relationship. Thus it is not the friendly group aspects of the environment that are associated with grades; it is rather a negative environmental press in this dimension that is related to grades. Grade-getting seems to emerge as a pretty hard-nosed business.

From these analyses we conclude that the direction of relationship stated in our fourth hypothesis is generally supported by the data. On the whole, environmental influences were more strongly related to the attainment of various objectives than were personality influences. Satisfaction appears to depend more on personality than on the environment, but the friendliness of the environment also has a good deal to do with students' satisfaction. Grades, which might be regarded as more or less neutral with respect to environmental press, are nevertheless associated with press to about the same degree as they are associated with personality characteristics.

In testing the final hypothesis, concerned with the relative impact of the total environment versus the environment of subcultures, the available data were examined in a number of ways.

First, each of the nine colleges was arranged in rank order according to its total IHA press. Then each of the nine colleges was arranged in rank order according to its students' ratings of progress toward the three objectives relevant to the IHA press. The correlation between the two rankings was .90. In colleges that have the strongest intellectual, humanistic, and aesthetic atmosphere, the students also make the most progress toward a broad cultural and literary education, understanding different philosophies and ways of life, and an appreciation and enjoyment of art, music, and literature. The rank-order correlation between scientific independent press and progress toward objectives relevant to it was .65. For the friendly, group welfare emphasis and its related objectives, the rank correlation was .57. For the practical, status-oriented emphasis and its relevant objective, the rank correlation was .28. Except for this last correlation, which is not significantly larger than chance, the relationships are clearly significant and, in one case, clearly substantial as well. By way of contrast, to note one example, we also looked at similar rank correlations within each of the four largest colleges between the IHE press of its various subgroups and the progress toward relevant objectives. These correlations were .40, .40, .24, and −.34.

Second, we looked at the range of differences between the total press scores of subgroups within each institution and compared this to the range of differences between the total press scores across the group of nine institutions. In all comparisons, and on all the press scales, the differences between institutions were much greater than the differences within institutions. On IHA press the range of differences between subgroups within an institution was, on the average, 4.5 points; but the range across institutions was 12.9 points. On the W press the typical range within institutions was 5.6 points, compared to a range of 15.3 points between institutions. On the SI press the corresponding figures were 3.9 (within) and 13.5 (between), and for the PS press the results were 4.2 (within) and 24.5 (between).

Third, we examined the data to see whether subgroups of a common type, such as physical sciences, might not be more similar to one another than to the colleges in which they happen to be located. Science is science, one might suppose, whether at one college or another. To test this supposition, the range of CCA mean scores for all similar subgroups across all colleges was compared with the range of composite mean scores across all colleges. If subgroups of a common type tend to be more similar to one another than to the colleges in which they are located, the differences between these common types of subgroups should be smaller than the differences between the colleges. In no case, however, was this true. Comparisons were made for all physical science groups, all biology and chemistry groups, all English, language, and literature groups, all social science groups, and all art, music, drama, and speech groups. In each set of comparisons, the range of mean scores across the presumably common type of subculture was almost identical with the range of mean scores across the colleges in general. In other words, science at College A is as different from science at College J as College A itself is different from College J.

From these three analyses we conclude that the total press of institutions has a greater bearing on students' attainment than the press of subcultures within the institution. Our fifth hypothesis is therefore not confirmed.

CONCLUSIONS

In the present research, we have regarded the college environment as a general stimulus, presumably having some kind of impact on the attainments and satisfactions of students. We have then broken this total stimulus into somewhat smaller segments, representing particular academic fields and particular circles of friends, to investigate what differential influences might be attributed to these sub-environments. At the same time, we have investigated characteristics of the students themselves, because it may well be that nature rather than nurture is the primary influence upon college attainment and satisfaction. The results of these studies can be seen as following a mass-action concept of educational impact.

As we move from the total environment to major subcultures within it, and then to particular aspects of these subcultures, we find that the relationships between environment and attainment are progressively smaller. The greatest impact is from the largest mass. The clearest differences in stimuli are those between the total environments of different colleges. Correspondingly, the clearest relationships between environment and attainment are those between the different colleges as a whole. Within the colleges, there are deviant sub-environments. Again at this level it is the total press of the subculture, rather than the press of any one aspect of it, that has the higher relationship to students' attainment of relevant objectives. Moreover, common types of subcultures differ from one another across colleges to as great a degree as the colleges themselves differ, indicating that the impact of a subculture depends more upon the college in which it is located than upon its presumed similarity to others of its kind.

In small colleges there are few differentiated subcultures. In more complex colleges the number is greater. We find not only environmental differences but also a roughly parallel distribution of like-minded students into the different subcultures. Where the characteristics of students and of subcultures are similar, or congruent, their combined mass influence on achievement is greater than the influence of either factor alone. When these factors are not congruent, achievement of relevant objectives is a little more frequently consistent with the press of the environment than with the personality of the students. In summary, the more massive, the more cumulative, and the more congruent are the stimuli, the greater is the impact they have upon the students.

In the general literature of social psychology there is impressive evidence of the influence of peer groups on the attitudes and performance of their members. Such evidence is found, for example, in the work of Asch (1952), Sherif and Sherif (1956), Hare *et al.* (1955), Cartwright and Zander (1960), Thibaut and Kelley (1959), and Newcomb (1950, 1961). But in our own studies we concluded that it was the college as a whole, rather than peer groups or subcultures within the college, that had the larger influence on students' attainment. This apparently contrary conclusion needs, therefore, to be examined more closely. There are differences in definitions, methods of analysis, and criteria which may account for the discrepancy.

Our studies can be seen as dealing with peer groups, membership groups, and reference groups in varying degrees of overlap and mixture. In answering the CCA, each student described the characteristics of his own peer group, i.e., his circle of friends and activities, but in our analyses we did not deal directly with these specifically defined peer group characteristics. Instead, we cumulated the responses of the students in an arbitrarily defined membership group, i.e., the major field or division to which the students belonged. This procedure was reasonable for our purposes, because we wanted to see whether the student atmosphere perceived by engineering students, for example, differed from the student atmosphere perceived by business students, and also, in each case, whether such atmosphere generally supported the academic atmosphere of the major field. Our classifications were of membership groups but not of precise peer groups. And we have been concerned with only one kind of membership group, namely, the academic department or division in which the student is majoring.

The college as a whole can be viewed as a larger membership group or as a general reference group. In small and fairly homogeneous colleges, the peer groups, membership groups, and reference groups may all be the same, sharing common values and characteristics. In larger, more complex and diversified universities or colleges, the students' academic membership groups may coincide only slightly with their peer groups, and neither kind of group may be as influential on their attainment as the larger reference group of the total institution, which exemplifies in its general atmosphere a strong or weak commitment to such values as intellectuality, reflectiveness, aesthetic appreciation, social welfare, privacy, vocational training, technical skill, personal gain, and so on. The four main dimensions of the environment measured by the CCA are of this large, and perhaps more pervasive, sort.

Moreover, the criteria of attainment and satisfaction in the present study involve general evaluations of the worth to the student of his entire experience in college. The nature of these criteria may also influence the kind of results obtained. In most peer group studies the outcome variables are more specific and limited in scope — a particular attitude or a particular performance. Thus, while subgroups influence specific attitudes and behavior, as previous research clearly indicates, more general evaluations of progress and development are more influenced by the total environment. Viewed in the perspective of the student's entire college experience, a specific peer group or membership group is a relatively small stimulus, and the impact of such a stimulus is perhaps best seen on attitudes and behavior that are correspondingly limited and pertinent to that stimulus. With more global criteria, more global influences are required.

Granted some validity to these explanations, we can see our results as compatible with previous studies; for what appear to be different results from different studies are merely results located at different points on a continuum of mass action and mass impact. Yet each is in line with the expectations at its place on that continuum.

Part III

Problems
and Prospects
in the Study of
College Peer
Groups

9

Peer Cultures
and Education in
Modern Society

JAMES S. COLEMAN

Since youth cultures stand as an intermediary between the larger society and youth, they constitute a kind of "intervening variable" in the framework of research. Both their sources and their effects are important matters of concern. From the perspective of social action, we are interested in the sources as a means of modifying the effects. To know the sources of variation in youth cultures without knowing their effects leaves us ignorant of which way to turn; to know the effects of various kinds of cultures without knowing their sources leaves us powerless to act. Thus the study of peer cultures in college must branch in both these directions. In order to "locate" the papers in this volume, to suggest how they contribute to the total study of college peer cultures, it is necessary to give them a framework of sources and effects. This will be done below by working backward, beginning with the kinds of effects that concern us, then examining the agents within the peer culture through which these effects occur, and finally looking at the factors that affect these agents of change.

THE EFFECTS OF YOUTH CULTURES IN COLLEGES
There are two important general effects of these youth cultures. One of these, discussed at length in the chapters of this

244

volume, is the effect on their members: the immediate and the continuing effects on individual college students. A second kind of effect is important as well: the student society as a force in itself, acting upon other institutions in society. This effect is more often upon the college, the formal institution that surrounds the youth culture. For example, these cultures can modify the goals of college administrators and of faculty, making them content with an athletic reputation for the college, even though their original goals were more academic. The cultures constitute a powerful "public opinion" that can shape the goals of the college, just as public opinion in the larger society can shape a nation's goals.

This force of the youth culture upon the surrounding adult institutions will be discussed only briefly. Of the chapters in this volume, only that of Clark and Trow touches upon the problem. The methodological tools presented in this book are not appropriate to it, but to the other problem, the culture's effects upon college students themselves.

EFFECTS OF THE CULTURE ON ITS MEMBERS

What kinds of effects does a student subculture have upon its members? This question is hardly less comprehensive than that of the effects a society has upon its members. For a student subculture is, at its strongest, nearly a society in itself. Its members are turned inward, looking to one another for their social rewards; their associations are almost completely with one another; and they have many of the accoutrements of a society, including a host of voluntary organizations and a highly developed stratification system.

Its major difference from a full-fledged subsociety within the larger one (such as some isolated religious sects in our society) is its temporary nature. Because of this, and because of its early position in the life cycle, its aftereffects are of special importance.

Thus two kinds of effects of the culture on its members are of concern: first, its immediate impact on the distribution of energies of its members, and second, the residual effect which its members take with them when they leave college. This residual effect has several components. One consists of matters they have learned, both intellectually and, in a broad sense, culturally: how to drink liquor socially; how to choose appropriate dress; how to carry on an intelligent discussion about a wide range of topics; how to exclude casually a person who aspires to one's group; how to put another person at ease or ill at ease; how to preside over a group. These are all learned at college, principally from one's immediate fellows and from the larger student culture. They are the product of the way one spends his energies at college, and thus their sources lie in those factors which shape the distribution of energies.

A second component of the residue that the college culture leaves may be termed *attachments*—attachments to others, to abstract beliefs or values, to oneself. Much of the research about "the effects of college" has concerned attachments to abstract values and their change during the college experience.[1] The way in which a college graduate relates to society and the people within it must be seen in part as a consequence of the college experience. Finally, his attitude toward himself, the general self-conception that he carries with him from college, is in part a residue of the roles into which he has been cast in the college society.

MECHANISMS OF CHANGE

In order to see just how these changes may be wrought by the college experience, and to see their relation to the agents of change in the culture, it is necessary to set down in brief the mechanisms of change. This statement follows in large part that by Newcomb in Chapter 1 (and to some degree that of LeVine in Chapter 4), in taking rewards and punishments as the crucial organizing concept. The youth culture, and various agents within it, provides rewards and punishments for various actions of its neophyte members. The responses made to these rewards and punishments include the following ones relevant to the focus

---

[1] See Jacob (1957), who finds little evidence of value change in a review of research in this area. In part, however, this reflects upon the research techniques, for surveys of the adult population show that a college education has a predictable effect on many kinds of attitudes and values in the area of public affairs.

of this book.[2] (1) The tendency to channel energy in those directions for which the student is rewarded. (2) The tendency to attach positive values to those directions in which his actions are going and to expect others to value them similarly. (3) The tendency to become positively attached to those who reward him and alienated from those who punish him. (4) The rewarding of, and attachment to, those who enter into a common effort with him, following the direction of his action. (5) Persons have needs for recognition, respect, and acceptance from other persons; thus in any totally encompassing community, the community itself holds a strong power of reward and punishment over its members.

It is through these mechanisms, and perhaps others, that the student culture has an effect upon its members. The need of the boy or girl for the recognition, respect, and acceptance of others means that such others hold a potentially powerful instrument of reward and punishment over him. By virtue of the first response listed above, they can shape the directions his energies take; by virtue of the second, they can implant values; by virtue of the third and fourth, they can shape his attachment to groups and people; and by virtue of the fifth, they can shape his attitude toward himself. Of course, differing talents among students, and diverse values from outside sources, will lead students to respond differentially to the rewarded and non-rewarded activities in a given subculture. Thus a girl whose values are strongly against drinking may become alienated from her sorority sisters instead of being converted to drinking. But whether she becomes converted or alienated, the culture has its impact upon her—in one case, upon her values, in the other, upon her interpersonal relations. Either response could have strong residual effects beyond college.

This is not to say that every boy or girl in a college is strongly affected in all these ways. In some non-residential colleges with what Clark and Trow term a "vocational culture," few such effects occur, for there is hardly a coherent student culture. The

[2] These responses as listed are supported by social psychological research, although there are social psychologists who would take issue with one or more of them.

point is, rather, that these are the kinds of effects, and the mechanisms of change, that some youth cultures have on some of their members. It remains for research of the types outlined in earlier chapters to specify in what kinds of cultures, and for whom, the effects occur.

THE AGENTS OF CHANGE

As earlier chapters of this book have made clear, the agents which affect students may be quite diverse: association with a roommate, pledging a fraternity, trying to win many friends — all these can be agents of change. The student society of a college is differentiated and often large; there are many points at which it touches the lives of its members. However, it is perhaps sufficient to consider three levels of social organization. These will serve to locate the research strategies discussed in earlier chapters.

The most comprehensive level of social organization is the total student body. It affects a student primarily through its status system. Having no material rewards to give or withhold, the student society has as its major rewards prestige and recognition. Such status in the total student society is ignored by some, shunned by some, but deeply desired by others. Desire for prominence or position is the lever by which the culture can exert its effect. Research is hardly needed to show some of the effects of this lever on the allocation of energy: in a school where the basketball team is adulated by the crowd, many boys will be drawn to basketball; in a school that has just selected a prom queen, many persons of both sexes will attempt to win her favor; in a college where dramatic presentations are important events, the drama club will have a large turnout. Many colleges are populated by people trying to "make good" — not in any long-range sense, but in an immediate social sense. If making good means grubbing as a reporter on the newspaper or pushing beans along a sidewalk as a pledge in a high-status sorority or doing odd jobs for a "big man on campus," there are many who will do so.

There are important questions about this overall status system. Is it a single unitary culture, with a generally recognized hierarchy of activities and of persons, or a set of rather distinct subcultures, each with its own status system? In any single status system, is there a complete hierarchy of activities, or are there a number of different activities that equally gain status? Is the culture more devoted to giving rewards for positive achievements or to meting out punishments for violations of norms? To characterize any such informal system of status adequately, these diverse aspects must all be considered. For example, unless one knows the relative amounts of reward for achievement and punishment for violation of norms, it is not possible to examine the system's effect on the amount of energy invested in college or to account for the differing numbers of psychological problems of students on different campuses.

The second level of organization in the student society is the host of voluntary organizations on campus: fraternities and sororities, activities clubs, service clubs, interest or hobby groups. Within each of these groups, there are positions of differing importance or prominence that channel student energies. Such groups often are exclusive, and mere admission into the group is an important reward that channels energy. The major point is that these groups within the larger student society have rewards and punishments of their own and can use these to mold the students who aspire to join or to remain in them.

Finally, at the lowest level, is interpersonal association: friends, roommates, classmates, dates. This interpersonal association is the most voluntary and selective of all the levels, for a boy or girl may search to find a compatible friend, but he must make peace with the larger student culture, whether compatible or not. Personal association can bring about all the changes discussed in the preceding sections, though its role is different from that of the culture as a whole. A close personal relation can have powerful rewards for its participants, as well as the threat of strong punishment if broken. Its potential effects are far greater than the more distant status system or even the fraternity, for the personal relationships themselves may provide sufficient social insulation to protect their members from the larger systems. Yet in their very selectivity lies their weakness as an agent of change—for if the compatibility is not initially great enough, the tension will be resolved not by change but by continuing the search for greater compatibility.

Each of these three levels in the organization of student societies has its own means of inducing change, as indicated above. Each has its set of rewards and punishments sufficient for channeling some energies and affecting some students. There is, of course, interaction between the levels: a boy may seek to gain status in his fraternity primarily for the aid it will give him in achieving campus-wide prominence; a fraternity may demand from its members behavior which will maintain its reputation on campus; two students may band together as mutual protection against the values of the student culture as a whole. Despite this interaction, it is useful to simplify the picture and look at each level alone, as in fact the chapters of this volume do.

THE PROBLEM OF MEASUREMENT

Measurement of the culture is essential to the study of the effects of the student society on its members or to the study of sources of variation. But what does one measure, and how does he go about it? Our knowledge of this problem is not nearly as far advanced as is our knowledge of individual measurement.

Chapter 6 by Selvin and Hagstrom, Chapter 7 by Rossi, and Chapter 8 by Pace and Baird, all attack the problem of measurement. Each chapter is something of an innovation; these are new approaches to the measurement of the culture of a group. They are not only new; they are three distinct and different approaches. Their first difference is in the level that they attempt to measure. Pace's College Characteristics Index (called the CCI, below) is designed to measure at the level of the college as a whole. It measures the "environmental press" of the college.[3] In contrast, Selvin and Hagstrom's approach by factor analysis has been used at the level of formal groups within the college

---

[3]As used until now, this has included the press from faculty and administration together with that from the student body. Pace indicates, however, that new research will measure separately the environmental press stemming from the student body. Thistlethwaite (1959) has already used parts of the CCI to measure student culture separately.

—residential groups, in the research they report here. Finally, Rossi's measures of interpersonal environment are designed (and were used in the Midwest College research he discusses) for the third level of social organization, personal association. Thus these are not three different approaches for measuring the same thing—they are designed for different, but complementary, purposes. However, this does not mean that the three approaches are perfectly compatible or that they join together to provide a perfect system for measuring the student culture in a college. They stem from quite different conceptual bases. It will be useful to explore these differences in some detail.

Perhaps the most fundamental difference is in the role of the person who responds to the questions. In Pace and Baird's approach, the respondent is reporting upon his environment. But in the approaches of Rossi and of Selvin and Hagstrom, the student is responding as part of the environment. Thus, the approach of Pace and Baird might be termed the anthropological approach, for the individual is used as an informant about the culture. The Selvin-Hagstrom and Rossi approaches might be termed examples of the survey approach, for the individual is treated as a respondent whose attributes constitute part of the culture.

In the extreme, the results of these two approaches might be exceedingly different. For example, an item of the CCI asks the student to agree or disagree with the statement "There is very little studying here over the weekends." The responses to this question may give a picture very different from that provided by an analogous question asked from the other perspective: "How much time on the average do you spend studying over the weekend?" To provide an environmental measure, this item is aggregated (over the formally defined group in the Selvin-Hagstrom case and over a set of persons with whom an individual is in contact in the Rossi case), and the aggregate response could logically be compared with a single response to the Pace and Baird question.

It is easy to see that the environment as measured by these two questions might be very different. There may be a great deal of studying but a perception by everyone that not much studying goes on—a kind of pluralistic ignorance. In a "collegiate" atmosphere, every boy may take pains to create an impression that he does less studying than he actually does; in a strongly academic atmosphere, everyone may take pains to exaggerate the amount of studying he does.

Thus the very discrepancy between the anthropological approach and the survey approach could give valuable information about the culture. The anthropological questions, at their best, measure public values or activities; the survey questions, at their best, measure private values or activities. The discrepancy between public and private may be an important one to distinguish.

These two different approaches have other important implications. Aggregation plays quite a different role in each of them. In the survey approach, aggregation is intrinsic to the approach, and if there is sampling within a group, then the sample must be carefully drawn according to prescribed rules.[4] In the anthropological approach, aggregation is necessary only to insure reliability of perception;[5] and the accuracy of sampling should be unimportant.[6] Thus in the use of this approach by Pace and Stern (1958), there has been little attention to the representativeness of the group from each college.

The smaller importance of sampling and representativeness is an important attribute of the anthropological approach. A further implication is perhaps of even greater practical importance: the CCI, and in general the anthropological approach, can be used when one's sample of students is spread throughout many colleges. By asking the student to report on the environment around him, it is possible to obtain a measure of this environment from him alone (if one disregards the projective distortion),

---

[4] It is the essence of Rossi's approach that the sample differs for measuring the environment of each individual and that the sample is weighted according to the frequency of the individual's contact with each member of the group.

[5] Ordinarily, in fact, psychologists use such descriptions of a situation as measures of perceptual distortion, i.e., as projective measures.

[6] If the accuracy of sampling *is* important — if the perception differs radically depending upon one's position in the system — then the basic assumption of a unitary culture must be discarded, and the questions would be best redesigned to refer to an explicit subgroup within which the culture is relatively uniform. If not, then the anthropological approach must be modified in the survey direction, toward obtaining measures of both the "average" culture in the college and the variance.

rather than from the environment itself. For example, Thistle-thwaite (1959), in following the National Merit Scholars into college, is able to use this approach with only a small, very unrepresentative group in each college.

I will turn now to the sociological substance of these three measurement approaches. The preceding sections of this chapter have important implications. They are the following. (1) The impact of the broadest level of the environment is through the awarding or withholding of informal status and recognition; that of the intermediate level of formal organizations on campus is through admittance, formal position, and informal status; and that of the level of personal association is through approval or disapproval and maintaining or breaking off the relation. (2) The activities for which such rewards and punishments might be applied could be of the most diverse sorts: studying hard, winning a football game, wearing a coat of a certain style, having one's hair cut a certain length, knowing Kafka's works, etc. (3) The principal effects of the culture are upon (*a*) the distribution of energies and, through this, upon what is learned; (*b*) attachments to abstract values; (*c*) attachments or orientations to other people or groups; and (*d*) the student's conception of himself. (4) At the broadest level, it is necessary to characterize a number of attributes of the system besides the content of the activities it rewards and punishes: its ascriptiveness, its singleness or substructuring; its cultural pluralism within a given unitary subculture; and its reward-punishment ratio.

It is evident that the concepts underlying the three measurement approaches under discussion are all quite different from this. Pace's CCI will be considered first, for it deals with the most complex level, the overall college culture. Pace's underlying model derives from Henry Murray's list of needs: need for achievement, need for abasement, etc. As Pace indicates, Murray's notion was that "just as the concept of need represented significant determinants of behavior within the person, the concept of press represented the significant determinants of behavior in the environment." Thus, for example, if the individual has a strong need for achievement, his behavior will include many attempts at achievement. If the environmental press has a strong achievement component, the people subjected to this press will similarly make many attempts at achievement.

This is a theoretical orientation about the way social systems affect their members that is radically different from the ideas discussed earlier. According to these ideas, the content and structure of the status system are the crucial motivating elements. Consequently, in a study of effects of peer culture, we would proceed to measure the attributes of the status system, as discussed previously (e.g., reward-punishment ratio, substructuring, specific content of activities rewarded and punished). This would give a measure very different from the CCI discussed by Pace. The important point to observe is that the difference in measures derives not from individual idiosyncracies but from a difference in the theoretical basis. If one accepts Murray's ideas about needs and the analogous environmental press, the CCI is appropriate, and the measure suggested above, inappropriate. If one accepts the idea that the status system is a society's motivating device, then the CCI is inappropriate. This is not to say that the CCI does not contain items useful for the "status system" conceptual scheme.

Similarly, it is important to know the specific content of activities or attributes that are rewarded and those that are punished. Such content may be quite specific to the situation, requiring investigation before it is measured. For example, one student culture may reward skill at squash but disdain all other sports; another may reward skill at all sports. It is important to catch this distinction in measurement if the impact of the culture is to be examined adequately.

Thus the set of attributes important to measure at the level of the college society as a whole consists of essentially those which characterize the status system—for it is the status system that provides the carrot and stick that motivates the society's members. In summary, the attributes are the following: (1) the content of activities rewarded and punished by the culture; (2) the ascriptiveness of the system, or, more fully, the degree to which status resides in particular achievements, in a formal office, or in particular persons with ascribed status; (3) the structuring into relatively separate subcultures; and (4) the monolithic or pluralistic nature of the system.

The elements of a status system, and perhaps others, are extremely important in considering both the sources and the effects of the student culture. To consider one example only: the reward-punishment ratio may be thought of as the degree to which the environment is supportive compared with the degree to which it is competitive. It is obvious that differences in this ratio may have an important impact upon the psychological health of students. Its sources may lie essentially in the structure of competition in a school. In a college with many premedical students, the competition is interpersonal, being focused around grades. In such a school, the competitiveness between individuals tends to reduce the number of rewards, and increase the number of punishments, with the culture acting to hold down effort. In a college having a strong program of intercollegiate athletics, a communal spirit is engendered, and the status system is probably more supportive, with a high reward-punishment ratio.[7] If this is the case, it is an extremely important matter to know, because it ties an important element of the status system to structural changes which might be made in colleges.

The CCI obtains measures which might be interpreted as measurement of rewards and punishments, for these concepts happen to coincide roughly with Murray's needs (nurturance, aggression). The important point, however, is that it is necessary to have a conception of how an informal status system functions and to derive one's concepts and measures from that, rather than to attempt to establish a parallelism between the psychological system and the social system, borrowing the concepts from one for use in the other.

The substantive assumptions of Selvin and Hagstrom's measurement approach are fewer than those of the CCI. They present a method which is relatively independent of substantive assumptions. The import of the preceding discussion, however, was that Pace's approach used the *wrong* substantive assump-

---

[7] For a theoretical discussion of differing reward-punishment structures and their consequences, see Coleman (1959).

tions, not that *no* substantive assumptions were necessary.

It was suggested earlier that the principal effects of a formal group on its members are through (*a*) the offices within the group, (*b*) selective entrance into the group, (*c*) the informal status system within the group, and (*d*) pressures toward consensus on matters toward which the group takes some unitary action. If this is true, it has implications for the ways groups must be characterized. One must discover what it takes to become a member, what qualities are important in holding a formal position, what are the principal types of actions the group takes as a unit, as well as all the attributes of the informal status system discussed above at the level of the college as a whole. This is in some ways easier, in some ways harder than Selvin and Hagstrom's approach of grinding questions through the mill of factor analysis to produce dimensions. For example, it is relatively easy to determine the formal and informal criteria for entrance into the group or for positions within it. It is more difficult, as the discussion of the CCI indicated, to measure the complex elements of the group's informal status system.

However, Selvin and Hagstrom's general approach seems to be directed toward another kind of effect groups have on their members—often the kind that sociologists and psychologists implicitly assume when they search for effects of groups on individuals: interpersonal influence through association. In other words, the approach of Selvin and Hagstrom is directed toward the lowest level of social organization, and the formal groups merely constitute convenient lines marking off boundaries between association-groups. (As the introductory section of Rossi's chapter indicates, it becomes extremely difficult to construct such boundaries from networks of informal association in an amorphous system.)

Taken from this perspective, one must consider the mechanisms through which interpersonal influence occurs and examine the approach relative to those mechanisms. We know, for example, that an important basis of rewards from another person is one's similarity to him on questions that require some mutual action. Thus there is a pressure toward interpersonal consensus on such questions, and when the large group takes action as a whole, a pressure toward overall group consensus. A measure of the amount of consensus on a given item within groups, relative to that between groups (see Coleman, 1957) gives a measure of this effect. There are problems in interpreting such a measure, however. Because of selective entrance into the groups, the consensus may derive either from an initial sorting-out or because students have modified themselves before gaining admittance to the group (through a process that sociologists call "anticipatory socialization"), rather than from changing after becoming members.

Another way that people are affected through personal association is by the expectations their associates hold for them. Thus another kind of measurement that should be constructed concerns these expectations. If the behavior of girls in different sororities is to be related successfully to their membership in the sorority, it must be viewed in terms of the expectations that their fellows hold for them. Their change in values becomes difficult to explain otherwise, and even more difficult to explain is the development of alienation, rebellion, or self-deprecation, all of which are responses to expectations held by one's fellows. As noted earlier, expectations are often toward behavior like one's own. Because of this the generally sloppy conceptual schemes we often use, looking merely for similarity of behavior in groups, can capture some effects due to expectations.

Despite the critique above, it is important that at this stage of social and psychological theory no rigid conceptual scheme be imposed upon group measurement. It is important to have a concept that will sensitize one to the measurement of things sometimes neglected, but the scheme should not block out other modes of measurement. Selvin and Hagstrom's approach is one that might prove extremely valuable (and has proved valuable in another study by Selvin [1960]). It delineates "types" of groups, according to the way they cluster on dimensions after the factor analysis of attitudinal items. Then the types of groups may be taken as independent variables in examining changes of members, or as dependent variables in examining how the groups came to be as they are. There is, however, a problem that arises in any development of complex "types." If only cross-sectional data are used, then many results of substantive interest are submerged in the development of types.

Rossi's approach to measurement of the "interpersonal environment" probably constitutes the greatest measurement innovation in this volume. But before examining the methodological departure that it takes, we want to look at its essential assumptions in relation to the framework of ideas presented above. These assumptions are quite independent of the methodological departure, and the two will be considered separately.

Earlier discussion in this chapter implied that personal association has its principal effects through the rewards of approval and continued association, or through disapproval and breaking off the relation, and that rewards are given for action in directions consistent with one's own. This is a far simpler set of notions than those behind the effects of the status system—and one with fewer problems for measurement. Rossi's scheme describes the frequency of interaction of A with ego, and the attractiveness of A for ego, as constituting a "weight" or "force" with which the content of A's interaction with ego shapes ego's interpersonal environment. Rossi's conceptual model is a kind of "communication model" in which ego is barraged by communications, each with its own force, and is thus subject to a resultant force that might move him (i.e., his opinion, attitude, value, or behavior). The imagery is somewhat different from that of the reward-punishment imagery expressed above but is generally consistent with it, for many social psychologists would agree that Rossi's concept of "interaction affectivity" constitutes the potential for reward or punishment that A has for ego. It would seem difficult to measure by this technique the relative amounts of rewards and punishments ego receives from another, but I know of no survey approach that has provided a systematic means of doing this. (The anthropological approach of Pace is able to do this by asking ego questions that indicate how supportive a person feels his environment is.)

Rossi's major innovation is not in his basic assumptions but in the structure of his measures. It has always been difficult to assess the "influence" that the social environment of individuals has upon them when that environment is not broken up into small, homogeneous association-groups with well-defined boundaries. Many attempts to define "clique" on the basis of sociometric measurement have hit obstacles, for reasons that Rossi shows. His approach starts from the opposite direction and says, in effect, "If we want cliques for nothing other than to measure their effect upon individuals within them, then why not build separate cliques around each individual?" This constitutes the individual's interpersonal environment, and we need not try to coordinate this environment with that of his associates.

Deriving from this basic approach are numerous statistical measures of his environment and of the aggregate environments of all members of the group or the student body. Averages and dispersions or variances of the associational concepts indicated above (frequency, affect, content) provide "environmental-level" concepts, and, after aggregation over the total student body or group, they provide concepts at the level of the total culture of the group. The potential they provide for examining effects of the lowest and simplest level of social organization, that of personal association (or the determinants of patterns of association) appears great; but it should be recognized that they cannot delineate the effect of the total student society.

This concludes my critique of the three measurement techniques presented in this book. They are doing for the first time a task that has stymied us in the study of society and its parts: providing systematic, quantitative measures of social units so that we can examine their effects on their members and how they came to be as they are.

RESEARCH STRATEGY IN THE STUDY OF EFFECTS

The three measurement techniques discussed above are most applicable to field studies, not experiments. In the study of the culture's effects upon its members, these measures are independent variables. The precise measurement of such variables is crucial for field studies that enter an ongoing situation. But in experiments, both in the laboratory and in the field, this measurement problem is less important. The experimental manipulation itself provides the independent variable in the research. So long as this manipulation is carefully and effectively done, then the only measurements necessary are those of the dependent variable—in this case, changes in the students who are subjects of the experiment.

It is such experiments with which Willerman's Chapter 5 is concerned. Appropriately, his focus shifts from questions of measurement to an examination of types of experiments—and types of variables manipulated by the experiments. Because the research discussed in this volume is research that takes as its focus a social system—the student society within a college—it is appropriate to ask where and how experiments can be fruitful. One of the attributes of a system is the complex interdependence of its parts. This interdependence spells dangers both for experimental and field studies, but dangers of different kinds.

The dangers for field research are well outlined by Willerman in the first part of Chapter 5; they can be summarized as the inability to sort out the effects of different processes in the system. For example, the potentially powerful effects of personal association are, as discussed earlier, weakened by the possibility of rejecting incompatible associates and searching until similarity is found. Thus a field study which discovers compatibility among associates is often stymied in its attempt to attribute this similarity to the effects of association or the effects of selection.

The dangers for experiments in the study of a system stem from a very different source. In the study of a complex system, it is important to discover two things: first, the effect of each process in the system, considered in isolation, and second, the way these processes are linked together—the structure of the system. The danger for experimental research is that the former goal will be met and the latter not. It is in the very nature of experiments that they intervene in the system, blocking off some of the processes to study others. As a consequence, their results do not pertain to the functioning of the system as an entity but only to particular processes within it. They uncover the operation of social psychological processes by fragmenting the system —and the danger is that these results will be seen as the ultimate results in the study of social systems.

There are several approaches to overcoming the twin dangers

of field studies and experiments. One is exemplified by works of Sherif and of Newcomb, and to a smaller extent, the "associational" experiments discussed in the section of Chapter 5 entitled "Experimental Studies of Selective Association": to devise experiments that initially fix certain experimental conditions but then have consequences, not through a single social psychological process, but through a complex system itself. Sherif's experimental separation of a summer camp into two cohesive groups allowed the systemic consequences of this separation to manifest itself. Newcomb's (1961) establishment of an experimental living unit blocked off the usual selection process in establishing living arrangements on campus and then watched, in microscopic detail, the development of the system of association and friendship that followed. The studies Willerman reports in the third section of Chapter 5 are similar, except that these studies have often sought out only an ultimate, long-range dependent variable, and have not traced out the system of association, friendship,, values, and allocation of energy that culminated in the ultimate effect.

Another answer to the twin dangers of experiment and field studies is similar, though at a different level: to treat colleges themselves as constituting experimental variations in those of their attributes which are fixed and independent of the student culture, such as size, type of curriculum, type of student residence, composition of student body, location relative to non-college population, etc. These variables and others are analogous to the media of the biologist's petrie dishes, within which he watches a culture develop. The sociologist can do the same — with the important exception that in most cases the cultures have already developed and he thereby misses valuable evidence.

Still another answer is perhaps the one that will be most often taken: that experimental studies and field studies be taken in conjunction, with explicit recognition of what each can best discover — experiments, for discovering the specific effects of separate social psychological processes; field research, for discovering how these processes are connected and the conditions which affect those connections. It is evident that experiments are most valuable for the problem upon which Chapter

5 focuses: that of establishing the effects of association as separate from the process of selection. These two processes are extremely difficult to separate in an ongoing system that lacks experimental manipulation.

SOURCES OF THE STUDENT CULTURE

The three chapters on measurement discussed earlier are concerned with description of the student culture at its various levels. Most of the other chapters of this volume are concerned with the problem for which this description acts as the independent variable: the problem of the effects of the culture. LeVine's chapter, for example, considers the effects of the culture from the perspective of the Miller-Dollard (1941) theory of socialization. I will not pretend to give a comment upon these other chapters treating effects of the culture but will instead turn to the one chapter that focuses on the other end of the problem of student cultures.

Chapter 2, by Clark and Trow, considers the side of the problem for which description of the culture is a dependent variable: the determinants of student culture. Such a focus provides an important perspective: without it, there is danger that the study of peer cultures in colleges will become nothing beyond a study of social psychological processes, rather than the study of student cultures.

The comments below will attempt to add to this perspective, as a kind of continuation of Clark and Trow's discussion. I have become intensely interested in the problem of what gives student cultures their character, in high schools as well as in colleges. It relates to interesting problems of social theory, as well as to important practical concerns of school administration. In social theory, it is related to the problem of how the environment of a social system affects its status structure; in school administration, it is part of the problem of how to create an institution that will encourage learning.

Earlier in this chapter, the student society was viewed much as an ordinary society and its status system examined in those terms. But it is actually different in an important way: the student society is a "subject nation," existing within the framework of an institution that makes demands upon its members and exercises some control over the student society's own institutions. The consequences of this for the status system of the student society are great. Some of these consequences can be suggested by situations that are roughly analogous: the workers' society in a factory; the prisoners' society in a prison; the enlisted men's society in an army. In all these cases, there is a large body of persons of roughly the same status, all with similar problems and similar life chances, within the framework of a larger organization: the factory, the prison, the army. The kinds of status systems that develop in these environments seem far more variable than those in ordinary autonomous societies. Casual observation of factories, prisons, and armies shows these polar types:

1. *A system with many norms designed to restrict production.* —In the factory, there are norms against "rate-busting"; in the army, constraints against volunteering and against the private who is "bucking for sergeant"; in the prison, strong norms against cooperation with the authorities; in the school, norms against the "grind." In such systems, there are few rewards for achievements, many punishments for disobeying the norm. The status system is nearly a negative thing, for there are few positive activities that can give status—or if there are such activities, these activities are different from those to which the constraining norm is applied. For example, a worker in a plant where rate-busting is negatively sanctioned may still have high prestige because he always wins on the horses.

2. *A system with many informal rewards for positive activity.* —In some army units in which there is an extremely high esprit de corps, the man with highest prestige is the toughest, most reliable combat soldier or the best performing parade soldier. In factories and other places of work, such esprit is less frequent but does occur in some cases with as much glorification as that given the Stakhanovite in Russia. In some work groups, particularly in small plants, there are informal rewards of prestige, deference, and respect paid to the worker who gets the most work out. In schools there are athletic heroes at the top of the status system, who are rewarded for achievement,

not punished for norm violation. Such status systems are nearly the reverse of those discussed in paragraph 1; attention is directed toward rewards for achievement, rather than punishments for violation of a norm. Quite apart from the ranking of different activities in these status systems, which may be identical to those in systems of the type discussed in paragraph 1, their structure differs greatly from that type. This is clearly evidenced by the relative amounts of rewards and punishments dispensed in the two cases, and should be reflected indirectly in many other attributes of the group—its "morale," its "mood," its "supportiveness," its energy, and others.

3. *A system that rewards activities directly antagonistic to the institutional goals.*—This is evidenced in prisons, where highest status goes to the prisoner who stands up most strongly to the prison guards; in some factories whose workers give highest status to the strike leader; in navies in which the sailors mutiny against the officers; in delinquent subcultures among adolescents; in beatnik subcultures among postadolescents; and in many colleges giving high status to the editor of the college paper who dares to fight the college administration.

These types illustrate the wide variation in the status systems of "subordinate societies" of the kind under discussion. It appears that the source of this wide variation lies in the superordinate institution and the "environment" it creates for these societies. The environment of an ordinary, autonomous total society probably varies much less, for it is determined by the demands of nature and technology, rather than the whims of a social institution.

A closer examination of these polar types indicates that they are characterized by two dimensions. The esprit de corps of paragraph 2 and the rebellion of paragraph 3 are systems that encourage and reward achievements, while the production restriction of paragraph 1 is a system that constrains achievement. Second, the individual activities that are being rewarded or constrained are, in the case of esprit de corps and restriction of production, moving in the direction of the goals of the surrounding institution; in the case of rebellion, they are opposed to it. This suggests a more systematic formulation in which these two dimensions are taken explicitly. This is done in Chart 9.1, below. Inside each cell is a label for the kind of social system produced by these two attributes. Type *d*, characterized by an individual opposition to the larger institution that is suppressed by the social system, is well exemplified by "obedient" systems among young children in school, in which each child may be individually impelled to disobedience by a teacher's demands, but the social system among the children constrains its members to obey.[8] Such systems may in fact show either high obedience or a great deal of unorganized violence and disobedience, depending on the degree to which individual activities develop in opposition to the institutional goals. However, if there is a strong social system, then the same institutional demands that generate individual opposition tend to generate a group defense mechanism, in which the group reinforces the opposition with rewards, to create incipient or active rebellion, a system of type *c*.

Perhaps the major reason that the status systems of sub-

		Individual activities, in relation to institutional goals	
		Toward	Opposed
Norms and values of the social system	Reward	Esprit de corps *(b)*	Rebellion *(c)*
	Constraint	"Restrict production" *(a)*	Obedient *(d)*

Chart 9.1 Social Systems Produced by Movement in Relation to Goals

[8] It may well be argued that, in such systems of reward, the children do not constitute a cohesive social system of the sort under discussion here. It seems that when there is a highly developed social system it will very seldom develop norms against individual actions and in alliance with institutional goals—unless, of course, there are other activities that give it an esprit de corps.

ordinate societies vary so widely is suggested by a particular contrast with a total autonomous society: every total society must carry out active efforts to support and maintain itself physically. Those persons who have traditionally held highest status in the society are persons such as physicians, military heroes, political leaders, and explorers,[9] whose activities contribute most to this need. (See Davis and Moore [1945] for an elaboration of this thesis.) But in subordinate societies within institutions, there are often no positive activities that will benefit the social system itself. In schools, scholastic efforts usually benefit only the individual;[10] in factories, greater work usually benefits only the individual and often harms others by comparison or by adjustment of work standards; in prisons, there is usually little positive activity possible. In armies, such a possibility for positive group-benefiting activity can occur in some situations (such as combat or in an elite corps which performs on special occasions) but not in others. When the superordinate institution fails to make possible such positive activity that can aid the group, then the subordinate social system can hardly be one that emphasizes rewards — unless the rewards are for activities irrelevant to or in opposition to the institution's goals.

One point discussed by Clark and Trow may be closely related to this. They note that prior to the introduction of organized interscholastic sports in colleges, the colleges were "full of student violence, directed at each other, at the faculty, the institution, and the townies." The status systems of these student societies were likely closest to type *c* or type *d* in Chart 9.1: individual activities opposed to the institution, either supported

[9] As societies grow large, public attention comes to be focused on those persons whose activities are carried over communication channels to which only a few gain access. Their status thus becomes disproportionately high because of their becoming widely known. The best example of this is movie and television stars; the best example in schools is the increasing status of cheerleaders as high-school size increases.

[10] There are several exceptions. In schools with scholastic fame, students whose efforts can add to that fame have high status. In high schools, this is often true of National Merit Scholars or students who place high on statewide examinations. Another exception is in interscholastic contests, such as debate, which win for the school as well as the individual.

by social rewards from the student society (*c*) or perhaps in some cases discouraged by them (*d*). The introduction of college sports moved these systems more nearly into cell *b*, with an esprit de corps built around the athletic teams. Thus the colleges, by broadening their goals to include those of organized athletics, were able to shift the status systems in a reward direction and in the direction of institutional goals.

If colleges wish to encourage the growth of student cultures with rewards in the direction of institutional goals, they must provide positive activities in accord with these goals. This is one of the directions that colleges have taken in recent years, with the development of numerous school-related extracurricular activities in which the school can surpass other schools. However, this has generally been done only by broadening the school's original goals — not by fostering positive activities within the core of educational goals. The pervasiveness and strength of the "collegiate" culture of which Clark and Trow write is testimony to the diversion from educational goals produced by these fringe activities.

It seems likely that the present organization of scholarly activity in undergraduate education allows positive group-aiding efforts only in special cases — particularly in those few schools which have special fame for their scholarship. However, there is incidental evidence that even there, "academic" cultures (using Clark and Trow's typology) are more nearly character-ized by punishments and interpersonal tensions than are col-legiate cultures. This is suggested by Pace and Stern (1958) in applying the College Characteristics Index to five colleges: Brooklyn College, Chicago, Colgate, Michigan State, and Syra-cuse. Chicago showed by far the highest orientation toward intellectual pursuits (the most "academic" in Clark and Trow's terms); Michigan State and Colgate, the most "collegiate."

In the CCI, there were two items that showed especially well the level of personal closeness or interpersonal tension. These items, and the responses by students in the five schools, are listed in Table 9.1 (data from Pace and Stern, 1958). In both these items, Chicago shows the least interpersonal closeness and Michigan State and Colgate the most, suggesting the correlation between an "academic" culture and interpersonal punishments.[11]

Other evidence is even less tangible. Occasional reports of students from the "new" academic culture of Harvard suggest its high competition. This contrasts with the expansiveness and exuberance of the "old" collegiate culture of Harvard before the war.

I suggest that academic cultures are often of type *a* ("restrict production") in Chart 9.1, while collegiate cultures are often of type *b* ("esprit de corps").[12] Whether this need be so or whether academic cultures can also be expansive and exuberant is another matter.[13] This hypothesis can easily be tested by extensive use of the College Characteristics Index, for this index contains scales both of the content of the culture and of other at-

[11] The scales of "nurturance" and "succorance" might also have been used to show these results, since Chicago is lowest of the five schools on these scales. However, they include several items not related to the students' interpersonal relations.

[12] To locate the other two of Clark and Trow's categories in Chart 9.1, the bohemian culture ordinarily rewards activities opposed to school goals and thus is usually the rebellious culture of type *c*. Their "vocational culture" really constitutes no society at all, being composed of part-time students living off campus, with much of their lives engaged elsewhere.

[13] See Coleman (1959) for suggestions on how the matter might be changed. Graduate education, with its very different status systems, shows other possibilities.

Table 9.1 The College Characteristics Index as Applied to Five Colleges

Characteristic	Per Cent Answering "Yes" to Characteristic				
	Chicago	Michigan State	Colgate	Syracuse	Brooklyn College
Personal hostilities are usually concealed or resolved as quickly as possible	41	81	74	73	62
Most of the students form lasting friendships here	59	80	86	66	76

tributes that can be reconceptualized as the amount of reward and punishment (succor, aggressiveness, and others).

It is not possible here to develop further the ideas discussed above about the determinants of the student culture, but these pages, and the discussion by Clark and Trow, show the way to interesting and important directions that research may take.

10

Comment

DAVID RIESMAN

Recently the Soviet authorities were happy to have an Americanized "White Russian," Wassily Leontief, return on an exchange visit that enabled them to learn about his input-output method of analysis, a technique useful in the planned society and with which their own economists were not familiar. Reading the papers for this volume, it has struck me that such programs of cultural exchange are equally desirable between the rival nationalisms of psychology and sociology and that these papers may serve modestly in this direction.

Indeed, as a relative newcomer and amateur sociologist, I have been struck for some time by the fact that Paul Lazarsfeld's methodological innovations percolate very lamely even in sociology, let alone in psychologically oriented social psychology (despite the fact that Lazarsfeld himself began his career as a psychologist). Thus, although Newcomb is familiar with Lazarsfeld's work, his general frame of thinking and his citations, like Willerman's, stay within the social psychological camp. This is even more striking in Pace and Baird's chapter and in their description of the Pace-Stern College Characteristics Index. Despite an "anthropological" effort to use individuals as informants rather than respondents, the material is nevertheless analyzed (as Selvin and Hagstrom observe) in individual psychological terms. I have pointed out previously (Riesman, 1959) in connection with Pace and Stern's work that "such a method may work with a college that is relatively homogeneous and where one is primarily interested in the students' ideology about the institution. But not all students are equally influential, either in determining the climate or the local legends about it, and of course few, if any, are aware of the full impact of college on them, along with, and in contradiction to, other agencies of socialization." Psychology suffers from its earlier methodological advances, and these—as Rossi's Chapter 7 and Selvin and Hagstrom's Chapter 6 suggest—may be too powerful for the subject at hand.

I had myself been somewhat inclined to lump factor analysis in this category and to regard it as largely a method of work preferred by the morally industrious and intellectually lazy who thought that data would "speak for themselves" and would never need to involve the researcher's own imagination and interpretation. But the Selvin-Hagstrom chapter makes me realize that factor analysis can be an adjunct of, not a substitute for, the imagination.

I did not need to be persuaded of the advantages of snowball sampling, as expounded in Rossi's chapter. Nearly ten years ago, in the Kansas City Study of Adult Life, I felt that this was the best way to understand the interpersonal environment of individuals (especially the relative isolation of older people) and to determine whether they regarded as friends those who were only "friends." Further, in my task as a consultant to the Harvard Student Study under the auspices of the University Health Services, I had hoped that snowball sampling could take the place of an attempt at larger coverage, especially since neither in the case of Kansas City nor in that of Harvard College is it at all clear what the boundaries of the sampling universe may be or whether they have any meaning beyond the cold comfort given by careful but irrelevant logistics.

Indeed, I would like to go farther than Rossi does—or than my Harvard colleagues have been willing to do—and use snowball sampling along with a sampling of particular subcultures chosen on the basis of their presumptive importance. That is, I would prefer to begin my snowball sampling by dipping first into a pool whose characteristics I know reasonably well and then, after taking one or two steps beyond the first respondent and his network, go and catch a fish in another such pool. It seems to me that this is what Selvin and Hagstrom in effect did when they selected residential units on the basis of theorizing about what attitudes toward civil liberties, school spirit, academic performance, and vocationalism might be associated with what residential patterns.

And here each college will present a different problem. The chapter by Clark and Trow makes great strides toward understanding such differences. It describes the constituencies which have a stake in a college, indicates how size, recruitment, selectivity, and tradition help create the climates within which peer groups are formed, and discusses the relative efficacy of these factors vis-à-vis other influences on students. For example, it is in their chapter that I believe one might find clues for interpreting the most startling single bit of knowledge I came across in this volume: the discovery reported by Wilson that Antioch students learn roughly the same amount no matter how they are taught or even if not taught at all in any formal sense. For Antioch is a college where the collegiate subculture is weak and the academic and nonconformist subcultures are potent. The image of Antioch is sharply defined and highly selective — the famous work program attracts the adventurous, rather than the vocationally minded, in the Clark-Trow sense.

Is it farfetched to suggest that Antioch students are mature enough to know how to study independently and that the whole Antioch program is a situation in which performance rises whatever the working conditions? Perhaps Antioch attracts some students who learn better without a teacher and others who, although they might prefer to have the TV of the professor's personality turned on, are nevertheless willing to learn just as much if he is not present. I am arguing, in line with Clark and Trow's own work, that the interpersonal environment of Antioch itself is more important than the chambered subgroupings into which Wilson divided his experimental and control groups, and that there is an interchange of attitudes and values among the groups that diminishes the effect of particular exposures.

When I read Phillip Jacob's (1957) study and some of the studies underlying it, I had the same impression that the lack of impact of various kinds of courses did not invariably reflect, as Jacob thought, the imperviousness of the student culture, but rather that at some of the colleges these courses influenced students who did not formally take them. Moreover, it may happen that at a campus where ideas are taken seriously, Professor A may recruit a few average disciples in his course while Professor B across the campus is helping polarize a number of other students in his course, some of whom are also taking A's course, against A. More generally, I sometimes wonder to what extent the lack of impact of a particular course or of the way it is taught reflects the fact that students have been exposed to American advertising and pitchmen ever since they could sit upright before a TV set and hence—quite apart from the resistances set up by the student culture itself—might have become fairly immune to formal efforts at indoctrination.

Even so, such tentative conjectures do not prevent a certain surprise at Wilson's finding. As far as the outsider can observe in casual visits, Antioch is not a college where the faculty is seen as a monolithic "they." Further, the ideology of close faculty-student contact seems to make learning in small discussion groups go with the grain of the student ethos and learning in isolation against it. It seems conceivable, however, that different students would profit from different conditions. Some might learn better free from the static of a group discussion, others through participation in such a discussion, and still others when undistracted by either students or staff. Determining this would require not only measures of grades and IQ but also measures of psychological style along the lines pioneered by Stern, Stein, and Bloom (1956) in their study at Chicago of stereotyped versus less authoritarian students.[1]

Certainly there is the strongest contradiction between Wilson's findings and the much less definitive and processed results of a study by Heath (1964; see also Heath, 1958). In the more recent of these two works, Heath describes his experiences as advisor for a group of thirty-nine students whom he saw on a weekly basis during their four years as undergraduates at Prince-

---

[1]Compare also a study by Loren Wispe (1951) indicating that students who generally prefer a permissive instructor who encourages their participation would nevertheless choose a directive and authoritarian one in a highly competitive and examination-oriented university.

ton (a Princeton man himself, he was teaching psychology there at the time).

At the beginning, he did a very rough and unscientific job of matching his freshmen advisees with other boys from comparable backgrounds who went on in the ordinary routines at Princeton. His book describes the way in which these advisees, only a few of whom were "reasonable adventurers," related to him and to each other and how these "modes of relatedness" to people had in turn their relevance for "modes of relatedness" to learning. The final result was that the men who had been Heath's advisees took a disproportionate share of the honors at Princeton. A number of them wrote honors theses, edited the college daily, the *Princetonian*, or took the lead in dramatics, athletics, and class affairs generally—all far beyond the group who did not have this experience with Heath. He also arranged for them to have experience with each other in the form of discussion groups of nine at his home.

I suggest, among possible interpretations of Heath's report, that the students at a highly competitive college like Princeton are rather fragile in their self-esteem and that their peer groups (to which of course not all students belong; many are isolates) are only a modest shelter against feelings of inadequacy. Heath seems to have given his students an "uncontaminated" response, that is, not contaminated either by the grading relationship or by the obligation to become or reject becoming a disciple of the faculty member or his field. Since Heath wanted nothing of his students beyond their development as "reasonable adventurers," he could get through to them in a way that faculty members seldom can, even under conditions of close contact at a place like Antioch. Of course, one must also ask how many faculty members are themselves "reasonable adventurers," rather than what Heath calls the "noncommitters," who often add insult to injury by protesting the conventionality and conformity of their students.

Heath's material implies that the student culture at Princeton does not foster strong and intense friendships that could support students' feelings of adequacy both in curricular and extracurricular enterprises. I get the same impression of thin and muted friendship, again without the author's explicit backing, in the studies of experimental groups touched upon by Newcomb and by Willerman. Indeed, I have the impression that as the major "academic" colleges and universities grow more competitive, and as the fear of homosexuality casts a shadow over same-sex friendships in the more sophisticated strata, there tends to be a decline in the close kind of chum relationship described by Harry Stack Sullivan and a commensurate rise in the importance and salience of cross-sex companionable "steady" ties.

Such inferences are at least not disproved by a participant-observer study made in 1959–60 of all Radcliffe freshmen in a particular dormitory (Haywood, 1960). Like the others in this volume the study noted the importance of propinquity for what passes for friendship at Radcliffe. All "best friends" relationships that did not antedate coming to Radcliffe were made within the dormitory, and mostly on the same floor. The study embraced all thirty freshmen in the dormitory, where they were mixed with upperclassmen, and examined through interviews and projective materials their conceptions of friendship on arrival and again six months later. At the outset, the definitions and ideals of friendship ran a wide gamut, but by March general agreement had been reached around a norm that Miss Haywood terms "company, comfort, and care." Those who asked more, or differently, of friendship became isolates (or in several cases maintained friendships outside the dormitory that had been formed before matriculation). It is striking that a consensus was achieved on this in the light of the accepted and powerful ideology that Radcliffe stands for "individualism" and *lack* of consensus. Despite great differences in background, fields of interest, and patterns of dating, the Radcliffe girls, like the "typical sorority" described by Selvin and Hagstrom, acted as if subjected to massive Sherif effects.

Even in as informal a study as that by Miss Haywood, this monograph would have been enormously helpful in giving leads for investigation and indicating the limits of possibility. For example, it would have been stimulating for her to try to find out where Radcliffe belongs in the Clark-Trow spectrum of subcultures. Is it really "academic," in view of the fact that, as at other women's colleges, graduate school beckons only a minority? Or is it, as it were, "academic" only through its ties to Harvard? Is it nonconformist, in spite of the diligence with which the academic program is pursued? And, if so, is its nonconformity again principally dependent on Harvard? Are there residues of the collegiate, in spite of the disdain with which obvious stigmata of this pattern are regarded?

These ethnographic leads could be supplemented by other materials from this volume. For instance, Miss Haywood sought to map the sociometric networks of all the girls, first, by asking them who their friends were — and then within the boundary of the dormitory going to those friends — and, second, by participant observation. Had the Midwest College study cited by Rossi been available, she would have had a basis for comparison with Midwest freshmen, whose networks of twenty other students seem much larger than those of the Radcliffe freshmen. It is likely that the impact of Radcliffe on the freshmen is to make them feel that to know as many as twenty other students well would reveal a lack of autonomy and an excessive gregariousness. Of course there are realistically many more distractions, academic and otherwise, in Cambridge than in the small city (*pop. ca.* 35,000) housing Midwest College, but I also suspect that in the Midwest ideology it is more desirable to spend time with a number of other students. In these respects, Radcliffe appears to be different from "Ivy College," as cited in LeVine's chapter, and appears to reflect at perhaps its most difficult the transition from dependence on parents "to a life in which self-reliance and personal freedom are greater." Of course, as Pace and Baird emphasize, the student's selection of Radcliffe operates as well as Radcliffe's selection of the student, but Miss Haywood's material indicates that the image of Radcliffe is rather unclear to a number of applicants who come longing for intense intellectual confrontations with their same-sex peers, something that they have missed in high school, and who are gravely disappointed to find themselves reduced to the "company-comfort-care" syndrome.

Another undergraduate honors thesis (Blackmer, 1960)

sheds further light on such attitude curves. In this study, Blackmer gave a questionnaire to Phillips Andover seniors whom he had divided into three groups: those bound for Harvard, those bound for Yale, and those bound for other colleges. The Harvard-bound Andover seniors formed a distinct subculture, negative toward Andover and its "Ivy" values, although not so alienated that they were unable to win important places in Andover's extracurricular activities. They looked forward to Harvard as a place where they would find more of their own kind. Six months after arrival at Harvard[2] the Andover graduates had a rather different image of themselves and of Andover. They had looked forward to an *intellectual* community at Harvard, but found themselves instead in the midst of an abrasively competitive *academic* one,[3] surrounded as it were by five hundred valedictorians.

At Andover, these students had rejected the going idea of well-roundedness as shallow and as fit only for Yalies, but in the Harvard atmosphere there seemed to be a choice only of being either a playboy or a grind (McCarley, 1959). In this setting Andover with its more humane ideals looked better in retrospect, and the respondents seemed to feel a stronger kinship even with their Andover classmates who had gone to more Ivy-type colleges. Such a feeling is perhaps not so very different from the kinship Americans may feel with other Americans abroad if there are few of them and they are put in a sufficiently uncomfortable milieu.

In instances such as those in the studies at Radcliffe and Harvard, what Rossi terms the interpersonal environment becomes a very complex phenomenon, including negative and positive as well as retrospective and prospective models. Moreover, the muted disaffection of the Andover graduates may reflect in part the increasingly democratic recruitment of Harvard, which selects not only students who resemble the high-status cliques

[2] This was not a longitudinal study, but I am treating it, as the investigation did, as if it were.

[3] "Academic" is employed here in a narrower sense than used by Clark and Trow. It refers to the pursuit of knowledge within particular scholarly disciplines in a specialized and rigorous manner. It implies pressure from the curriculum. See Jencks and Riesman (1963).

in James Coleman's Illinois high-school study and who are used to frequent interaction, but also students of lower social origins, who in Rossi's words "are involved in much looser and less intense informal groups or not in such groups at all." In an earlier day a few such low-status students could be socialized into accepting the conceptions of friendship and cliquishness of the majority, but there may now be much less clear-cut predominance and very little of what Rossi calls climate consensus.[4]

It would be very interesting to compare the views of Harvard seniors on the effects of agents of change during their college careers with the study of agents of change at Antioch. Although many Harvard students hold summer jobs, they do not have the intense work experience which helps many Antioch students discover their vocational aptitudes and interests, and helps also, I would assume, to give them a feeling of confidence in facing the curriculum, a confidence possibly reflected in the high figures for self-development in Wilson's Tables 3.4–3.6. At Harvard I would expect faculty members to exert slightly less influence, books perhaps slightly more, and fellow students certainly no more.

As already implied in my discussion of the Andover students' reactions to Harvard, none of these studies, or the formulae of Rossi, seems to me to be able to cope with the problem of negative models—the students who help, in Erikson's terms, frame a negative identity for other students. For instance, Willerman's study (Chapter 5) does not discuss possible negative changes in Group B, who moved away from their imposed membership group rather than toward it. Nor does he discuss the possibility that the dissimilar roommates he mentions in his section entitled "Manipulating Similarity and Difference in Academic Ability" were negative models for each other, as possibly the "low similars" were also. Pace's discussion of subcultures may also be interpreted in terms of negative models. At the University of Kentucky the negative model is the north-

---

[4] Radcliffe in these respects is very different from Harvard, since it is one-fourth as large and has many fewer scholarships. Thus it draws on a much wealthier and more academically selective student body.

erner who makes southerners feel much the same whether in the liberal arts or engineering or education, and at San Jose State College, the oldest state college in California, the liberal arts students and the engineers view each other with strong feelings of social distance: they live in different worlds, and they seem to thank God for it.

Newcomb and Wilson, in the Preface to this volume, state their assumption that "educational practices can be more wisely —because more realistically—determined with than without documented information on the nature and extent of college students' influence upon on another." One group who can say amen to this are the architects who are now engaged all over the land in laying out dormitories or even whole campuses. On recent occasions I have been consulted by such men about what social science could contribute to their handling of questions of layout and size of unit, and I have felt how limited my information was. I would cite Newcomb's (1943) study of Bennington, the study by Festinger *et al.* (1950) at MIT, and one or two others. But then I would have to add that none of these would be conclusive for the institution in question, for which Rossi's index of gross affective climate, Clark and Trow's categories, or similar studies, were not available. As Rossi's formulae indicate, some students have a larger interpersonal environment and much more sociable energy than others; they are more "there" than others, more visible.[5] Or, to give another example, Haverford authorities recently consulted social scientists, including me, about whether they would lose the impalpable ethos that has characterized the College if they in-

[5] It is striking that none of the chapters says anything about appearance as a factor in interpersonal influence on a campus. Compare in this connection the very interesting experiment by Scodel and Mussin (1953) at Ohio State University, where they brought together more or less look-alike students who stood respectively high and low on the F-scale and asked them to talk about a neutral subject like the movies. They found that the high authoritarians tended to assume that other students, visibly like them in externals, also must share their right and proper views, while the low authoritarians realized that there was a difference, although they underestimated its extent. In such a research, one can almost see at work LeVine's brilliant observation that students will tend to overestimate their differences from others only on those attitudes or values that are salient for them.

creased numbers beyond the four hundred and fifty who could not quite squeeze into the College Chapel. My own impressionistic response was that this could not be answered as an abstract exercise in sociometric span of control. If Haverford students believe that they can and should know everybody, then they will make the effort to do so, within a considerable margin. Even so, I feared any tampering with this margin that might give both students and faculty members the sense that the place was becoming big and impersonal even though, had it started at a larger size, it would still seem manageable to its denizens.

Had I had Clark and Trow's paper to give them, I would have urged them to consider other ways of clustering students to avoid impersonality, possibly by subcolleges as at Wesleyan. But this paper would also have put them on notice how rapidly subcultural constellations can change, so that in a very short time a once-collegiate place can go academic (if it is private and much sought after), just as it can go vocational (if it is public and under constituency pressures). Conceivably, as the curriculum tightens and the drive to get into graduate school, already strong, comes to resemble that at Reed or Swarthmore, students may no longer value the effort needed to know everyone on campus. Indeed, they may come to think of themselves as psychology majors or physicists (and Haverford already has a student body of very high academic aptitude) before they think of themselves as Haverford students. And they may respond to this academic pressure by using a Bryn Mawr girl as countervailing power to establish their own adequacy at least in one salient area.

In turn, the Bryn Mawr girls may come to feel much like the Radcliffe freshmen who told Mary Haywood that friendship with girls, though they gave lip service to its importance, was a waste of time compared to studies or dating, both of which directly prepared one for the future.

Such a comment brings us back to the issue raised most directly by LeVine's chapter: the role of the peer group as an intermediate stage between the family and the larger postcollege world. Talcott Parsons (1961) and with him S. N. Eisenstadt

(1955) see the peer group in just this functional way; and in a recent essay (Lipset and Lowenthal, 1961), Parsons and Winston White argue that student peer groups serve on the one hand to support mobile, achievement-oriented youngsters whose families and backgrounds would hold them back from high attainments and, on the other hand, to cool off and offer consolation prizes to those youngsters whose parents hold out too high hopes for them. They maintain, however, that American society is still achievement-oriented and that neither the peer group nor the family permits or encourages self-fulfilling pleasures, their emotional orientations being primarily toward the maintenance of the human equipment for the larger society.

I would think that their interpretation helps explain the thinness in friendship and even in roommate ties that appears in Willerman's research. But I have also indicated my belief that, at the high-pressure colleges, friendship may have become too weak a reed to support the looming pressure of postcollege performance. In other words, while in the "typical sororities" studied by Selvin and Hagstrom at Berkeley, the academic (whether vocational or not) doesn't get in the way of the social, there are a few other influential institutions where the wheels, not of intellectual, but of academic advance are racing so fast they disorient the social psychological motors of student life.

Of course even at the latter institutions there are "consummatory" subcultures, whether beat or otherwise rebellious, that reject exploitation either by the curriculum or by the larger society, which they see as a rat race. However, it is not my impression that these nonconformist subcultures develop a great deal of solidarity. It may happen in the next decades that faculties, having first sought out social scientists to discover how to diminish the influence of the collegiate culture as a drag on academic pursuits, may come around asking us how to restore a vanished harmony of interests. Compare, in this connection, the work of Stouffer (1949) and of Stouffer and Toby (1951). I gather from these articles, which used Harvard students as subjects, that many of them apparently lack any great sense of solidarity with their friends—at any rate, they would turn them in to the authorities for cheating or other offenses if by not doing so they might endanger their own standing. Perhaps they deprecate themselves unduly; possibly they are cynical about "friends." In discussion, Stouffer has indicated his agreement with my surmise that students at other universities would be more inclined to say that they would go down the line for friends, even at the cost of some risk to themselves. In correspondence, Toby has pointed out that the Harvard students are genuinely caught in a conflict between the morality of universalism (they value scholarship and academic competition too highly to condone cheating per se) and the morality of particularism, that is, of friendship itself. And they can rationalize being influenced by the danger of discovery by relying on the universalistic side of the dilemma which would confront them if they let their friends escape.

Research on peer groups must confront the possibility (which underlies so much of Durkheim's thinking) that loyalty to the ideal of individualistic academic excellence, favored in general by faculty members, may be at odds with loyalty to the group, to the college, or to any larger entity.

References

ALLEN, P. J. Childhood backgrounds of success in a profession. *Amer. sociol. Rev.,* 1955, **20,** 186–90.

ALLPORT, G. A. *Personality: A psychological interpretation.* New York: Holt, 1937.

AMERICAN COUNCIL ON EDUCATION. *A fact book on higher education.* Washington, D. C.: American Council on Education, n.d. (Loose-leaf portfolio.)

——. *College testing: A guide to practices and programs.* Washington, D.C.: American Council on Education, 1959.

ANASTASI, A. *Psychological testing.* New York: Macmillan, 1954.

ANGELL, R. C. *The campus.* New York: D. Appleton and Company, 1928.

ANTIOCH COLLEGE. Experiment in independent study, 1957–1958. Yellow Springs, Ohio: Antioch College, September, 1958. (Mimeographed.)

ASCH, S. *Social psychology.* New York: Prentice-Hall, 1952.

ASTIN, A. W. Dimensions of work satisfaction in the occupational choices of college freshmen. *J. appl. Psychol.,* 1958, **42,** 187–90.

AUSUBEL, D. P., SCHIFF, H. M., and GOLDMAN, M. Qualitative characteristics in the learning process associated with anxiety. *J. appl. Psychol.,* 1953, **48,** 537–47.

BALES, R. Small-group theory and research. In R. MERTON (Ed.), *Sociology today.* New York: Basic Books, 1959. Pp. 293–305.

BARRETT, D. M. Aptitude and interest patterns of art majors in a liberal arts college. *J. appl. Psychol.,* 1945, **29,** 438–92.

BARTON, A. H. The concept of property-space in social research. In P. F. LAZARSFELD and M. ROSENBERG (Eds.), *The language of social research.* Glencoe, Ill.: Free Press, 1955. Pp. 40–53.

BARZUN, J. Where are the disciples? *Antioch Rev.,* 1960, **20** (Spring), 5–14.

BECKER, H. S., and CARPER, J. W. The development of identification with an occupation. *Amer. J. Sociol.,* 1956, **61,** 289–98.

BERELSON, B., LAZARSFELD, P. F., and McPHEE, W. M. *Voting.* Chicago: University of Chicago Press, 1954.

BEST, S. The relationship between the College Characteristics Index and other measures of the college environment. M.A. thesis, Syracuse University, 1962.

BLACKMER, A. The transition from Andover to Harvard. Distinction thesis, Social Relations Library, Harvard University, 1960.

BLAU, P. Orientation of college students toward international relations. *Amer. J. Sociol.*, 1953, **59**, 205–14.

——. Formal organizations: Dimensions of analysis. *Amer. J. Sociol.*, 1957, **43**, 58–69.

BLOOMGARDEN, L. Our changing elite colleges. *Commentary*, 1960, **29** (February), 150–54.

BOGUE, D. J. *The population of the United States*. Glencoe, Ill.: Free Press, 1959.

BORGATTA, E. C., JR., and MEYER, H. J. On the dimensions of group behavior. *Sociometry*, 1956, **19** (December), 223–40.

BORGATTA, E. F., and COTTRELL, L. S., JR. On the classification of groups. *Sociometry*, 1955, **18** (December), 409–22.

BROOM, L., and SELZNICK, P. *Sociology*. (3rd ed.) Evanston, Ill.: Row, Peterson, 1963.

BROWN, J. C. An experiment in role-taking. *Amer. sociol. Rev.*, 1952, **17**, 587–97.

BUROS, O. K. (Ed.) *The fifth mental measurements yearbook*. Highland Park, N.J.: Gryphon Press, 1959.

CAMPBELL, D. T. Factors relevant to the validity of experiments in social settings. *Psychol. Bull.*, 1956, **54**, 297–312.

——. Social attitudes and other acquired behavioral dispositions. In S. KOCH (Ed.) *Psychology: A study of science*, Vol. **5**. New York: McGraw-Hill, 1960.

CAPLOW, T., and McGEE, R. J. *The academic marketplace*. New York: Basic Books, 1958.

CARLSON, H. B. Characteristics of an acute confusional state in college students. *Amer. J. Psychiat.*, 1958, Vol. **14**.

CARTWRIGHT, D., and ZANDER, A. (Eds.) *Group dynamics: Research and theory*. Evanston, Ill.: Row, Peterson, 1960.

CATTELL, J. M. A study of the occupational background of men listed in the first edition of *American Men of Science*. *Science*, 1906, **24**, 732–44.

CATTELL, R. B. Types of group characteristics. In H. GUETZKOW (Ed.), *Groups, leadership, and men*. New York: Carnegie Press, 1951. Pp. 16–52.

CATTELL, R. B., SAUNDERS, D. R., and STICE, G. F. The dimensions of syntality in small groups. *Hum. Relat.*, 1953, **6**, 331–56.

CHRISTIE, R., and MERTON, R. K. Procedures for the sociological study of the values climate of medical schools. In *The ecology of the medical student*. A report of the Fifth Teaching Institute. Evanston, Ill.: Association of American Colleges, 1958.

CHURCHILL, R. Preliminary report on reading course study. Yellow Springs, Ohio: Antioch College, September, 1957. (Mimeographed.)

CHURCHILL, R., BASKIN, S., and JOHN, W. Experiments in independent study, 1957–1958. Yellow Springs, Ohio: Antioch College, September, 1958. (Mimeographed.)

CLARK, B. R. College image and student selection. In Field Service Center and Center for the Study of Higher Education, *Selection and educational differentiation*. Berkeley: University of California, 1960. (a)

——. *The open door college*. New York: McGraw-Hill, 1960. (b)

——. Faculty authority. *Bull. Amer. Ass. Univ. Profs*, 1961, Vol. **47** (Winter).

——. *Educating the expert society*. San Francisco, Calif.: Chandler Publishing Co., 1962.

COLEMAN, J. S. Relational analysis: The study of social organizations with survey methods. *Hum. Organization*, 1958–59, Vol. **17** (Winter), No. 4.

——. Academic achievement and the structure of competition. *Harvard educ. Rev.*, 1959, **29,** 350–51.

——. The adolescent subculture and academic achievement. *Amer. J. Sociol.*, 1960, **65,** 337–47.

——. *The adolescent society*. New York: Free Press of Glencoe. 1961.

——. *Social climates in high schools*. ("Cooperative Research Monograph Series.") Washington, D.C.: Government Printing Office, 1961.

COLEMAN, J. S., and ROSSI, P. *Determinants and consequences of college choice*. (Prepared for the College Entrance Examination Board by NORC and the Department of Social Relations, Johns Hopkins University.) Chicago: NORC, 1964.

COOPER, J. M. Catholics and scientific research. *Commonweal*, 1945, **42,** 147–49.

COTTRELL, L. S., JR. The adjustment of the individual to his age and sex roles. *Amer. sociol. Rev.*, 1942, **7,** 617–20.

CRONBACH, L. J., and GLESER, G. C. *Psychological tests and personnel decisions*. Urbana: University of Illinois Press, 1957.

DAVIE, J. S., and HARE, A. P. Button-down collar culture: A study of undergraduate life. *Hum. Organization*, 1956, **14,** 13–20.

DAVIS, J. A. *Great books and small groups*. New York: Free Press of Glencoe, 1961.

DAVIS, J. A. Group variables. *Amer. sociol. Rev.,* 1962, **28,** 814.

DAVIS, K., and MOORE, W. E. Some principles of stratification. *Amer. sociol. Rev.,* 1945, **10,** 242–49.

DEMORATH, N. J. Adolescent status demands. *Amer. sociol. Rev.,* 1943, **8,** 513–18.

DEVANE, W. C. Quoted in *New York Times,* Sunday, June 5, 1960.

DEWITT, N. Soviet science education and the school reform. *School and Soc.,* 1960 (Summer), pp. 297–300.

DEXTER, E. S., and STEIN, B. The measurement of leadership in white and Negro students. *J. abnorm. and soc. Psychol.,* 1955, **51,** 219–21.

DORNBUSCH, S. M. The military academy as an assimilating institution. *Soc. Forces,* 1955, **33,** 316–32.

DOUVAN, E. Social status and success strivings. *J. abnorm. and soc. Psychol.,* 1956, **52,** 219–23.

DRESSEL, P. L., and MAYHEW, L. B. *General education: Explorations in evaluation.* Washington, D.C.: American Council on Education, 1954.

DRUCKER, A. J., and REMMERS, H. H. Citizenship attitudes of graduated seniors at Purdue University, U.S. college graduates and high school pupils. *J. educ. Psychol.,* 1951, **42,** 231–35.

DURKHEIM, E. *Suicide.* Trans. J. A. SPAULDING and G. SIMPSON. Glencoe, Ill.: Free Press, 1951.

EARNEST, E. *The academic procession.* Indianapolis: Bobbs-Merrill, 1953.

ECKERT, R. E. *Outcomes of general education.* Minneapolis: University of Minnesota Press, 1943.

EISENSTADT, S. N. *From generation to generation.* Glencoe, Ill.: Free Press, 1955.

EISMAN, B. Some operational measures of cohesiveness and their inter-relations. *Hum. Relat.,* 1959, **12,** 183–89.

ELKIN, F., and WESTLEY, W. The myth of adolescent culture. *Amer. sociol. Rev.* 1955, **20,** 680–84.

ERIKSON, E. H. *Childhood and society.* New York: Norton, 1950.

——. The problem of ego identity. *J. Amer. psychoanal. Ass.,* 1956, **4,** 56–121.

FESTINGER, L. Informal social communication. *Psychol. Rev.,* 1950, **57,** 271–82.

——. Laboratory experiments. In L. FESTINGER and D. KATZ (Eds.), *Research methods in the behavioral sciences.* New York: Dryden Press, 1953. Pp. 136–72.

——. A theory of social comparison processes. *Hum. Relat.,* 1954, **7,** 117–40.

FESTINGER, L., BACK, K., SCHACHTER, S., KELLEY, H. H., and THIBAUT, J. *Theory and experiment in social communications.* Ann Arbor: Institute for Social Research, University of Michigan, 1950.

FORSYTH, E., and KATZ, E. A matrix approach to the analysis of sociometric data. *Sociometry,* 1946, **9,** 340–47.

FRENCH, J. R. P., JR. Experiments in field settings. In L. FESTINGER and D. KATZ (Eds.), *Research methods in the behavioral sciences.* New York: Dryden Press, 1953.

FRENCH, J. R. P., JR., and ZAJONC, R. B. An experimental study of cross cultural norm conflict. *J. abnorm. and soc. Psychol.,* 1957, **54,** 218–24.

GARDNER, E. F., and THOMPSON, G. G. *Social relations and morale in small groups.* New York: Appleton-Century-Crofts, 1956.

GERTH, H. H., and MILLS, C. W. (Eds.) *From Max Weber: Essays in sociology.* New York: Oxford University Press, 1946.

GOETSCH, H. P. *Parental income and college opportunities.* ("Teachers College Contributions to Education," No. 795.) New York: Columbia University, 1940.

GOFFMAN, E. On the characteristics of total institutions. In WALTER REED ARMY INSTITUTE OF RESEARCH, *Symposium on preventive and social psychiatry.* Washington, D.C.: Government Printing Office, 1958. Pp. 43–84.

GOLD, D. Some comments on "The Empirical Classification of Formal Groups." *Amer. sociol. Rev.,* 1964, **29,** 736–39.

GOLDSEN, R. K., ROSENBERG, M., WILLIAMS, R. M., JR., and SUCHMAN, E. A. *What college students think.* Princeton: Van Nostrand, 1960.

GORDON, R. L. Interaction between attitude and the definition of the situation in the expression of opinion. *Amer. sociol. Rev.,* 1952, **17,** 50–58.

GORDON, W. C. *The social system of the high school.* Glencoe, Ill.: Free Press, 1957.

GOTTLIEB, D., and HODGKINS, B. College student subcultures. *School Rev.,* 1963, **71** (Autumn), 266–90.

GOULDNER, A. W. Cosmopolitans and locals: Toward an analysis of latent social roles, I and II. *Admin. Sci. Quart.,* 1957, **2,** 281–306, 444–80.

GROSS, N., and MARTIN, W. E. On group cohesiveness. *Amer. J. Sociol.,* 1952, **57,** 546–54. (a)

———. Rejoinder [to Stanley Schachter]. *Amer. J. Sociol.,* 1952, **57,** 562–64. (b)

GUETZKOW, H. (Ed.). *Groups, leadership, and men.* Pittsburgh: Carnegie Press, 1951.

288

College Peer Groups

GUILFORD, J. P. *Personality.* New York: McGraw-Hill, 1959.
GUILFORD, J. P., and LACEY, J. I. *Printed classification tests.* ("Army Air Forces Psychology Program Research Report," No. 5.) Washington, D.C.: Government Printing Office, 1947.
HAGGERTY, M. E. The effective college curriculum. In COMMITTEE ON EDUCATIONAL RESEARCH, *The effective general college curriculum.* Minneapolis: University of Minnesota Press, 1937. Chapter 1, pp. 3 – 11.
HAGSTROM, W. O. *The scientific community.* New York: Basic Books, 1965.
HAGSTROM, W. O., and SELVIN, H. Determinants of support for civil liberties. *Brit. J. Sociol.,* 1960, **11** (March), 51 – 73.
——. Two dimensions of cohesiveness in small groups. *Sociometry,* 1965, **28** (No. 1; March), 30 – 43.
HALBWACHS, M. *La théorie de l'homme moyen.* Paris: Felix Alcan, 1912.
HALL, R. L., and WILLERMAN, B. The educational influence of dormitory roommates. *Sociometry,* 1963, **26** (September), 294 – 318.
HALPIN, A. W. *The leadership behavior of school superintendents.* Columbus, Ohio: Ohio State University, 1956.
HALSEY, A. H. British universities and intellectual life. *Universities Quart.,* 1958, **12** (February), 144 – 52.
——. The changing functions of universities in advanced societies. *Harvard educ. Rev.,* 1960 (Spring), **30,** 118 – 27.
HARE, A. P., BORGATTA, E. F., and BALES, R. F. (Eds.) *Small groups: Studies in social interaction.* New York: Knopf, 1955.
HATCH, R. W., and LANDIS, P. H. *Social heritage as a factor in college achievement.* "Research Studies of the State College of Washington," Vol. **10,** No. 4. December, 1942.
HAVEMANN, E., and WEST, P. *They went to college.* New York: Harcourt, Brace, 1952.
HAYWOOD, M. Had we but world enough and time. Undergraduate distinction thesis, Department of Social Relations, Radcliffe College, 1960.
HEATH, G. R., JR. Personality and student development. In *New dimensions of learning in a free society.* Pittsburgh: University of Pittsburgh Press, 1958, Pp. 225 – 45.
——. *The reasonable adventurer.* Pittsburgh: University of Pittsburgh Press, 1964.
HEMPHILL, J. K., and WESTIE, C. M. The measurement of group dimensions. *J. Psychol.,* 1950, **29,** 325 – 41.

HILL, W. F. Learning theory and the acquisition of values. 1959. (Mimeographed.)

HOCHBAUM, G. M. The relation between group members' self-confidence and their reactions to group pressures to university. *Amer. sociol. Rev.*, 1954, **19,** 678–87.

HOFFMAN, L. R. Homogeneity of members' personality and the effect on group problem-solving. *J. abnorm. and soc. Psychol.*, 1959, **58,** 27–32.

HOFSTADTER, R. Part one: The development of higher education in America. In R. HOFSTADTER and C. DE W. HARDY, *The development and scope of higher education in the United States.* New York: Columbia University Press, 1952.

HOFSTAETTER, P. R. A note on group cohesiveness. *Amer. J. Sociol.*, 1952, **58,** 198–200.

HOLZINGER, K. J., and HARMON, H. H. *Factor analysis.* Chicago: University of Chicago Press, 1941.

HOMANS, G. D. *The human group.* New York: Harcourt, Brace, 1950.

IFFERT, R. E. *Retention and withdrawal of college students.* "United States Department of Health, Education, and Welfare Bulletin," No. 1, 1958. Washington, D.C.: Government Printing Office, 1957.

JACOB, P. E. *Changing values in college: An exploratory study of the impact of college teaching.* New York: Harper, 1957.

JACOBS, W. Need more diversity. *Princeton Alumni Wkly,* 1958 (February 7), p. 11.

JENCKS, C., and RIESMAN, D. Patterns of residential education: A case study of Harvard. In N. SANFORD (Ed.), *The American college.* New York: Wiley, 1962. Pp. 735–36.

JOHNSON, B. *Campus versus classroom.* New York: I. Washburn, 1946.

KAHL, J. A. Educational and occupational aspirations of "common man" boys. *Harvard educ. Rev.*, 1953, **22,** 186–203.

KATZ, D. Field studies. In L. FESTINGER and D. KATZ (Eds.), *Research methods in the behavioral sciences.* New York: Dryden, 1953. Pp. 56–97.

KATZ, E., and LAZARSFELD, P. F. *Personal influence.* Glencoe, Ill.: Free Press, 1955.

KELLEY, H. H., and SHAPIRO, M. M. An experiment in conformity to group norms where conformity is detrimental to group achievement. *Amer. Sociol. Rev.*, 1954, **19,** 667–77.

KELLEY, H. H., and WOODRUFF, C. L. Members' reaction to apparent group approval of a counternorm communication. *J. abnorm. and soc. Psychol.*, 1956, **52,** 67–74.

KELMAN, H. C. Three processes of social influence: Compliance, identification and internationalization. Paper read at the meetings of the American Psychological Association, Chicago, August 30, 1956.

KENDALL, R., and LAZARSFELD, P. F. Problems of survey analysis. In P. F. LAZARSFELD and R. K. MERTON (Eds.), *Continuities in social research: Studies in the scope and method of the American soldier.* Glencoe, Ill.: Free Press, 1950. Pp. 133–96.

KERR, C. *The uses of the university.* Cambridge, Mass.: Harvard University Press, 1963.

KLOPF, G. *College student government.* New York: Harper, 1960.

KLUCKHOHN, C. Have there been discernible shifts in American values during the past generation? In E. E. MORISON (Ed.), *The American style.* New York: Harper, 1958. Pp. 145–217.

KNAPP, R. H., and GREENBAUM, J. J. *The younger American scholar: His collegiate origins.* Chicago: University of Chicago Press, 1953.

KUHARICH, J. L. Quoted in *The Oregonian* (Portland), April 22, 1960.

LAU, J. B. Attitude change as related to change in perception of the group norm. Unpublished Doctoral Dissertation, University of Michigan, 1954.

LAZARSFELD, P. F., and MENZEL, H. On the relation between individual and collective properties. Unpublished manuscript, 1956.

——. On the relationship between individual and group properties. In A. ETZIONI (Ed.), *Complex organizations.* New York: Holt, Rinehart, and Winston, 1961.

LAZARSFELD, P. F., and MERTON, R. K. Friendship as a social process: A substantive and methodological analysis. In M. BERGER, T. ABOL, and C. H. PAGE (Eds.), *Freedom and control in modern society.* New York: Van Nostrand, 1954. Pp. 18–66.

LAZARSFELD, P. F., and THIELENS, W., JR. *The academic mind.* Glencoe, Ill.: Free Press, 1958.

LEARNED, W. S., and WOOD, B. D. *The student and his knowledge.* New York: Carnegie Foundation for the Advancement of Teaching, 1938.

LEONARD, R. C. The incidence-intensity fallacy in sociological research. *Berkeley J. Sociol.,* 1959, **5**, 111–18.

LIFTON, R. J. Thought reform of Chinese intellectuals: A psychiatric evaluation. *J. soc. Issues,* 1957, **13**, 5–20.

LINDZEY, G., and BORGATTA, E. F. Sociometric measurement. In G. LINDZEY (Ed.), *Handbook of social psychology.* Cambridge, Mass.: Addison-Wesley, 1954.

LIPSET, M., AND LOWENTHAL, L. (Eds.) *Culture and social character.* New York: Free Press of Glencoe, 1961.

LIPSET, S. M., LAZARSFELD, P. F., BARTON, A., and LINZ, J. The social psychology of voting. In G. LINDZEY (Ed.), *Handbook of social psychology.* Cambridge, Mass.: Addison-Wesley, 1954.

LIPSET, S. M., TROW, M., and COLEMAN, J. S. *Union democracy.* Glencoe, Ill.: Free Press, 1956.

LUCE, D. C. Connectivity and generalized cliques in sociometric group structure. *Psychometrika,* 1950, **15,** 169–90.

LUCE, D. C., and PERRY, A. D. A method matrix analysis of group structure. *Psychometrika,* 1949, **14,** 95–116.

MCARTHUR, C. Personality differences between middle and upper classes. *J. abnorm. and soc. Psychol.,* 1955, **50,** 247–54.

MCCARLEY, R. A walk around the yard: A study of the freshman year at Harvard. Undergraduate thesis, Department of Social Relations, Harvard University, 1959.

MCCONN, M. *College or kindergarten?* New York: New Republic, Inc., 1928.

MCCONNELL, T. R. *The study of selected institutions.* Berkeley, Calif.: Center for the Study of Higher Education, 1963.

MCCONNELL, T. R., and HEIST, P. Do students make the college? *College and University,* 1959, **34,** 442–52.

MCKEACHIE, W. J. Students, groups, and teaching methods. *Amer. Psychologist,* 1958, **13,** 580–84.

MCNEMAR, Q. *Psychological statistics.* New York: Wiley, 1955.

MACRAE, D. Direct factor-analysis of sociometric data. Chicago: University of Chicago, n.d. (Mimeographed.)

Mademoiselle STAFF. Is education on the way out? *Mademoiselle,* 1960 (May).

MEREI, F. Group leadership and institutionalization. *Hum. Relat.,* 1949, **2,** 23–29.

MERTON, R. K. Continuities in the theory of reference groups and social structure. In R. K. MERTON (Ed.), *Social theory and social structure.* (2nd ed.) Glencoe, Ill.: Free Press, 1957.

——. The self-fulfilling prophecy. *Antioch Rev.,* 1948, **8,** 193–210.

MERTON, R. K., and ROSSI, A. S. Contributions to the theory of reference group behavior. In R. K. MERTON (Ed.), *Social theory and social structure.* Glencoe, Ill.: Free Press, 1957. Pp. 225–80.

MERTON, R. K., READER, G., and KENDALL, P. (Eds.) *The student physician: Introductory studies in the sociology of medical education.* Cambridge, Mass.: Harvard University Press, 1957.

MILLER, N. Academic climate and student values. Paper read at American Sociological Society, Chicago, September, 1959.

MILLER, N., and DOLLARD, J. *Social learning and imitation.* New Haven: Yale University Press, 1941.

MILLS, E. S. Abnormal psychology as a selective factor in the college curriculum. *J. educ. Psychol.,* 1955, **46**, 101 – 11.

MILNER, E. Effects of sex roles and social status on the early adolescent personality. *Genet. Psychol. Monogr.,* 1949, **40**, 235 – 325.

MOFFETT, M. Social background and activities of teachers college students. Teachers college, Columbia University, 1929.

Monthly Labor Review, 1963, **86** (January), 9, Table 4.

MORENO, J. L. *Who shall survive?* "Nervous and Mental Disease Monograph Series," No. 58, 1934.

MUELLER, K. H., and MUELLER, J. H. Socio-economic background of women students at Indiana University. *Educ. and psychol. Measmt,* 1949, **9**, 321 – 29.

MULLIGAN, R. A. Social-economic background and college enrollment. *Amer. sociol. Rev.,* 1951, **16**, 188 – 96.

——. Social characteristics of college students. *Amer. sociol. Rev.,* 1953, **18**, 305 – 10.

MURDOCK, G. P. *Social structure.* New York: Macmillan, 1949.

MURPHY, G. *Personality: A biosocial approach to origins and structure.* New York: Harper, 1947.

MURRAY, H. A. *Explorations in personality.* New York: Oxford University Press, 1938.

NEWCOMB, T. M. *Personality and social change: Attitude formation in a student community.* New York: Dryden, 1943.

——. *Social psychology.* New York: Dryden, 1950.

——. An approach to the study of communicative acts. *Psychol. Rev.,* 1953, **60**, 393 – 404.

——. The prediction of interpersonal attraction. *Amer. Psychologist,* 1956, **11**, 575 – 86.

——. *The acquaintance process.* New York: Holt, Rinehart, and Winston, 1961.

NICHOLSON, H. *Good behaviour.* Boston, Mass.: Beacon Press, 1955.

OBERLIN COLLEGE. Report on independent studies experiment at Oberlin College. Oberlin, Ohio: Oberlin College, 1958. (Duplicated.)

OLMSTEAD, M. S. *The small group.* New York: Random House, 1959.

ORLANS, H. *The effects of federal programs on higher education.* Washington, D.C.: Brookings Institution, 1962.

OWENS, W. A., and JOHNSON, W. C. Some measured personality traits of collegiate underachievers. *J. educ. Psychol.,* 1949, **40**, 41 – 46.

PACE, C. R. Psychological differences between college environments. Paper presented at the annual meeting of the Western Personnel Institute, Pasadena, California, November 4, 1959.

——. Five college environments. *College Board Rev.*, 1960, **41,** 24–28.

——. The influence of student culture and faculty values in the American college. In G. Z. BEREDAY and J. A. LAUWERYS (Eds.), *Higher education: The year book of education.* New York: World Book Company, 1959.

PACE, C. R., and STERN, G. G. An approach to the measurement of psychological characteristics of college environments. *J. educ. Psychol.*, 1958, **49,** 269–77.

PARSONS, T., and WHITE, W. F. The link between character and society. In S. M. Lipset and L. Lowenthal (Eds.), *The sociology of culture and the analysis of character.* Glencoe, Ill.: Free Press, 1961.

PELZ, D. C. Some social factors related to performance in a research organization. *Administrative sci. Quart.*, 1956, **1,** 310–25.

RAVEN, S. Perish by the sword. *Encounter*, 1959, **13,** 37–49.

RETTIG, S. Multiple discriminant analysis: An illustration. *Amer. sociol. Rev.*, 1964, **29,** 398–422.

RIESMAN, D. *Constraint and variety in American education.* Lincoln, Nebr.: University of Nebraska Press, 1956.

——. The influence of student culture and faculty values in the American college. In G. Z. BEREDAY and J. A. LAUWERYS (Eds.), *Higher education: The year book of education.* New York: World Book Company, 1959.

——. College subcultures and college outcomes. In *Selection and educational differentiation.* Berkeley, Calif.: University of California Field Service Center and Center for the Study of Higher Education, 1960.

RIESMAN, D., and JENCKS, C. The viability of the American college. In N. SANFORD (Ed.), *The American college.* New York: Wiley, 1962.

ROBINSON, D., and ROHDE, S. Two experiments with an anti-Semitism poll. *J. abnorm. and soc. Psychol.*, 1946, **41,** 136–44.

ROETHLISBERGER, F., and DICKSON, W. J. *Management and the worker.* Cambridge, Mass.: Harvard University Press, 1940.

ROSENBERG, M. Factors influencing change of occupational choice. In P. F. LAZARSFELD and M. ROSENBERG (Eds.), *The language of social research.* Glencoe, Ill.: Free Press, 1955. Pp. 250–59.

——. *Occupations and values.* Glencoe, Ill.: Free Press, 1957.

ROSS, I. Group standards concerning the admission of Jews. *Soc. Problems*, 1955, **2,** 133–40.

Rossi, P. H., and Rossi, A. S. Background and consequences of parochial school education in the United States. *Harvard educ. Rev.*, 1957, **27**, 168–99.

Sanford, N. (issue Ed.). Personality development during the college years. *J. soc. Issues*, 1956, Vol. **12** (No. 4).

Schachter, S. Comment on Gross-Martin paper. *Amer. J. Sociol.*, 1952, **57**, 554–62.

———. *The psychology of affiliation*. Stanford, Calif.: Stanford University Press, 1959.

Schachter, S., and Burdick, H. A field experiment on rumor transmission and distortion. *J. abnorm. and soc. Psychol.*, 1955, **50**, 363–71.

Schmidt, G. P. *The liberal arts college*. New Brunswick, N. J.: Rutgers University Press, 1957.

Schnore, L. F. Urbanization and economic development. Paper read at the 54th annual meeting of the American Sociological Association, Chicago, Ill., September 3, 1959.

School Review staff. Social climates in school and college. *School Rev.*, 1963, Vol. **71** (Autumn).

Schutz, W. D. *FIRO: A three dimensional theory of interpersonal behavior*. New York: Rinehart, 1958.

Scodel, A., and Mussen, P. Social principles of stratification. *Amer. sociol. Rev.*, 1945, **10**, 242–49.

Sears, R., Maccoby, E. E., and Levin, H. *Patterns of child rearing*. Evanston, Ill.: Row, Peterson, 1957.

Selvin, H. C. The logic of survey analysis. Berkeley, Calif.: University of California, February, 1954.

———. *The effects of leadership*. Glencoe, Ill.: Free Press, 1960.

Selvin, H. C., and Hagstrom, W. O. Determinants of support for civil liberties. *Brit. J. Sociol.*, 1960, **11**, 51–73.

———. Reply to Davis. *Amer. sociol. Rev.*, 1962, **28**, 814.

———. The empirical classification of formal groups. *Amer. sociol. Rev.*, 1963, **28** (June), 399–411.

———. Reply to Gold. *Amer. sociol. Rev.*, 1964, **29**, 739.

———. The dimensions of cohesiveness in small groups. *Sociometry*, 1965 (Spring).

Sherif, M. *The psychology of social norms*. New York: Harper, 1936.

Sherif, M., and Sherif, C. W. *An outline of social psychology*. New York: Harper, 1956.

Siegel, A. E., and Siegel, S. Reference groups, membership groups and attitude change. *J. abnorm. and soc. Psychol.*, 1957, **55**, 360–64.

Sokal, S. R., and Sneath, P. H. A. *Principles of numerical taxonomy*. San Francisco and London: W. H. Freeman and Co., 1963.

SPENCER, H. *The study of sociology.* New York: D. Appleton and Co., 1891. P. 13.

STERN, G. G. The ecology of the American college student: Varieties of constraint in American education. Syracuse, N.Y.: Psychological Research Center, Syracuse University, 1959. (Mimeographed.)

——. Environments and learning. In N. SANFORD (Ed.), *The American college.* New York: Wiley, 1962. Pp. 690–730.

STERN, G. G., and PACE, C. R. *College characteristics index, form 1158.* Syracuse, N.Y.: Psychological Research Center, Syracuse University, 1958.

STERN, G. G., STEIN, M. I., and BLOOM, B. S. *Methods in personality assessment.* Glencoe, Ill.: Free Press, 1956.

STOUFFER, S. Analysis of conflicting social norms. *Amer. sociol. Rev.,* 1949, **14,** 707–17.

——. *Communism, conformity, and civil liberties.* Garden City, N.Y.: Doubleday, 1955.

STOUFFER, S., and TOBY, J. Role conflict and personality. *Amer. J. Sociol.,* 1951, **56,** 395–406.

STRANG, R. *Behavior and background of students in college and secondary schools.* New York: Harper, 1937.

SUSSMAN, L., *Freshman morale at M.I.T.* Cambridge, Mass.: Massachusetts Institute of Technology, 1960.

TAGIURI, R., and PETRULLO, L. (Eds.) *Person, perception and interpersonal behavior.* Stanford, Calif.: Stanford University Press, 1958.

THIBAUT, J. S., and KELLEY, H. H. *The social psychology of groups.* New York: Wiley, 1959.

THISTLETHWAITE, D. L. College press and student achievement. *J. educ. Psychol.,* 1959, **50,** 183–91.

THORNDIKE, R., and HAGEN, E. *Measurement and evaluation in psychology and education.* New York: Wiley, 1955.

THORNER, I. J. Nursing: The functional significance of an institutional pattern. *Amer. sociol. Rev.,* 1955, **20,** 531–38.

TROW, M. Some implications of the social origins of engineers. In *Scientific manpower.* Washington, D.C.: National Science Foundation, 1958. Pp. 67–74.

——. Reflections on the recruitment to college teaching. In J. W. GUSTAD (Ed.), *Faculty supply, demand, and recruitment.* Winchester, Mass.: New England Board of Higher Education, 1959.

——. Cultural sophistication and higher education. In *Selection and educational differentiation.* Berkeley, Calif.: University of California Field Service Center and Center for the Study of Higher Education, 1960. (a)

——. The campus viewed as a culture. In *Research on college students.*

Boulder, Colo.: Western Interstate Commission for Higher Education, 1960. (b)

TROW, M. Student subcultures and administrative action. In R. L. SUTHERLAND et al. (Eds.), *Personality factors on the college campus.* Austin, Texas: Hogg Foundation for Mental Health, 1962.

UNIVERSITY OF CALIFORNIA. Regulation on student government. Berkeley, Calif.: University of California, 1959. (a)

——. *University Bulletin,* 1959, **8** (Nov. 2), 66. (b)

VEROFF, J., WILCOX, S., and ATKINSON, J. The achievement motive in high school and college age women. *J. abnorm. and soc. Psychol.,* 1953, **48,** 108–19.

WALLACE, W. L. *Student culture: Social structure and continuity in a liberal arts college.* Chicago: Aldine, 1966.

WARNER, W. L., HAVIGHURST, R. J., and LOEB, M. B. *Who shall be educated?* New York: Harper, 1944.

WARNER, W. L., MOEKER, M., and EELLS, K. *Social class in America.* Chicago: Science Research Associates, 1949.

WATSON, J., and LIPPITT, R. *Learning across cultures.* Ann Arbor, Mich.: Institute for Social Research, 1955.

WENKERT, R., and SELVIN, H. C. School spirit in the context of a liberal education. *Soc. Problems,* 1962, **10,** 156–68.

WHITE, H. C. Unpublished manuscript, Department of Sociology, University of Chicago.

WILLERMAN, B. Roommate relations in a college dormitory. Unpublished study, 1951.

——. Communication between friends and strangers. Unpublished study, 1959.

WILLERMAN, B., and SWANSON, L. Group prestige in voluntary organizations: A study of college sororities. *Hum. Relat.,* 1953, **6,** 57–77.

WILSON, W. The spirit of learning (1909). In *Selected literary and political papers and addresses of Woodrow Wilson,* Vol. 1. New York: Grosset and Dunlap, 1925. Pp. 244–65.

WINCH, R. F. Heuristic and empirical typologies: A job for factor analysis. *Amer. sociol. Rev.,* 1947, **12,** 68–75.

WISPE, L. Evaluating section teaching methods in the introductory course. *J. educ. Res.,* 1951, **45,** 161–86.

WOLFBEIN, S. The need for professional personnel. In S. MUSHKIN (Ed.), *Economics of higher education.* Washington, D.C.: Government Printing Office, 1962.

ZETTERBERG, H. L. *An American college for adults.* New York: Columbia University Bureau of Applied Social Research, 1958. (Mimeographed.)

Indices

Author
Index

Subject
Index